Counseling
through
Group Process

Joseph Anderson, D.S.W., A.C.S.W., is Professor and Chairperson of the Social Work Department at Shippensburg University. He received his doctoral degree from the University of Maryland, where he has also taught. Dr. Anderson was president of the Central Pennsylvania Chapter of the National Association of Social Workers, and a member of the Commission on Accreditation of the Council on Social Work Education. Currently, he is a member of the Academy of Certified Social Workers, the Educational Planning Commission of the Council on Social Work Education, and the Editorial Board of *Social Work with Groups*. Dr. Anderson is the author of *Social Work Methods and Processes* and numerous journal articles on group counseling and social work practice and education.

Counseling through Group Process

Joseph Anderson, D.S.W., A.C.S.W.

Springer Publishing Company
New York

Springer Publishing Company, Inc.
200 Park Avenue South
New York, New York 10003

84 85 86 87 88 / 10 9 8 7 6 5 4 3 2 1

Library of Congress Cataloging in Publication Data

Anderson, Joseph.
   Counseling through group process.
   Bibliography: p.   Includes index.
   1. Group counseling. I. Title.
BF637.C6A48   1984   158'.3   84-1302
ISBN 0-8261-4620-1

Printed in the United States of America

To my favorite group . . .
Chris, Angie, Laurie, Rachel,
and our newest member, Erin

Contents

Part II. The TACIT Model

Preface

This book is about skills for counseling through group process. It presents a model of group process and of generic skills for a variety of helping professionals. The model promotes the enabling of stages of group development in counseling groups. The group's growth toward mutual aid, facilitated by the developmental functions and skills of the counselor, is the medium through which individual members' needs are met.

Research on group process and outcome variables, counselor/leader variables, and the stages of group development ground the approach in tested knowledge. The approach is called TACIT, an acronym for the sequential stages of counseling group process: *Trust, Autonomy, Closeness, Interdependence,* and *Termination.* Each of these stages, based on research, informs particular counseling functions and skills. Counselors facilitate the group process, especially in time-limited and theme-centered groups, through the disciplined and creative use of these skills. The methodology addresses all major elements of counseling group process—the members ("I"s), the group ("We"), and the content ("It")—and presents the TACIT skills in operational terms. As in all effective professional practice, readers can find direction in the model's principles, concepts, and skills, but each reader must find his or her own unique way of using this model.

I wrote the book especially for classroom and practicum learning situations. I have found it a most fruitful resource for teaching group counseling through involvement in a classroom learning group in which students take turns co-facilitating the group process with me, either before or during a field experience in working with a counseling group. The TACIT model also served as the conceptual base for consultation with students establishing their first counseling groups in the field. The methodology also provides a framework for the advanced practitioner's continual professional development through self-study, consultation, supervision, and/or advanced training work-shops and seminars.

One cannot write a book on groups without having learned from many others. My many others are too numerous to name and too significant for me to separate from my current understanding of group process. These include leaders in learning and personal growth groups in which I was a member, fellow members in these groups, and members in groups which I facilitated, who worked so hard on behalf of the group and themselves. In these groups, and in my family, I learned what I consider my greatest lesson: our thrusts for mutual aid are very alive and well, even in a society growing evermore alienating and depersonalizing. I only hope this book helps others discover this potential for mutual aid.

Joseph Anderson, D.S.W., A.C.S.W.

1

Introduction: Core Concepts

This book presents a developmental skill model for *counseling through group process:* Counseling refers to the helping process for persons who are experiencing current and specific problems in personal and social living. Its focus is upon these immediate reality-oriented problems. Its objective is more effective coping with these problems in the person's current life situation in a way that stimulates the person's growth process. Group counseling is a methodology for learning to cope more effectively with these problems and for stimulating the growth process through participation in a group process. The central element of influence is the member's interaction with others toward achieving common and individual goals: in a word, interdependence. The group becomes a social microcosm for each member—a slice of life. The assumption is that learning how to live differently and to grow inside the group can be transferred to living differently and growing in one's life outside of the group.

The *process* perspective spotlights certain developmental elements of the counseling group experience. There are three interrelated elements at work and through which the work gets done. These are the individual's, the group's, and the counseling process. Process connotes a natural progression of gradual changes that lead toward a particular result. It implies forward movement or development in its natural, ideal state—a condition never really existing but only approximated for human process. An understanding of process provides the direction for both the group's and the counselor's parallel work.

The process model developed in this text views individual problems as immediate obstacles to normal growth and development. The major underlying objective for each group counseling member is growth toward self-actualization. Likewise, group process is developmental. As the group grows toward its own potential as a mutual aid system, members' needs are met in such a way that their individual goals are achieved. They grow. And yet it is not so simple as this.

A recent cartoon depicts two men standing outside of their psychiatrist's office. The one tells the other, "Dr. Wise says I am not rich enough to have problems. . . . I just have troubles." There is more than a semantic difference reflected in the psychiatrist's comments. Most consumers of counseling services provided by helping professionals are not the typical person depicted (at least by assumption) in theories of counseling—the upper-middle-class, articulate, insightful, white female who is seeking a "talking cure" to perceived specific problems. Rather they tend to be persons, many of whom may be poor or nonwhite or both, who are troubled (or "in trouble") by a variety of personal and life conditions and who have sought help, or who have been somehow forced to use help, for improving some particular aspects of their personal and social living. The assumption of this text is that particular helping processes are more effective than others for working with these troubled and often alienated persons who receive professional counseling services.

Basic Premises

This text presents a generic model derived from research-supported hypotheses for group counseling with these consumers. In this model, the group has a specific purpose and is time-limited (has an established time for beginning and ending the overall process). It translates its purpose into group goals through a common theme and session subthemes. As all members are engaged in these shared purposes, goals, and themes and the limited time for their work together, they, as research suggests, achieve their individual gains. The "I," the "We," and the "It" of the group process combine. It works.

While the work gets done by the members themselves, as it must, it is the counselor who is responsible for enabling group process in behalf of the members. This book is written in such a way that it can be used for learning to be an effective member in group process, as, for instance, in a class designed to learn about groups as a prerequisite for working with them. However, the primary audience I address are those who can develop a special expertise to enable group and member growth—the counselor. I focus particularly on what I call the TACIT skills for counseling through group process.

The theory presented in this text, like any useful theory of counseling, includes three general parts. They are: (1) the basic

philosophical assumptions and theoretical premises about the people
to whom counseling is directed (the *knowledge* and *values* of individual and group process); (2) the specific theory for instructing the
goals and the basic means of influencing these people (the *knowledge*—theory and research—and *values* of the helping process); and
(3) the procedures and techniques for achieving selected goals with
those involved (the *skills* of the helping process). No theory is adequate without all three of these. We can know everything we need to
know about our goals and plans for the counseling process, but we
must be able to do, to have procedures and techniques which can be
used to translate our knowledge and values into action in behalf of
those we serve. In short, this theory needs to teach skills.

TACIT skills provide a way of translating group development
knowledge and values into a practice model. These skills meet several criteria deemed significant for teachable group practice (Gill &
Barry, 1982). These criteria are:

1. *Generic*. The behavior which constitutes the skill is essential
   for group counselors in *most* settings with *most* group clients
   for enabling the achievement of *most* group counseling goals.
2. *Appropriate*. The skill is attributed reasonably to the role
   and functions of the group counselor.
3. *Empirically supported*. The skill is consistent with existing
   research findings on group counseling process and outcomes.
4. *Definable*. The skill is described in terms of operations to
   perform it.
5. *Observable*. Both experienced and inexperienced observers
   can identify the skill when it occurs as repeated in like form
   by different counselors in different settings.
6. *Measurable*. Objective recording of both the frequency and
   quality of the skill can occur with a high degree of agreement
   among observers.
7. *Developmental*. The skill is placed within the context of a
   progressive relationship with other skills, all contributing to
   the group's process. Effectiveness of later stage behavior in
   the counseling process depends upon the effectiveness of the
   skills used at earlier stages.
8. *Group-focused*. The target of the skill is the group, or more
   than one participant. The behavior which constitutes the
   skills relates to the interaction between two or more participants and serves to facilitate interaction, to encourage
   shared responsibility for the group process, and to invite

mutual aid in using the group's resources in decision making and problem solving.

In individual counseling, we find some generic skill models which meet all of these criteria except for *group-focused*. Shulman (1979) in social work and Carkhuff (1969) in counseling are two excellent examples. The models for group counseling in social work tend to meet some of these criteria but fail particularly in defining empirically supported skills in measurable, observable, and/or development terms (Garvin, 1981; Henry, 1981; Klein, 1972; Schwartz, 1971; Tropp, 1972). The counseling literature tends to operationalize skills for working with groups more effectively in observable and measurable terms, but it has yet to produce an empirical base and/or a developmental perspective of these skills for group counseling purposes (Corey, 1981; Dyer and Vriend, 1977; Fullmer, 1971; Ivey, 1973; Lieberman, Yalom, & Miles, 1973; Ohlsen, 1977; Yalom, 1975). The TACIT skills borrow from these cited works, among others, in developing a model which meets all eight of the above criteria for teachable group counseling skills.

The basic premises of the TACIT model are that:

1. Individual development occurs in microcosm in group development.
2. Group process, or group development, recapitulates and reciprocates individual development.
3. Group counseling occurs through group process.
4. Group process has its own inherent "curative factors." The essence of these factors is the "mutual aid" system that evolves in the maturing group; that is, a group that evolves through the stages of group development.
5. The primary learnings in group process are interpersonal, related to the growth of autonomy ("I") and interdependence ("We") in relation to the content ("It") of counseling group process.
6. Natural, evolving group process has these curative factors and the potential for establishing a mutual aid system that develops autonomy and interdependence for members. It is a slice of life wherein one can learn to live up to the foremost commandment for healthy living; that is, "Love thy neighbor as thyself."
7. The counselor can either facilitate or obstruct this process.
8. The process in general is the tacit dimension of all group

experience and interpersonal growth. In fact, TACIT seems a useful acronym (and perhaps a mnemonic device) for the stages of group development: Trust, Autonomy, Closeness, Interdependence, and Termination. TACIT reflects the major interpersonal themes in all sequential personal growth and in group process.

9. An understanding of TACIT is the basis for the counselor's use of skills for helping through group process.

10. The TACIT foundation, as supported by existing research on counseling group process and outcomes and counselor functions and skills, provides a framework for effective counseling through group process.

These premises suggest that the core theoretical concepts of the TACIT model are related to the interpersonal themes in social living. These themes—autonomy and interdependence as balanced in responsibility—are the basis for individual and group process which combats alienation and promotes self-actualization.

Core Theoretical Concepts

Alienation

Members often begin counseling groups alone. From the extroverted "social butterfly" to the introverted "wallflower," our groups increasingly include those experiencing alienation. In our industrial society, interpersonal alienation is a priority social problem whose victims will continue to need counseling services, among others.

The antidote for this alienation is responsibility. The two sides of this responsibility are autonomy and interdependence. Autonomy refers to taking responsibility for one's self. Interdependence is the ability to relate responsibly to others in cooperative mutual aid. A significant medium for the development of this responsibility, the balance of autonomy and interdependence, is experience in intensive face-to-face small groups in which one is helped to establish empathic, caring connections with other members (Anderson, 1978). Providing this experience to ameliorate alienation is a major objective of counseling through group process.

Whenever the theme of alienation is found, whether in the humanities or the social sciences, central to its definition is the idea that people have lost their identity, or "selfhood." There is the implicit or explicit assumption that this self-alienation obstructs self-actualization.

Less explicit, however, is the theory for how we achieve this selfhood. One answer comes from the symbolic interactionists, especially Cooley (1956) and Mead (1962). They argue that we develop a self through interaction with others. To Cooley this is a process of acquiring a "looking glass self," or seeing ourselves as others see us. To Mead, it is by "taking the role of the other," or through empathy. If one discovers a self in interaction with others, then a loss of selfhood is a social as well as an individual problem. This means that a person experiencing alienation is not only cut off from the springs of one's own creativity but is thereby also severed from groups of which one would otherwise be a part. Those who fail to achieve a meaningful relationship with others are deprived of some part of themselves. Alienation is at base, then, a problem in human relations.

In this view, alienation is a vicious circle of feelings which leads to a sense of futility in responsibly communicating one's needs to others and in trusting others' ability to understand. Its central dynamic is loss of faith in people—the self and others.* After an extensive review of the theory and research, Hobart (1965) defines alienation in this circular process. A feeling, whether correct or not, that others "don't understand" results in fewer and less forthright attempts to communicate one's needs to others; less communication results in others' understanding less, and thus in a deeper sense of social isolation and loneliness—the state of alienation wherein the person feels that no one else could possibly understand (Garland, 1981).

What one does makes no difference. Thus, one loses one's sense of autonomy, which is necessary for initiating and building interdependent relations with others. This results in feelings of self-estrangement which are manifested in behavior toward oneself and the events in one's life demonstrative of powerlessness, meaninglessness, normlessness, and isolation (Seeman, 1959). The person experiences the self and others as "things" to be manipulated and to manipulate (Israel, 1971) rather than as autonomous persons who can be involved through empathy and caring with others and with the events in one's life.

Combating alienation, therefore, requires a breakdown in the

---

*Keniston (1965), for instance, found his scale of "distrust"—"expect the worst of others and you will avoid disappointment"—as the most predictive measurement for alienation of the thirteen scales he used in his classic study.

circular process leading to self-estrangement. In brief, the "alien-ated" need experiences in being understood and in understanding—to assume more fully their responsibility for the self and others. They need to develop both autonomy and interdependence in their human relations.

Experience in intensive small groups has been found to contri-bute significantly to increased feelings of being understood, an in-creased sense of personal autonomy (perceived responsibility for one's own life), increased empathy toward others, and decreased feelings of alienation (Anderson, 1978; Dunnette, 1969; Koziey, Loken, & Field, 1971). These group experiences appear to help mem-bers validate themselves and others—to help self-perceived nobodies to become somebodies in interpersonal transactions. Counseling groups, because of their use of members as the source of each other's help, can provide this antidote to alienation. There seems to be no more powerful affirmation of one's self than to be needed to under-stand another.

Autonomy

Autonomy and interdependence are two significant concepts in a number of group approaches. In the approach of this text, however, they are the central organizing themes of both the group process and the counseling process. Individual autonomy is an existential given. At the core of existence each of us is unique, separate, alone, and therefore responsible for our own life choices. In the counseling group, responsibility must go along with choice so that members are confronted with the ultimate in freedom: each person is responsible to oneself and cannot escape this responsibility by projecting it onto others.

Individual autonomy therefore refers to the "I-ness" of my ex-perience, to self-awareness and selfhood. As the individual "re-sponse-able" for the perception of the outside world emanating to me (I feel good and/or bad about what I receive), I am at the center of my universe. I, in my awareness of you, am still at the center of my universe, although you are now a part of this. I am autonomous with regard to you in that I can choose the kind of relationship I want with you and can attempt to create it. You are autonomous in that you can choose whether to accept, reject, or modify my definition of our relationship. Autonomy, therefore, relates to self-awareness, self-responsibility, and self-actualization. It is being captain of one's own ship—one's self.

In development, it is only through becoming an "I" that one can truly become part of a "We," or interdependence. Therefore, in developmental processes, autonomy themes precede interdependent ones, while both are a part of our basic nature as human beings. Autonomy, underdeveloped, is selfishness, an alienated state of irresponsibly using others for one's own gains. It leads to the manipulation and control of others that we see most often in early stages of group development. Autonomy, developed, is the basis for interdependent relationships with others. As the aphorism attributed to Rabbi Hillel goes: "If I am not for myself, who will be? If I am only for myself, what am I?" Self-actualization, then, is a balance of autonomy and interdependence. But the ability to "Love thy neighbor as thyself," the basis of interdependence, is grounded, as Fromm (1956) has proposed, in the ability to love one's self—in autonomy.

Interdependence

While existentially we are separate, we are also connected. Donne's classic "No man is an island entire of itself; everyman is part of the continent, a part of the main . . . I am involved in all mankind; and therefore never seek to know for whom the bell tolls; it tolls for thee . . ." remains a most poetic statement of this human connectedness. Interdependence is based on this connectedness and exists because my autonomy is not sufficient to the satisfaction of all my needs. Without others with whom I can get close, I will feel lonely and alienated and many of my most important needs will go unmet. The other does not have to be you. To the extent that I feel *only you* can satisfy my needs, I have exchanged my interdependence for symbiosis—an uncut umbilical cord, a defensive fusion, a dependency not *inter*dependency. There do, however, have to be others.

Therefore, autonomy and interdependence are both existential givens. They can be denied only at the expense of one's fundamental sense of and responsibility toward reality. Their denial is the deep, dark hallway through which alienation lurks. The person who claims helpless and passive dependence in the role of "victim" blots out his or her sense of autonomy and is all alone in a malevolent universe, just as the isolated, alienated, highly mistrustful paranoid is blind to a sense of interdependence. The group approach of this text requires the counselor throughout the process to provide both the experience and the awareness of autonomy and interdependence of each member, as balanced in their development of responsibility. Such group experiences can enable those experiencing alienation to accept the responsibility that social living and psychological growth entail. In turn, this responsibility combats the behavioral consequences of their increased interpersonal alienation.

Responsibility

Responsibility as a concept of growth and of therapy is found earlier in the individual psychology of Alfred Adler (1956) and more recently as a central dynamic in Glasser's Reality Therapy (1965), Frankl's Logotherapy (1965), and existential psychotherapy (Yalom, 1980). Adler maintained that the human personality is much more than the passive product of either internal or external forces, while embedded in a social context. He saw persons rather as the creative center of their world and, as such, to an important extent, the creator of themselves. Problem behavior, therefore, for Adler was not "sick" but "irresponsible." Responsibility is based upon our evolutionary thrusts for social interest, participation, social embeddedness, or what Adler called *Gemeinshaftsgefuhl*. Responsibility is our contribution to others, to the commonweal. Adler believed that the only salvation from our continuously driving inferiority feeling is the knowledge and the feeling of being valuable to the common welfare. Social interest was Adler's antidote to alienation. This social interest is the sense of belonging, of being an integral part of the human enterprise through assuming responsibility.

Adler continuously attenuated the self-centeredness of his patients by reaching for their strengths for getting out of themselves and involved in some constructive ways with others. To him "the iron clad logic of social living" was found in the wisdom of the teachings of all of the great world religions in one form or another. For instance, his paradoxical warning that the self is lost unless it is given away, invested in others, is made throughout the Bible, perhaps no better than in the New Testament parable of the talents in Matthew 25, verses 14 to 30. In this source, we are told that he who risks himself garners more. But he who seeks before all to secure what he has finds himself bereft of even that with which he began.

Glasser similarly believes that people do not act irresponsibly because they are ill, but rather that they are ill because they are acting irresponsibly. To Glasser: "Responsibility, a concept basic to Reality Therapy, is defined as the ability to fulfill one's needs, and to do so in *a way that does not deprive others of the ability to fulfill their needs.* . . . A responsible person also does that which gives him a feeling of self-worth and a feeling that he is worthwhile to others" (p. 41). On the other hand, an irresponsible person does what one feels like, what is most convenient, and what is most profitable to oneself. To Glasser, this person gains no one's respect, including one's own, and in time brings down suffering on oneself and others.

Therefore, Reality Therapy is based upon a concerned involvement with patients, the challenge of the reality of irresponsibility, and the help to make and live up to their own commitments to their own standards of what is right versus what is wrong. Responsible, "right," or moral behavior in therapy is defined as acting in such a way that one gives and receives love and feels worthwhile to the self and others. For Glasser, if standards and values are not stressed, the most that therapy can accomplish is to help people become more comfortable in their irresponsibility. Because his effort is always directed toward helping people fulfill their needs, Glasser insists on their striving to reach the highest possible standards. He sees the job of therapy not to lessen the pain of irresponsible actions but to increase the person's strength so that he or she can bear the pain of a full life as well as enjoy the rewards of a deeply responsible existence.

Glasser views those who are not responsible, as having a "failure identity." A person who has adopted a failure identity lacks a concept of self as a loved and worthwhile individual. This person will not work for any long-term goals. His life is full of pain and he lives in a haphazard, erratic struggle to get rid of the pain. The failure identity can be replaced by a "success identity" only through learning to assume responsibility for the self and others.

Frankl's Logotherapy also holds a central place for responsibility. He writes (1965): "Logotherapy is ultimately education toward responsibility" (p. xiv), and is "always responsibility for the actualization of values" (p. 84). Responsibility is concomitant with our basic autonomy. In Logotherapy this autonomy is not freedom from the limits imposed on an individual by biological and social conditions, but "rather freedom to take a stand on whatever conditions might confront him" (p. 16). To Frankl, we do have genuine choices. With this autonomy comes the responsibility to choose in ways that actualize our values to refrain from harming the physical, mental, and emotional integrity of others; to observe good faith of our contractual and personal relations; and to attempt to render unto others what is due them and fosters their well-being. In this sense, our social life results from our individual conscience. Logotherapy attempts to help people do what they "ought" to do.

In existential psychotherapy (Yalom, 1980), responsibility also evolves from the fact that we constitute our own worlds, that each of us is the author of our own story. In Yalom's words, "To be aware of responsibility is to be aware of creating one's own self, destiny, life, predicament, feelings, and, if such be the case, one's own suffering" (p. 218). The inability to face responsibility is one of the primary existential themes for psychotherapy patients. In this view, much behavior—compulsiveness, conformity, "acting out" or losing control, and indecisiveness, among others—reflects fears of facing the existential guilt for not having lived up to one's own potential. Patients are patients because they refuse to become their own parents and to face the basic autonomous and separate nature of their being and becoming.

Yalom (1975) places this concept of responsibility in the perspective of group therapy. The group as a social microcosm ignites individual member's conflicts. Conflict with authority and autonomy activate so many different individual interpersonal issues in the group that Yalom conceives the therapy group as a miniature social universe for each of its members. In the here and now of this group process, members confront responsibility directly in their behavior and awareness. First, members learn how their behavior is viewed by others in the group through feedback and self-observation. Second, they learn how their behavior makes others feel. Third, they learn how their behavior creates the opinions others have of them (valued, disliked, respected, avoided, exploited, feared, and so on). Fourth, they learn how their behavior influences their opinions of themselves; they evaluate their behavior on the basis of how they are as against what they wish they were to others. Fifth, they choose, decide, or take responsibility to change this behavior. In other words, group members comprehend that through autonomy one is responsible for how others see, regard, and treat one as well as how one regards oneself. In this process, owning one's responsibility in the group is the vestibule for change in assuming individual responsibility in life outside of the group.

Responsibility in Group Counseling

Effective group counseling uses the members themselves and their process together as the major agents of help. Assuming responsibility outside of the group begins with this requirement to assume it within. Each member is responsible for the conduct of the group. Research

(Lieberman et al., 1973) has shown that the group does not revolve around the solitary sun of the leader. The real stars are the members themselves, as patients have indicated when they review their successful therapy group experiences and cite primary "curative factors" of relationships with other members—support, resolved conflict, acceptance, or most often, the experience of having been helpful to members (Butler & Fuhrman, 1980; Dickhoff & Lakin, 1963; Freedman & Hurley, 1979, 1980; Hill, 1975; Kapp et al., 1964; Long & Cope, 1980; Maxmen, 1973; Rohrbaugh and Bartels, 1975; Sherry & Hurley, 1976; Yalom, 1975).

Therefore, the counselor's responsibility is to create a social system in which the group and its members are the agents of change. This requires acute sensitivity to the location of responsibility in the group, particularly on how much is projected onto the counselor as perceived "leader" and how much the leader may blindly assume. It also requires that the counselor understand the stages of group development as these reflect group progress. This counselor can then help members learn about their own developmental process and encourage their active choice to progress as individuals and as a group toward creating the interdependence necessary for meeting their needs and achieving their goals. In all of the specific skills available for this facilitation of group process, the underlying strategy is encouraging members to take responsibility for their lives through learning to take responsibility for their counseling.

This concept of responsibility, as found in the works of Adler, Glasser, Frankl, and existential psychotherapy, has been studied extensively as an *"internal* locus of control" (expectancies of control over one's own life). These studies have identified *external* locus of control (wherein one sees life beyond one's control or responsibility) as correlates of failure identities and alienation (Hamsher, Geller, & Rotter, 1968; Joe, 1971; Lefcourt, 1976; Rotter, 1966). Several of these studies (Diamond & Shapiro, 1973; Felton & Biggs, 1972; Felton & Davidson, 1973; Foulds, 1971; Foulds, Guiran, & Worehing, 1974; Smith, 1980) support the hypothesis presented in this chapter: A basic point of individual growth process in life and in the intensive small group experience (such as the counseling group) is the development of an increased internal locus of control, or a sense of self-autonomy. When this autonomy is balanced with interdependence in responsible relations with others, the here-and-now social microcosm of the group becomes the reality for learning to be responsible for oneself in the there-and-then of one's wider social world. The challenge of one's growth becomes a friend and the security of alienation an enemy.

Therefore, the most salient point about problems in personal and social living is alienation, which is derangement of social (interpersonal) relationships. The capacity to form responsible relationships with others is the primary index of growth and development. The healthy person engages actively and responds freely in interpersonal transactions. Maintaining one's sense of self-identity and autonomy, this person enjoys close relationships and acknowledges the need for them. He or she belongs to groups and participates in group activities. This person recognizes his or her interdependence with others, with a sense of both support and challenge, and is capable of love and compassion.

The objective of group counseling, then, is enabling the person's capacity to enter into relationships. The person must be helped to free himself from the conflicts of autonomy and interdependence—through their balance in the individual and group process—and to assume responsibility for himself and others in mutual aid relationships. The counselor's function is to facilitate the process in which this can occur. The counselor influences the development of the group to the point that the person is able to risk closeness with others, to cooperate, and to find security in interpersonal relationships instead of in alienation.

This task requires that the counselor help group members balance all major points in their group experience—the members' autonomy, interdependence, and content. In Figure 1.1 these significant elements of the group process are labeled the "I-We-It triangle" (Cohn, 1972; Shaffer & Galinsky, 1974, pp. 242–264). This triangle provides the general framework for counseling through group process.

Autonomy and Interdependence in Group Counseling: "I-We-It" Triangle

The "I-We-It" triangle represents the significant elements of all interaction, such as in group process. The "I" encompasses the individual. "I" is the unique experience of each member at any one point in time in terms of needs, feelings, thoughts, and behavior. Without "I's" there would be no group. The "We" reflects the group. "We" is the interrelationships within the group at any one point in time and the awareness of members that they are a distinct, unique group with its own particular patterns of relationships, interconnections, and concerns. "At any one point in time" denotes that these concepts stand for processes that are changing moment to moment. Both the "I" and

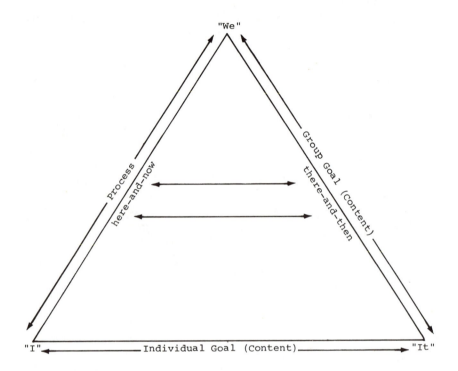

FIGURE 1.1   I-We-It triangle.

the "We" are developing in parallel and sequential stages throughout the group process. Therefore, the "I" aspect of the triangle symbolizes autonomy; the "We" aspect, interdependence.

The "It" point of the triangle refers to the individual and common goals, or the theme, for which the group meets. "It" determines much of the group's specific focus. Whether stated or not, "It" is always present in groups. For instance, the implicit theme of a counseling group in the beginning is often: "I want to feel and function better"; of an encounter group: "I want to get more in touch with the world inside me and outside me"; of a community action group: "I want more of this community's resources allocated to us." In effective counseling groups, common goals reflect individual goals in the "It" (the theme). This theme is clear and explicit. All effective groups balance their attention to all three points of this triangle. Ineffective groups arise when one or two points of this triangle are left un-attended for too long.

"Content" is a traditional term for what is here called "It"; whereas "process," which is often contrasted with "content," is embraced by the "I" and "We." All counseling groups attend to certain of these three points more than to others at times. Often in the early stage of group development, content, or "It," predominates. For example, parents of emotionally disturbed children in a counseling group might use much of their early time together talking about the difficult parental situations they share in common. While there is some attention to the "I" in this interaction (as members will likely include at least a few of their own personal thoughts and feelings about the problems they face at home with their specific children), the "It" may be in the forefront.

Later, "We" aspects may gain salience, as members engage in a discussion of what is happening in the group. For example, a female member of the parents' group might observe that it is the women in the group who have participated most; another might wonder whether this is because they, as mothers, feel more closely related to the child; and still another might suggest that the counselor is a woman and therefore they sense more support in the group. An incipient "I" focus may tinge this "We" at those moments when a member begins to elaborate on his or her personal reactions to the group process. The "I" focus, with minimal attention to the "We" or "It," occurs when an individual member, with little overt reference to either the stated theme or the other group members, talks about his or her life outside of the group.

In later group process, the content and process often coincide. Members dovetail thematic and interactional motifs in their here-and-now interaction. If "I-We-It" has been balanced earlier in group process and this dovetailing evolves, the group effectively assumes responsibility for mutual aid and members' growth. Let us say, for instance, that in the parents' group Jill describes herself as an over-protective parent. Jack then points out to her that he also sees her playing the "mother-hen" role in the group, trying to protect all other members from harm in any direct confrontation. Several other members agree, and one of them, Nancy, states that this behavior irritates her. At this point Jill begins to talk about her chronic anxiety, which she believes is related to her compulsive concern with the welfare of others. In this segment of the group scenario, the "I" (Jill and her anxious feeling in and out of the group), the "We" (the other members' feedback about her behavior in the group and the feelings this engenders in them), and the "It" (Jill's overly anxious treatment of her child) all intersect. We can sense the power and excitement of what Jill and other members learn through this interaction.

The "I," "We," and "It" are not all-or-none phenomena; they are a matter of more or less. For instance, at a point where a mother in the above group talks about the problems of all parents of emotionally disturbed children, she is relatively abstract and therefore primarily centered on the "It." Nevertheless, her statements include some inevitable (while diminished) attention to the concrete "I"; it is *her* statement and *her* thought. When she expresses her deeper feelings about her particular situation and her child, the "I" focus looms larger and balances more with the "It." When she leaves the content theme altogether and discusses an experience she had on the way to the group meeting that upset her, the "I" focus becomes even larger, while the "It" begins to diminish. If, after a few minutes, another member interrupts her in order to express current feelings toward her, the "We" focus, which has thus far remained fairly dormant but has always been there (after all, she is speaking in *this group*), starts to enlarge. In other words, while one or two of these triangle points may diminish or enlarge, they are all always present to some degree. Figure 1.1 diagrams the interrelationship of these points as they are omnipresent in the triangle of group process.

Conclusion

The "I" and the "We" are always directly related in the here-and-now TACIT dimension of group process. These are the points in which individual developmental themes (the "I") reciprocate and inter-weave with group developmental themes (the "We"). The counselor who understands the nature and characteristic of this development is in a position to help balance, through members' awareness, these triangular points in the group for facilitating members' social learn-ing and growth. This understanding and its use, as it develops re-sponsibility and combats alienation, is the purpose of this book.

Part I, which follows, presents the research foundation for the group counseling model of this text. It covers elements of the "I," the "We," and the "It" in counseling-like groups. Upon this foundation, I build the "counseling through group process" TACIT skill model in detail in Part II.

PART I
RESEARCH BASE

2

Member and Group Variables

In counseling we want to be effective. We want what we do to make a difference in the pain and suffering of others' lives. Any approach we learn for this awesome responsibility to contribute effectively to others' lives must promise some efficacy. But how are we to know what approach may be more effective than others—may help most and hurt least? The fact is that our help can be for better or for worse (Carkhuff, 1969). We need some knowledge which we can trust will help and, like the first principle of medicine, *primum non nocere,* "do no injury."

We do not have this knowledge with certainty. We do know from well-designed research, however, that some elements of group process and of the counselor's behavior in the group do make a difference both ways. That is, we have some empirical evidence of what contributes to members' growth as well as what contributes to injury in a wide variety of counseling-like groups. This chapter and the next two in Part I review this research as it has influenced the TACIT group counseling model.

The research selected here has met the rigors of scientific design and has considered how process elements (the group, the leader/counselor, and individual members) relate to outcomes (changes for good or for ill in members) (Fike, 1980; Parloff & Dies, 1978). There is a dearth of such research in the group counseling field, even while growth and counseling groups and those studying them have burgeoned.

Most of the research focuses on self-reports of group members and singularly on outcomes (Benson & Blocker, 1967) rather than on process–outcome relationships (Zimpfer, 1968). We have thousands of those who complete intensive small group experiences telling hundreds of students of these experiences that they are effective; at the least, they seem to provide members an opportunity for satisfying some relationship needs in contrast to too many other life experiences that offer little more than increasing awareness of their alienation. As Dunnette (1969) notes in referring to his extensive review (Campbell & Dunnette, 1968) of this loosely designed research of sensitivity training groups: "If we give evaluative weight to testimonial and antecdotal evidence and expressions of elation, we must conclude that the hopes of most participants have been more than fulfilled" (p. 28).

These testimonials and the self-reports of outcome-only research do reflect the power of an intensive small group experience. But all powerful instruments can be a double-edged sword, can remove or create the pain. More controlled research, however, suggests that these experiences are not the royal road to existential bliss for everyone, that actual outcomes tend to be more limited for most members, and that some members even become casualties. Those aspects of the group experience that this better-designed research finds are related to actual positive outcomes and to injuries are reviewed in this chapter and the next and are used as guidelines in the counseling methodology presented in the text. This review includes a variety of growth group or counseling-related group research. This chapter focuses on member and group variables. The next chapter reviews the findings relevant to the leader/counselor functions and roles.

Process and Outcome Variables

In general there have been three sets of independent variables studied in relation to therapeutic outcomes in this research (Fike, 1980; Parloff & Dies, 1978). These are: (1) the *members,* especially what they have brought to the group in particular personality characteristics and value and attitude orientations; (2) the *group,* especially such characteristics as size, methodology used, and aspects of group structure, group climate, and group process; and (3) the *leader/counselors,* especially their functioning and styles as these impact upon outcome. The outcomes studied have been changes in values and attitudes, self-concept, behavior, view of environment, and interpersonal orientations and relationships.

Outcomes

Most of these studies reveal that the major changes are in values, attitudes, and awareness toward the self, others, and the world, rather than in specific behavior (for major reviews of this research, see Anderson, 1969; Bednar & Lawlis, 1971; Buchanon, 1965; Campbell & Dunnette, 1968; Fullmer, 1971; Gazda & Peters, 1975; Gibb, 1970; Gundlach, 1967; Harrison, 1967; Lieberman et al., 1973; Ohlsen, 1970; Pattison, 1965). The greatest changes appear in values and attitudes. These self-attitudes include increased self-acceptance, self-esteem, and a sense of self-autonomy (felt more in charge of self). There tends to be more value placed on the "real self," on feelings, and on one's own growth toward self-actualization. In relation to others the greatest attitude increases are in trust and acceptance (Smith, 1979). There seems to be less stereotyping and more individualizing and humanizing of others and more acceptance and understanding of those who are different from one's self. Participants come to value openness with others more and person-to-person rather than role-to-role relationships. Similar attitude and value changes occur in relation to one's environment; there is an increase in valuing and perceiving opportunities for open communication with others in one's life situation and for environmental resources to meet one's needs.

The greatest behavioral changes reflect the living of some of these value and attitude changes. There is an increase in more trusting, open, and honest behavior. Each person hides less of himself as experienced inside, discloses this self more, and gives and requests more feedback in interpersonal relationships. There appear to be more behaviors oriented toward coping with problematic situations by confronting them and making choices rather than by denying or evading them. The studies also suggest that behavior changes may not be maintained for members as much as changes in values and attitudes, and some of the changes in openness and honesty may increase rather than solve interpersonal problems outside the group. The highest level of maintained openness seems related to those who perceive adaptive openness as curvilinear: too much or too little jeopardizes relationships with others. In keeping with the rule of the golden mean, they discovered a "happy medium" for openness in interpersonal relationships.

The Lieberman et al. (1973) study of 179 Stanford University studies in seventeen different growth groups researched most of these outcomes with similar findings to those studies of numerous others. They found that the most important and stable areas of change were in values and attitudes and in self. Participants were more likely to become change-oriented and growth-oriented. Their self-images moved toward perceiving themselves as more lenient and toward increased congruency between their ideal self and their real self. Behavioral changes appeared to be less stable. Although at termination participants had increased their coping adequacy and perceived their behavior as more interpersonally adequate, only the latter maintained the significant difference in the long run.

While their data on all participants reveal these changes as statistically significant, they also discovered that only 16 percent of those involved were high changers who increased in five or more of the outcome areas (values and attitudes; self-concept; behavior; view of environment; and view of others) without offsetting negative change. Nine percent were deemed as casualties from the group experience, that is, they were not just negative changers but were "psychologically injured."

In sum, intensive small group experiences, such as counseling and other growth groups, are supported by research as potentially effective. They increase members' awareness of their growth needs and the growth process in themselves, others, and their world, and enable members to learn to choose, on the basis of this awareness, to act differently to promote this process. Sometimes, too, they hurt more than they help some members. The research also suggests that the specific outcome—growth or injury—is related to what members bring to the group, what evolves in group process, and what the leader/counselor does to enable, obstruct, or harm. It behooves us to know what these variables are and how they contribute to positive or negative change in intensive small group experiences. Then we will have a stronger foundation on which to build our counseling approach for promoting growth and preventing casualties. We can be more effective.

Member Variables

There are certain characteristics which members bring to therapeutic groups that contribute to the positive or negative nature of what they may take from the experience. These include some significant *personality characteristics* (Abramowitz & Abramowitz, 1974; Baekeland & Lundwall, 1972; Bednar & Lawlis, 1971; Catrell, 1948; Koran & Cartell, 1973; Van Dyck, 1980; Woods & Melnick, 1979); *interpersonal needs* (Melnick & Woods, 1976; Schutz, 1958; Van Dyck, 1980; Woods & Melnick, 1979); and *expectations* for the experience (Bednar & Kaul, 1978; Frank, 1959; Melnick & Rose, 1979; Melnick & Woods, 1976; Taylor, 1954; Van Dyck, 1980; Woods & Melnick, 1979). The knowledge of these indicates some important guidelines for group composition, member orientation, and what has been called "pretraining" (Ahumada, Abiuso, Baigueura, and Gallo, 1974; Bednar &

Battershy, 1976; Bednar & Lawlis, 1971; Bednar, Melnick & Kaul, 1974; Cartwright, 1976; Curran, 1978; Gauron & Rawlings, 1975; Imber, Lewis & Loiselle, 1979; Piper, Doan, Edwards & Jones, 1979; Ribner, 1974; Rooney, 1975, 1977; Strupp & Bloxom, 1973; Waxer, 1977; Yalom, 1975).

Personality Characteristics.   Those most likely to benefit from an intensive small group experience have some sense of their evolving personality and identity and some willingness to venture change. There is enough personal identity to risk its exposure in the challenge of learning through experimentation with others (Melnick & Rose, 1979; Thelen & Harris, 1968). There are fears *and* also expressed wishes for becoming more aware of who one is, and can be, with others. The personality is in some flux and the person is at least dimly aware of this current process within (Abramowitz & Abramowitz, 1974). In brief, the person experiences and demonstrates some openness to know and understand his or her self better and to form and firm it more. This openness is the opening to the group and for the group.

Interpersonal Needs.   Interpersonally, the potentially growing member reflects some need to get closer to others. There is the need for belongingness and acceptance reflected in some behavior which reaches out to others, discloses, and seeks feedback. "Some" is used to indicate more than "none." The point is that at least the beginnings of the need for others is reflected in orientations toward others (Van Dyck, 1980; Woods & Melnick, 1979). The need, of course, is always there in human growth and development, but those who have defended against experiencing it so strongly that they verge on autistic relationships with others are not candidates for constructive group experiences. The stronger the awareness of and the acting on this need, as well as the awareness of the complexities and difficulties of getting closer to others, the higher the potential benefit for a member beginning a counseling group.

     Schutz (1958) views these interpersonal needs as inclusion and affection versus control in his FIRO model of personality. His research supports the importance of these needs in composition to maximize positive outcomes for members. Slavson (1951) labels these "social hunger" and presents this need as the primary variable for group composition. By this he refers to a basic reaching out for others, wanting to be with others more and alienated less, and having enough fidelity to connect through communication with group members (Stava & Bednar, 1979). These basic interpersonal needs also include some desire to gain insight, or awareness and conceptual understanding, about the self and others in interpersonal relationships (Woods & Melnick, 1979). In other words, one not only wants to learn about oneself but also wants to learn more about others and about people in general.

Expectations.   The expectations of those more likely to benefit from the group experience are not so incompatible with what the actual process may be (Frank, 1959). The difference most often is in expecting less rather than more of what might be accomplished. The research of those who achieved high outcomes and identify what contributed to them invariably show members noting a world of learning experiences in the group that exceeded original expectations: perceiving and conceiving self and others differently; feedback; a sense of interdependent community; being accepted; expressing strong emotions; taking responsibility for oneself, or a sense of mastery; and the sheer pleasure of being close to others and caring for them and being cared for by them (for review, see Hill, 1975). The major compatible expectation, however, is that the group is a medium through which one can learn how to relate and live. It is not perceived at first as real living but as the place to experiment with and learn different living outside of the group. This expectation appears to permit the member to use the experience in ways that can become more "real" than some of the life outside of the group as more of the real self (not the socialized role-related self) is expressed and accepted in the here and now of the group process. It is the member who expects to learn more about how the here-and-now events in the group can be transferred to the there-and-then world outside of the group who does so (Bednar & Kaul, 1978; Bugen, 1978).

Casualties

Casualties, as well as dropouts who often, too, may be casualties (Baekeland & Lundwall, 1972; Bednar & Kaul, 1978; Melnick & Woods, 1976; Rosenzweig & Folman, 1974), are psychologically injured primarily by aspects of leader/counselor behavior and group structure and process. However, these variables are involved in a subtle interplay with the individuals' personality characteristics, interpersonal needs, and expectations (De Julio, Bentley, & Cockayne, 1979; Grotjahn, 1972; Koran & Costell, 1973; Stava & Bednar,

1979; Woods & Melnick, 1979; Yalom, 1975). Knowledge of these and their use in group composition, orientation, and perhaps pretraining, as well as the counselor and group variables covered later, may prevent this psychological damage.

Personality Characteristics.   Those who have more potential to be harmed by an intensive small group experience tend to have a more rigid, closed, or controlled personality (Grotjahn, 1972). They hold firmly onto an identity that is not fluid, or they are experiencing so much flux that they have little sense of who they are or want to be (in the colloquial, they appear to be "dizzy" or "airheads"). The former tend to be extremely self-controlled and fearful of emotional expression in groups; the latter tend to be overstimulated by the emotional events (Taylor, 1959). Both types of personalities appear fearful of rejection yet often assume deviant, noncontacting roles in the group (Cartell, 1948; Haythorn et al., 1956; Koran & Costell, 1973; Woods & Melnick, 1979; Yalom, 1975).

Interpersonal Needs.   Their interpersonal needs reflect wishes for closeness but far more fears and therefore strong needs to control others and the situations in which they relate to others (Schutz, 1958). Their interpersonal goals often are unrealistic. They wish to break through a schizoid straitjacket to learn "to feel" and get more in contact with others while they fear getting in touch with their inevitable feelings and revealing certain things about themselves (Grotjahn, 1972). They hold on tightly to their controls in interpersonal relationships (and in the group), not disclosing, not reaching out to make more emotional contact, and not opening opportunities for feedback (Lee & Bednar, 1977). Out of this fear and their control of aspects of their feelings and themselves they tend to inhibit everything. Thus, they are stripped of their spontaneity and awareness and unconsciously monitor all their responses lest they let their "secrets" slip through.

Very often these "secrets" are their experiences of anger and fears of intimacy that seem very contrary to the group's norms for openness and honesty in disclosure, feedback, and other communication. The fears of anger and intimacy may be so distorted in expressions early in the group that rather than promote understanding they may invite rejection from other members or the leader/counselor. For instance, research suggests that some of this may be expressed as too early aggressive disclosure (a desperate attempt to break through) or as extreme concern about the group's expression of anger (from fearing one's own) or as expressing a desire for instant early intimacy (from fear of closeness and/or self-disclosure) (Bednar & Kaul, 1978; Lieberman et al., 1973; Melnick & Woods, 1976).

Expectations.   The beginning expectations of those who may become group casualties are unrealistic (Baekeland & Lundwell, 1972; Bednar & Kaul, 1978; Koran & Costell, 1973; Woods & Melnick, 1979). In brief these people most often expect dramatic, quick change. They expect the leader/counselor to enable their breakthroughs from control to feelings and spontaneity at the snap of his or her fingers. They expect other members to reach out to them to create instant intimacy without any anger, attack, or rejection and without their having to risk disclosing their fearful feelings and feared self. They expect the group to be a substitute for life outside, rather than a medium for learning to live differently in the outside world.

Unfortunately, the research demonstrates that these expectations are not clarified before the experience, that leaders/counselors and other members often react with rejection rather than support for these members' early forays into the group, and that while counselors/leaders do not seem aware of this harm to certain members to predict the casualty possibility, other members are almost always and accurately aware of this damage during the experience. Group members do know who is being hurt. In fact, the research on casualties to date suggests that the group members themselves rather than counselors knew best who were hurt (Schopler & Galinsky, 1981). As Lieberman et al. (1973) note in the part of their study of casualties and dropouts: "Thus, if a subject is perceived as having been hurt by more than one member of his group (or so perceived himself), it is highly probable that he represents a casualty of the group experience" (p. 176). Counselors need to use their own understanding and the members' perceptions more to prevent casualties and dropouts and to actualize maximally the potential of growth for all members. Both leaders/counselors and the group members in their process together greatly influence the positive and negative outcomes for participants. Let us now examine the research on how the group itself relates to these.

Group Variables

The group variables found most closely related to outcomes are the *structural* ones of group positions, statuses, roles, and norms; the *climate* ones of group involvement (or belongingness), intensity, and harmony (or warmth); and the *process* ones of cohesiveness, self-disclosure, feedback, empathy, and interdependent mutual aid. The research suggests that each of these variables either separately or in combination can significantly influence the group as a medium for learning. This learning, as related to these variables, again, can lead to personal and interpersonal growth or to increased awareness of alienation—that is, they can be for better or for worse.

Structural Variables

Position. Position is one's place in the group, as perceived by both one's self and by others. Members experience position, and it is measured by how "in" or "out" of the group they perceive themselves to be. Basically, there are central, peripheral, and outside positions in groups (Leavitt, 1951). Those in the center and on the immediate periphery and outer edges who move toward the center during the group experience have access to the growth-promoting group resources. Their chances for positive change are high. Those on the outside, in positions of the neglected "isolate" or the rejected "scapegoat," do not have access to these resources. If they are not brought "in," their chances of growth are very low and the chances of injury very high.

Status. Status relates to position but refers specifically to the rank one gives oneself and is given by other members in the group. Status is also experienced (and measured) by what rank an individual member assigns himself and is assigned by other memebers of the group as compared with these others. In general there can be high-, middle-, and low-status members in all groups. The specific status is usually closely correlated with one's position and roles and the group norms (Cartwright, 1951). As members assume positions and roles which promote and establish group norms, they tend to be granted and to perceive certain statuses. High-status members in the group experience higher self-esteem; low-status members experience painful self-doubts. Casualty often relates to members with high self-esteem needs having low status and therefore extreme threats to their basic self-confidence and feelings of worth. Members who learn that everyone, including themselves, can get higher and more equal status by assuming helping roles, coming "in" or involving themselves in the group, and living up to the group norms seem to change more positively. If any member has both an outside position and very low status for any length of time in the group, the odds are extremely high that he or she will drop out, feel a failure, and be hurt.

In regard to both statuses and positions, the research demonstrates that members are sensitively and accurately aware of who is ranked where and who appears to be valued more or less by themselves and others. Leaders/counselors very often are not. For effective groups leaders/counselors either must be more aware of these structural variables, as experienced and perceived by members, or discover from members what is happening, or both.

Roles. Roles are the behavioral expectations one has for oneself and perceives others to have for one in conjunction with particular positions and statuses (Cartwright, 1951). In general there are active–passive, leader–follower, and influencer–deviant role continua in groups. It is through assuming one's roles as these meet needs and help to achieve group goals that one experiences whether one belongs or not in the group. In small groups, the research indicates that high positive change comes from members' sharing roles which support group norms, influence the group's work, and permit spontaneous, authentic, and frequent activity (Ohlsen & Pearson, 1965). In other words, for positive outcomes all members need at times to assume active, leader, norm-influencing roles and receive other members' support for these. Those who assume passive, follower, and/or deviant roles for any length of time and are entrenched in these by other members' expectations do not achieve positive outcomes. They do not experience belongingness to the group. In fact the research of members' roles and statuses indicates that high changers increase their active, leader, influencer roles during the growth group experience (Lieberman et al., 1973). Negative changers and casualties decrease these roles. The role variable most predictive of failure in these groups is the combination of deviance and a low sense of belongingness. To be perceived as and to perceive oneself as a "nobody" in a group of "somebodies" is a personally devastating experience which must be prevented in every possible way by group leaders/counselors.

Norms. Norms are the shared ideas of appropriate behavior in a particular social system (Psathas & Hardert, 1966). In groups, norms are the members' consensus of what best protects their fears and promotes their wishes in relation to what they do in movement toward goals. Norms are often measured by a high proportion (such as two-thirds) of members' agreement on what "do's" and "don'ts" are "in force" in the group. Norms are also related closely to positions, statuses, and roles. The leader and high-status members are often in positions to influence most the establishment and changing of norms and often embody the most significant norms in their behavior. In effective groups all members influence these norms, and this influence relates to their more central positions, equal statuses, and active leadership roles, which reciprocate with developing norms supportive of this equality and opportunity structure.

Group norms do significantly relate to positive and negative changes in growth groups. As Lieberman et al. (1973) express it: "Norms *do* make a difference in the prediction of outcomes—a contribution at least as powerful as that of specific leader [counselor] behavior" (p. 270). The norms which contribute most to member growth are those of member peer control (versus leader/counselor control) of the group. Peer control norms disapprove of both domination and withdrawal by any member and permit loose boundaries for what are appropriate content and behavioral ranges. Groups with norms which permit the discussion of there-and-then as well as here-and-now material have higher yields, as well as those that approve of a range of intimacy-seeking behavior and support more moderate expression of emotions and of more hostile, judgmental confrontations. Also, groups with a larger number of norms, regardless of the content of these norms, tend to have higher changers and lower casualties. In sum, norms which support members to be honestly and spontaneously who they are yet challenge them to change in behalf of their needs and the needs of the group help each member a great deal and very likely will not hurt any of them in the process.

Most significantly related to negative change and casualty are norms against peer control. When leader-control norms dominate, growth is limited and some members are highly vulnerable to injury. It appears that in growth and counseling groups the member-control, or peer-oriented, norms which prohibit manipulation and domination, discourage withdrawal and indifference, and promote an open and equal opportunity structure may well be needed to protect members from negative outcomes or injury. The medium for change and growth needs to be the group members' psychosocial relationship processes with each other. Norms need to support this interdependent mutual aid system.

The research on growth group norms also indicates the leader/counselor relationship to their development and contribution to outcomes (Hall & Watson, 1970; Lieberman et al., 1973; Psathas & Hardert, 1966). For instance, if the counselor's expected norms become the actual group norms, groups have a higher potential for members' growth. If the counselor's expectations and members' expectations of the group experience closely match, they have a high probability of becoming the group's norms and of influencing a higher growth yield (De Julio et al., 1979). Counselors/leaders appear to be able to obstruct the development of group norms and harm some members, but they do not seem to be able to fully impose their own norms onto the group if these do not match members' expectations. Counselor influence on group norm development tends to be largely restricted to strengthening existing members' expectations for the group or to converting uncertain expectations into decisive group norms. This research strongly suggests the importance of early clarification and negotiation of counselor and members' expectations in forming an explicit contract, including possible normative "ground rules" for the group (Hall & Watson, 1970). The importance of this contract and attention to member peer-oriented and open-boundary norms is weighted even more by one other finding in relation to growth group norms: they are the most systematically related variable to the actual behavioral changes of members. Members must act in the group as they might outside for the group to make a difference in what members *do* in learning from it. Group norms, if appropriately developed, provide both support and challenge for this experimentation with behavior that might be viewed as more appropriate, problem-solving, need-meeting, and growth-promoting in the wider social worlds.

Climate Variables

Involvement. Involvement refers to the members' investment in the group. It reflects their commitment to membership and their sense of belonging. A group in which most or all members have a high level of involvement is a group that takes on significance for members and therefore becomes a potent resource for influencing them (Bassin, 1962; Mezzano, 1967). The climate for growth and development or for painful rejection is more intense.

If this involvement builds a climate for acceptance and belonging, there is more potential for members taking the risks to open the doors to change and possible growth (Scheidlinger, 1964). Research (Lieberman et al., 1973) demonstrates that the sense of belonging and involvement of members does not necessarily guarantee successful outcomes for them. The lack of belongingness and low levels of one's own and others' involvement does, however, correlate highly with failure in growth groups.

Intensity. Intensity is a climate variable that refers to the level of emotional expressiveness (Snortum & Myers, 1971). High-intensity groups ignite spontaneous interchange of anger, fear, pain, grief, love, and joy. Low-intensity groups spark only surface feelings in expression. A certain level of emotional intensity appears to be necessary for change. If the climate is not intense enough, members do not risk deeper emotional disclosures and do not make the affectual investment so vital for corrective emotional experiences and for shifts in behavior and self-concepts (Bach, 1965). Intensity best creates a climate for change when it increases during the development of the group (Levine, 1971; Zimpfer, 1967). Too much emotional intensity early in the group creates churning and excitement but also fears and hurts which prevent the necessary trust and stable relationships necessary for a "corrective emotional experience," or the acceptance and closeness responses to the expressions of feelings. Once a solid, coherent group has evolved, this intensity seems a necessary variable in the climate for change.

Harmony. Harmony is the experience of warmth in the atmosphere of group members' relationships (Zimpfer, 1967). It reflects a basic mutual regard for each member and such factors as compatibility, congeniality, fellowship, friendship, and cooperation. This variable is closely related to cohesiveness and includes the sense of group bond and consensus. Harmony does not imply no conflict, as conflict is inevitable in all group process (Cowger, 1979; Frank, 1955; Hulse, 1950). It does, though, include an underlying agreement to disagree—to face conflicts, stick them out, and resolve them in a way that benefits all parties involved and the group as a whole. In growth and counseling groups, research demonstrates that when anger is expressed early and is lessened later and harmony develops, there is higher group yield (Gazda & Peters, 1975; Lungren, 1977). Conversely, sustained intense anger and conflict and low harmony are greatly related to low group yield and to members' getting psychologically injured. These are important climatic conditions of the group.

Process Variables

Cohesiveness. Cohesiveness refers to members' feelings about the group, particularly the feelings of the group's specialness and their attraction to it. Cohesiveness is most often measured by an aggregate score of individual attraction measures. A cohesive group takes on significance for members as the *sine qua non* of growth and change.

In the therapeutic research, cohesiveness has been found analogous to the relationship in individual counseling or therapy (Yalom, 1975). It establishes the foundation and is the medium in which problem solving and growth occur. In the major experimental studies of growth and counseling groups (Anderson, 1978; Bednar & Lawlis, 1971; Dies & Hess, 1971; Evans & Jarvis, 1980; Frank, 1957, 1959; Heckel, Holmes, & Rosencrans, 1971; Lieberman et al., 1973; Taylor, 1958; Yalom, 1975; Yalom & Rand, 1966), cohesiveness appears as a most significant independent variable related to positive or negative outcomes. The movement to higher rather than lower cohesiveness during the development of the group tends to assure group effectiveness. Low-cohesive groups, or groups which begin with relatively high cohesiveness and drop sharply during the process (especially found in groups where leaders/counselors use structured exercises extensively for group activity), tend to assure negative change and casualties.

Some other significant findings in relationship to cohesiveness have been discovered in this research. Two studies (Anderson, 1978; Lieberman et al., 1973) report that the presence of the cohesiveness variable in group process has a beneficial effect on outcome, independent of leader/counselor style or methodology. That is, the best protection from ineffective and potentially harmful leaders/counselors for the group is the development of its own cohesiveness. One study found cohesiveness very closely related to members' feelings of being understood by other members (Anderson, 1978). In this study it did not matter whether, in fact, members were actually understood by others. What mattered most and correlated greatly with cohesiveness and positive outcomes was that they *felt* understood—they believed that others in the group were capable of understanding them. It appears that only in cohesive groups does this dynamic of basic trust and closeness take place and provide the catapult for risking and experimenting with change and potential growth (Evans & Jarvis, 1980). All the relevant research confirms that this cohesiveness is strongly, significantly, and independently related to group yield. It could be that the greatest skills a counselor can have in working with groups are those which enable the group to develop its processes toward cohesiveness.

Self-disclosure.   Self-disclosure is the expression of intense personal feelings and the sharing of deeply personal material in the group. Most often, this refers to feelings and material in the here and now. The research of this process variable indicates that it is not independently related to outcomes (Anchor, 1979; Cozby, 1973). In connection with other processes, however, it tends to be a mechanism of change in group process (Brammer & Shostrom, 1976; Culbert, 1968). For instance, the findings do not support emotional expressivity per se as a major growth dynamic (Anchor, 1979). Members tend to feel better about themselves when they express intense personal feelings and do believe in *post hoc* reports that this expressivity was instrumental to their growth. This correlation is not supported by the research, which suggests rather that feeling expression is a clearing of the underbrush, an opening of the path to growth, that must then be traveled for fruition. The member needs to have these feelings responded to in a "corrective emotional experience" (Frank & Ascher, 1954) of new insight into the self and others and to *work* for this growth.

Likewise, the disclosure of deeply personal material appears to have utility only within the interpersonal context in which it occurs. It seems most useful for change and growth when this self-disclosure is understood, appreciated, and accurately interpreted by the group (Anderson, 1978). It becomes dialogue. Then, the perspective gained from this material, the new cognitive insight, appears to make a difference in terms of learning from self-disclosure.

Self-disclosure, when effective, is also closely related to autonomy. As members develop their autonomy in the group and begin to experience themselves as masters of their own fate within and outside (Diamond & Shapiro, 1973), they are more likely to engage in the self-disclosure which helps them to achieve some cognitive mastery over their own actions (Bean & Houston, 1978). This disclosure, then, is marked by increased awareness, insight, responsibility, and choice. This choice is more likely to be based on one's will to grow and will promote this growth.

Conversely, intense self-disclosure based on early dependency rather than autonomy can be disastrous for members. It can lead to embarrassment, shame, doubt, and self-effacing without the group ready to understand, appreciate, and empathize with these feelings and material. It almost tends to assure a group casualty (Anchor, 1979). Leaders/counselors would do well to prevent this early extreme exposure of members rather than to encourage it out of a misguided belief that intense emotional expression of deep personal material is always good for the group and for individual members. The sparks that this inappropriate disclosure creates may set fire to the group momentarily but may burn forever in the pain of those who are left exposed and not understood.

Feedback. Feedback generally refers to giving information to others about one's perception of them and to the receiving of such information about oneself (Jacobs, 1974). In the research, the focus is on feedback as the process of receiving information about oneself from others—information that the receiver believes is important and useful (Berzon, Pious, & Farson, 1963; Yalom, 1975). Participants in growth group experiences almost universally rank feedback in conjunction with cathartic self-disclosure high (second only to cohesiveness) in their assessment of helping mechanisms in the group (Butler & Fuhriman, 1980; Freedman & Hurley, 1979, 1980; Hill, 1975; Long & Cope, 1980; Maxmen, 1973; Rohrbaugh & Bartels, 1975; Sherry & Hurley, 1976; Yalom, 1975). Feedback can be positive, negative, or generally neutral (as in advice or cognitive information). In actual outcomes, feedback does not relate directly to results (Clark & Culbert, 1965). There is, however, a trend for high changers receiving a mixture of positive and negative feedback and for those with little or negative change to receive mostly negative or cognitively oriented feedback, if any (Martin & Jacobs, 1980). Feedback is a process mostly tapped as a mechanism of change when it follows self-disclosure. When self-disclosure precedes rather than follows feedback, more likelihood of change ensues. This difference in the effectiveness of feedback stems in all probability from the fact that using one's autonomy to increase awareness and to achieve cognitive mastery (self-disclosure) to arrive at self-understanding with the help of others is a different experience than achieving such understanding through the action of others (feedback). Furthermore, feedback is most useful when one is ready for it, as reflected in self-disclosure (Goldstein, Bordnar, & Yandell, 1979). The leader/counselor would do well to reach for feedback in the group when the member has extended his or her hand in readiness through self-disclosure.

Empathy. Empathy is the ability to put oneself in another's skin and life space and to perceive the world as the other does. Empathy is the wings of care, concern, or love (Chessick, 1965). In research it is defined and measured as perceiving another at least as accurately as the other perceives him- or herself (Carkhuff, 1969). In groups it extends to accurate perception of the differences between the self and other members and among other members and therefore is open to individualized information about each person (Dunnette, 1969; Scheidlinger, 1964). The research on the development of empathy processes in groups (Anderson, 1978; Carkhuff, 1969; Dunnette, 1969; Myers et al., 1969) indicates a relationship of greater empathy to higher outcomes. Empathy correlates highly with cohesiveness but tends to be a separate process for what members achieve (Anderson, 1978). In fact, one of the major outcomes from growth and counseling groups might be transferring learned empathy to interpersonal relationships outside of the group (Anderson, 1978). Being the recipient of empathy increases growth, but high changers are those who learn to be givers—who develop their own ability to empathize (Anderson, 1978; Carkhuff, 1969; Lieberman et al., 1973). Lieberman et al. (1973) discovered, for instance, that "a major distinction . . . is that learners appeared to be people who could take the role of others, who could step into another person's shoes and feel with him, as well as get some perspective for themselves through this process and some useful analogies to their own cases" (p. 376). In other words, high changers develop their ability to empathize through group process.

Empathy, as well as the other group process variables, strongly supports the hypothesis that the essence of the small group experience and the major agent for change is the group itself—the members' psychosocial relationships with each other and the system they build together. Together, they compose the environment for learning and growth in the group. Leaders/counselors must not only model this empathy in their behavior in the group but must reach for, permit, and expect the development of empathy in all members if the group is to be an effective environment for interpersonal learning and the agent of individual growth.

Self-disclosure invites the feedback which triggers and increases this empathy. The empathy, in turn, triggers the deepening of cohesiveness and the climate variables of involvement, intensity, and harmony. It blazes the trail for the process of interdependent mutual aid. To be effective in the group, empathy must be active. Feeling understanding of another is not enough. This understanding must be expressed for the other to be understood. Again, the key dynamic in growth is increased awareness; in empathy, this awareness includes increased understanding of others as well as of oneself.

Interdependent Mutual Aid. Mutual aid is a phrase first coined by Kropotkin (1925) in his study of animal and human evolution. It refers to the basic interdependence between the person and the group that he found in species that have survived and progressively developed in evolution. In therapeutic group research, interdependent mutual aid has been examined as a basic curative factor in group process under the concept of "altruism," which refers both to a group process and the unique social climate experienced in the therapeutic group (Dreikurs, 1951). The research on curative factors relates altruism to cohesiveness (Hill, 1975). It refers to a "being together" in such terms as "the group helps me because it is good to belong to a group of people that is together and cares about each person in the group" (Long & Cope, 1980, p. 393). This variable moves from being helped to be together (cohesiveness) to being helped *by being together*. Altruism is experiencing one's own role in the group as being helpful to others and contributing to a climate in which the major norms are helping and being helped. Mutual aid is dependent upon whose needs are most dominant, not on the dominance of particular positions, statuses, and roles embedded in group structure. The structure here is based on equity and interdependence and evolves from these needs of both members and the group as a whole.

The operational definition and measurement of altruism requires members to rate such statements as "Giving part of myself to others"; "Helping others and being important in their lives"; "Forgetting myself and thinking of helping others"; "Putting others' needs ahead of mine"; and "Helping others has given me more self-respect" (Yalom, 1975, p. 78). Graduates of growth groups rate these factors most highly as curative processes for them (Hill, 1975; Long & Cope, 1980). While less highly ranked, these curative factors are also revealed as important by patients who leave psychotherapy groups (Yalom, 1975). Groups with the development of high levels of interdependent mutual aid, as perceived by members, have higher yield (Lieberman et al., 1973); those with low levels produce negative change and injury. Leaders/counselors need to find ways to help the group tap its potential for the evolution of this mutual aid system.

Conclusion

These group process variables together constitute the major "curative factors" in successful groups. Whether these factors have been studied by data derived from outside judges (Berzon et al., 1963), from leaders/counselors (Corsini & Rosenberg, 1955), or from members themselves (Dickhoff & Lakin, 1963; Yalom, 1975), they support the notion that the agent of change is truly the group. The effective group is one that moves toward cohesiveness, self-disclosure, feedback, empathy, and interdependent mutual aid. These processes flow as the sea against the sands of members' growth needs, rippling into streams of awareness of the contact boundaries of the waves on the shore—the self in relation to others.

The leader/counselor can enable or obstruct this flow. If we stay with the metaphor of the sea, the leader/counselor can dig some paths in the sand through which the ripplets of waves may flow and can illuminate the process by encouraging those on the beach to stop, look, and listen—to grow more aware. Or the leader/counselor can pile up the sand and harden it to the point that the remainder of the ebb and flow of the tide is dammed. When he or she enables and illuminates these core group processes, the group works and the members grow; when he or she obstructs them, the group falters and members not only do not grow, they can be damaged. The next chapter reviews the research on the leader/counselor variable in group process with special attention to what is done that promotes, restricts, or harms the growth of the group and its members.

3

Leader/Counselor Variables

What leader/counselors do has great impacts on the group experience. These behaviors have been comprehensively studied experimentally by Lieberman et al. (1973). They found particular leader styles reflected in those who assumed basic leader/counselor functions to different degrees. They also discovered how these functions related to outcomes. While other studies are included (Ashkenas & Tandon, 1979; Gurman & Gustafson, 1976; Parloff, Waskow, & Wolfe, 1978; Peters & Beck, 1982; Schopler & Galinsky, 1981; Sibergeld, Thune, and Manderschied, 1979; Truax & Mitchell, 1971; Weinberg et al, 1981; Winter, 1976), this chapter primarily summarizes the Lieberman et al. (1973) findings. In addition, the use of structured experiences with groups has been studied as a correlate to group outcomes (Anderson, 1980). This research, too, is considered as it delineates what the counselor can do and can try not to do to enable group process in behalf of members.

Leader/Counselor Style and Functions

What leader/counselors do in specific situations does not make a significant difference in group process. Rather, their general stance toward group process and their style has impact on the group for good or ill. This style relates to four basic leadership functions which Lieberman et al. (1973) discovered by factor analyzing all of the behavior of the leaders/counselors in the therapeutic groups that they studied. All of the specific behaviors of these leaders/counselors clustered statistically into these four functions, and their particular style reflected the consistency of carrying out these functions. These functions are: emotional stimulation, meaning attribution, caring, and executive function. The definition and description of basic leader/counselor behavior within each of these functions is presented below.

This section is followed by the findings of how these functions related to outcomes. These functions, as carried out to various degrees by leaders/counselors, further factor into six different types or styles of leadership. These styles are then presented and reviewed as they relate to outcomes of both positive change and casualties. This review then concludes with an examination of the research on the use of structured experiences or exercises by leaders/counselors as these tools have gained prevalence in leader behavior in groups. Finally, the chapter considers the major implications for practice desired from the research reviewed in Chapters 2 and 3.

Functions

Emotional Stimulation. The emotional stimulation function is used to catalyze the expression of feelings in the group to spark intensity in group climate and carthartic experiences for members. Most often the leader/counselor behaviors within this function are those directed toward releasing emotions by demonstration. High risk is modeled by expressing anger, warmth, or love. The leader/counselor's own self-disclosure, if used frequently and with intensity, functions to create a leader-centered experience wherein the major interactions are between the leader/counselor and individual group members and the rest of the group tend to be spectators to this main event. The leader/counselor uses his or her own charismatic influence to make the sparks fly and to fire the group through intensive emotions. Moderate use of this function reflects less frequent and consistent self-disclosure. There is more reaching for others' feelings and emotional interchange among members to energize them and the group as a whole.

Meaning Attribution. The meaning attribution function is used to teach members to develop awareness and cognitive insight into themselves, others, and the group. It includes processing what is occurring and helping to give meaning to group events. The high use of this function reflects frequent and consistent behavior that is directed toward interpreting experienced reality. The leader/counselor provides concepts for how to understand, explain, clarify, and interpret behavior and events. He or she names feelings and translates these feelings and emotional interchanges into concepts (or cognitive insights) about the self, others, and people in general. He or she also provides conceptual frameworks for how members and the group can change. The meaning attribution function requires that the leader/counselor's expertise about human behavior and growth and about group process and growth is offered to the group as a resource for its needs. He or she does not teach in the traditional sense of "lecture-listen" but serves to guide members' experiential and cognitive learning.

Caring. The caring function is used to provide support to the group and its members through establishing a basic nurturing relationship. The leader/counselor who frequently and consistently provides this caring function expresses considerable warmth, acceptance, genuineness, and a real concern for all members. He or she acts on this expressed concern by protecting members from harm; offering friendship, love, and affection; and frequently inviting members to seek feedback as well as support, praise, and encouragement. The behaviors are group- and member-centered and not leader-centered. A low-level caring function is assumed by those leaders/counselors who remain aloof, who place total responsibility for what happens onto the group and then abandon it, and/or who support certain members who act up to their expectations of behavior in the group and reject others. The caring behaviors often function to express actively that "I'm O.K. and you're O.K. and if we use this support to challenge each other to grow, we'll all become more O.K." This message is not only delivered by the leader/counselor, but received by the group members.

Executive Function. The executive function is used to direct the group into certain behaviors that the leader/counselor deems important for change. The leader/counselor who frequently and consistently carries this executive function sets limits, suggests rules, establishes goals, sets norms or directions for movement, and manages time—sequencing, pacing, stopping, blocking, interceding, and so on. He or she also often invites or elicits and questions; gives many suggestions for exercises and procedures; requests feeling expressions through questions and suggestions rather than through demonstration; and asks the group to process and interpret its reality rather than provides concepts for illuminating meaning. High executive function is similar to the director of the play, who already knows the script, has the scenario planned out in his or her own mind, and now must have the actors strut their parts to his or her satisfaction. Low executive function is the laissez-faire message to the group that they are free to "do their own thing," and if they are overwhelmed with frustration and fail, it is their own faults. Moderate executive function is more like the navigator on a ship that the group itself sails. The leader/counselor keeps some firmness of direction against the rough and changing winds and sea and guides the ship safely toward its destination as the members themselves control the sails. This direction comes from knowing the territory and the map of it and suggesting from this expertise how the ship may proceed, feeding back when the compass reveals that members have sailed off course; where they are; and what they can do to get where they want to go faster. The navigator becomes the captain only when the members are abandoning the sails and/or threatening an internal mutiny, which can drown them all in the deep sea of discouragement or wash them up with exhaustion on a deserted shore. The moderate director first waits to see whether the floundering, off-course group will find its own will to captain the ship again and rediscover their direction by using the help of the navigator before he or she grabs the helm.

Relationship of Functions to Outcomes. Lieberman et al. (1973, pp. 226–267) found a direct relationship of these leader/counselor functions to outcomes. Effective leaders/counselors (those with groups of high changers and low or no casualities) were high in caring and meaning attribution and moderate in use of emotional stimulation and executive function. The curvilinear, or "golden mean," relationship of emotional stimulation and executive function to outcomes indicates that there is a medium use of these required for effectiveness. Both too little and too much use contributed to negative outcomes. Too little of both resulted in a laissez-faire group in which members floundered and played too safe to change. Too much of both created a highly charged leader-centered group in which change was low but casualties were high. The leader/counselor risks wasting members' time when these are not used much and risks harming members when these are used extensively. Effective counselors must understand these functions and the nature of their moderate use in enabling group process.

Caring was a central function in members' growth. The data analysis concludes that the more caring, the better. All of the effective leaders consistently carried out the caring function. Similarly, effective leaders/counselors used at least moderate, at best high, meaning attribution. On the other hand, ineffective leaders/counselors (those with groups of low changers, negative changers, and casualties) were routinely neglectful of assuming the meaning attribution function. In fact, high meaning attribution was the most significant function in the Lieberman et al. (1973) study. They discovered that while the caring function is critical (the higher, the better), high meaning attribution and moderate caring are more effective than high caring and low meaning attribution.

These functions determine particular leader/counselor styles in groups. The different degrees of consistently carrying out each of these functions create a cluster of six basic styles. Lieberman et al. (1973) label leaders/counselors with these styles as (1) providers, (2) social engineers, (3) energizers, (4) laissez-faires, (5) impersonals, and (6) managers.

Styles

These six leader/counselor styles are described in Table 3.1 by the degree of assumption of each of the four functions (H = High; M = Moderate; L = Low) and related to the change (H, M, L) and casualty (H, M, L) outcomes.

Again, the most effective style was that of the providers, who were high in meaning attribution and caring behaviors and moderate in emotional stimulation and executive function. They enabled high change with low to no casualties. Next were social engineers, who were high in both meaning attribution and caring, moderate in executive function, and low in emotional stimulation. They, too, enabled high change but contributed to more casualties. The only

TABLE 3.1
Leader/Counselor Styles by Order of Effectiveness

Style	Function				Outcome	
	Meaning Attribution	Caring	Emotional Stimulation	Executive	Degree of Change	Degree of Casualty
Providers	H	H	M	M	H	L
Social engineers	H	H	L	M	H	M
Energizers	L	H	H	H	M	H
Laissez-faires	M	L	L	L	L	L
Impersonals	L	L	H	L	L	M
Managers	L	L	H	H	L	H

other style which influenced change was that of the energizers. They were high in caring, emotional stimulation, and executive function, but low in meaning attribution. They valued experience and made things happen through leader-centered dynamics. Their groups had moderate change but at the cost of relatively high casualties. None of the other styles were effective, but laissez-faires (moderate on meaning attribution and low on all other functions) did less harm. Impersonals, who stimulated emotional expression but did not assume much of the other functions, did moderate harm while not effecting positive change. Manager styles are the most dangerous of all. Managers were high in emotional stimulation and in executive function and low in meaning attribution and caring. They influenced the most dependent, leader-centered groups wherein members were directed toward intense emotional expressions almost for their own sake and then were left hanging, on the rope the managers had made into a noose. As expected, their groups had very little positive change, high negative change, and high casualties.

This research finds support in other studies of leader/counselor behaviors. Scheidlinger (1980a), after an extensive review of the theory and research, concluded that the ingredients of the effective group leader/counselor are somewhere on the axis between genuine empathy and caring and an organized cognitive theory of growth and development which is communicated to members. Other research (Singer & Goldman, 1954; Tompkins 1972; Weinberg, Hall, Samuels & Dale, 1981; Winter, 1976) discovered leader/counselor style related to members' development of involvement and cohesiveness. Those leaders/counselors who used more group-centered caring and democratic learning styles and less leader-centered executive structuring and emotionally stimulating styles increased member involvement and group cohesiveness, which, in turn, increased positive outcomes. These studies suggest that some leader-initiated (or executive) structure is initially helpful but, if not curtailed in favor of group-centered functions, is detrimental in the long term.

One of these studies (Singer & Goldman, 1954) discovered that emotional stimulation, if overused, can actually decrease, rather than increase, involvement. It defeats one of the basic purposes for which it is designed. This finding is especially strong in the detrimental use of emotional stimulation and executive functions as attempts to draw in silent members and to increase their level of participation in the group. This research suggests that leaders/counselors need not be so desperate to break through silence as has historically been the case. The uninvolved group member, not the silent one, may best receive the attention of leaders/counselors. The degree of emotional involvement in the group, as evidenced by body movements, facial expressions, and other nonverbal communication during the critical hours of the group's therapeutic events, are the best guide to this involvement, rather than the number of comments made or not made by any particular member. The research clearly demonstrates that this involvement, not the level of verbal participation per se, is the key variable to a member's gain in therapy, growth, and counseling groups.

The research by Carkhuff (1969) and Truax (1961; Truax, Carkhuff, & Kolman, 1965) also attests to the singular importance of the effect of leader/counselor caring on the group process and its outcomes. In a series of well-designed studies, this research significantly demonstrated that high levels of leader/counselor empathy, warmth, and genuineness were predictive of successful outcomes. Equally predictive were high levels of these among members in the group process. A group climate of high levels of empathy, warmth, and genuineness contributed to high cohesiveness and interdependent mutual aid (Dickenson & Truax, 1966; Truax 1968a & b; Truax & Carkhuff, 1967), which, in turn, increased favorable outcomes (Truax & Carkhuff, 1967). It appears that the leader's shadow does loom large over the group and sets the tone for the behaviors of members. Those leaders who project high levels of caring (through empathy, warmth, and genuineness) and meaning resonate with the members' ability to care and to learn. Together, they produce results.

There were some other interesting, and perhaps informative, findings about the leader/counselor style as related to outcomes in the Lieberman et al. (1973) study. Two of the groups were leaderless in that they were instructed by a tape recorder. The taped directions had built in high support for intermember caring, high meaning attribution, moderate executive function, and low levels of emotional stimulation. These groups were the third and eighth highest yield groups of the seventeen and the safest of all. In both groups there were a high proportion of moderate change for members and no casualties. This finding, corroborated in other studies that compared leaderless to leader/counselor groups (Anderson, 1978), is a humbling one for those of us who work with groups. The functions themselves appear more important for outcomes than having a leader/counselor present to carry them out. There is some truth to this, but the day is far away, if ever, that computers and other machines can replace us as counselors. Provider-led groups had by far the greatest proportion of the highest changers and very low casualties in this study (Lieberman et al., 1973). Also, the greatest outcomes related to specific leader/counselor styles were in the realm of members' changes in values and attitudes. The tape-led groups were lowest in their overall changes (most of which were moderate in degree) in this very area of values and attitudes. It would appear that leaders/counselors especially make a difference in the group when the functions they carry out and the style through which these functions are manifested live the values and attitudes that members can learn in the group and transfer to life outside. As leaders/counselors embody high caring and meaning-seeking as well as moderate value for and expression of feeling and use of structure, members learn to carry out these functions themselves in the group process and in their own life process.

Another finding was that effective leaders (the providers) and the tape-led groups influenced interpersonal outcomes and self-esteem most. Members of these groups felt a greater sense of their own autonomy and adequacy and were more accepting of others and willing to establish interdependent relationships with them. The two most important group process variables that these members attributed to their growth were feedback and cohesiveness, or closeness.

In these groups members truly discovered that they themselves and others are people rather than stereotypes in positions, statuses, and roles. The group, through its members, unlike a group centered on the leader/counselor, became the real agent of change.

Finally, Lieberman et al. (1973) also report an alarming finding in their data. *The leaders/counselors rated the highest in competency by members were the least effective in actuality!* These leaders/counselors were those high in both emotional stimulation and executive function. They used an extraordinary amount of structured exercises to carry out these functions. The members of their groups, including some of their high casualties, became their proselytes. They manifested conversion behavior and perceived themselves as "turned-on" by a "together," "charismatic" leader. This startling finding of the power of the leader/counselor and his or her structured exercise techniques to fulfill members' needs for a fantasied omnipotent leader (who in actuality may be hurting them more than helping them) warrants special attention to the use of structured exercises in groups.

Leader/Counselor and Structured Exercises

Definition

There has been more theory than research on the use of structured exercises, or experiences, in groups (Anderson, 1980). A structured exercise is the leader/counselor's intervention in group process that involves a set of specific orders, instructions, or prescriptions. These prescriptions specify certain group members' behavior alternatives at a particular moment in the group. For example if the leader/counselor says, "Pick out the member of the group you feel most different from and we'll go around for each of you to tell that person how you feel and why you think you feel that way," he or she is using a structured exercise. Each group member can choose whether or not to carry out the directive; however, if he or she chooses to participate in the exercise, the behavior alternatives are limited by the instructions. These structured exercises are often used by leaders/counselors in their assumption of emotional stimulation and executive functions. High use of these functions almost inevitably means high use of structured exercises. The research of their use does suggest some principles as guidelines for the moderate rather than too high or too low carrying out of emotional stimulation and executive functions through these structured exercises.

Research

Lieberman et al. (1973) did a *post hoc* analysis of the effects of structured exercises on group process and outcomes and came to the following conclusions regarding the impact of structured experiences: First, as noted above, the leaders/counselors who used a greater number of structured exercises were most popular with their group members. The members rated them as more competent, more effective, and more perceptive than those who used these exercises sparingly. Yet the high-structured-exercise groups had significantly lower outcomes for members than did the group using the least-structured experiences. In other words, the high-structured-exercise groups had fewer "high changers," fewer "positive changers," and more "negative changers." Moreover, the high changers of the high-structured-exercise groups were less likely to maintain their change over time, once the group had ended.

In short, the finding suggests that if leaders/counselors want group members to think they are competent and know what they are doing, then they should use an abundance of structured exercises. In fact, for this outcome, too much does not seem to be enough. In this kind of "leading," in providing many explicit directions for members, in assuming this total executive function for the group, they seem to be fulfilling the group members' fantasies of what a leader should do. However, the outcome of the group experience for members will not be improved; in fact, the evidence indicates that these techniques, when overused, are less effective than the less-structured approaches.

Second, Lieberman et al. (1973) looked at other differences between high- and low-structured-exercise groups. Each group was similar in the amount of members' self-disclosure and in emotional climate. There were significant differences, however, in the themes attended to in these groups. The high-structured-exercise groups focused almost exclusively on the expression of positive and negative feelings. The lower-structured-exercise group had a greater range of concerns: setting of goals, establishing procedures, and determining norms regarding closeness versus distance, trust versus mistrust, genuineness versus phoniness, and affection and isolation.

It seems, then, that many of the common themes with which most groups must deal in order to forward their own growth are simply not considered in groups led by many structured exercises. The leader/counselor's activity "settles" these issues for the group. The experiences appear to plunge the members into a greater degree of expressiveness in what proponents have viewed as an "enlivened" atmosphere, but the group might pay an exacting price for its speed. It circumvents many group development tasks, and it obstructs the development of a sense of autonomy and potency, as other research on short-term growth group experiences suggests (Anderson, 1978). In fact, members may feel less autonomous and less understood and more alienated as a result of this artificial palliative to their own struggle for more autonomous and interdependent interpersonal relationships (Anderson, 1978).

Third, Lieberman et al. (1973) discovered that group leaders consistently overestimated the actual impact of their structured exercises on the group. Almost all of the leaders in the project used some structured exercises. Even the more effective leaders, who used fewer of these, tended to attribute a large measure of their success to those experiences used. However, the very same structured exercises were as highly valued by the ineffective leaders as by the effective leaders. Clearly, as the above review pointed out, there were more leadership variables at work than the exercises themselves, but the leaders'

giving erroneous credit to their potency as a facilitative technique
tends to perpetuate the growing myth of the importance of emotional
stimulation and executive functions for working with groups. As
Lieberman et al. (1973) conclude this part of their research report:

> On balance, exercises appear at best irrelevant in that they do not yield
> markedly different results whether they are used or not; more likely, it
> can be inferred that they are less effective in general than more unstruc-
> tured strategies. Unfortunately, too many other factors of climate and
> leader strategy enter into such an equation to speak conclusively about
> the singular contribution of exercises in relationship to an individual's
> learning [p. 419].

These other findings were explicated in this chapter in some of
their other major findings. The evidence suggests that of central
importance are the group's psychosocial member-to-member processes. In other words, the data failed to support the implicit hypotheses
behind the frequent use of structured exercises that the group re-
volves around the solitary sun of the leader and that the leader/
counselor's techniques for direct interaction with each member are
central to members' outcomes.

Other research comparing the outcomes of structured exercise
and nonstructured exercise groups has resulted in findings similar to
those of Lieberman et al. (Levin & Kurtz, 1974). In these studies,
groups in which leaders used structured experiences at the beginning
of each group session were compared to groups in which no structured
exercises were used. The comparison was in relation to specific outcomes as well as to the participants' self-concepts and satisfactions
about the experience. All structured exercise groups were assessed by
members as more cohesive, more involving, and more satisfying and
as having more significant positive effects on their personalities.
None of the structured experience groups, however, differed significantly in actual effects on outcome measures. Moreover, in the Levin
and Kurtz study, leaders got strong pressure from members to dis-
pense with the structured exercise and to move toward an unstructured format halfway through the group sessions. The leaders re-
sisted this pressure for the sake of the research, but its emergence
suggests that the participants in the structured groups did not wish
to depend on the experiences in order to function (Kurtz, 1975).

O'Day's (1974) research challenges the efficacy of highly structured exercises in groups. He discusses their potential for obstructing
the group's working through of the authority theme of group process,
which is a requisite for group development and for members' gaining

increased skills for autonomous and interdependent functioning. O'Day found that the most effective leader used few structured exercises; however, the least effective leaders used many. In fact, the most effective leader was the least active (in total *number* of interventions) in the early sessions, focused directly on the "counterdependent" hostile components of the member–leader relationship that his little activity aroused in an interpretive, self-confident way, and tended to ignore (and therefore not reinforce) direct instances of member dependency. The leader's effectiveness was directly related to this combination of frustrating members' attempts to establish a familiar "authority" relationship early in the group and then responding to the consequent member hostility in a personally confident and accepting way at the point of conflict regarding authority and control in the group process. This finding has been corroborated in earlier work on the styles and techniques of effective group leadership (Miles, 1970).

The conclusion of this research seems clear. If groups are to be vehicles for interpersonal and personal change, then it is necessary to permit group conditions that do not feed the myth of the leader/counselor's charisma through overuse of structured exercises but that can actually permit members to challenge and rebel against the leader. It may be precisely through this process that members experience the power of collective human energy and will, the exhilaration of taking control over an uncomfortable and frustrating situation, the courage to confront authority directly, and, most importantly, the meeting of each other as autonomous and interdependent peers in collaborative relationships instead of competing as subordinates as the leader's "best child" through involvement in his or her structured exercises. It is these attitudes and skills that have the most potential for members' influencing their social systems outside of the group (Fisher, 1974; Frank, 1955; Hulse, 1950).

This research indicates that through the leader/counselor's help in confronting his or her authority, group members can come to realize that the important themes of the group—autonomy and interdependence—are also the important themes of their families, organizations, and communities. It appears that without this confrontation at critical points of group process, this learning is lost and dependencies are increased. Therefore leaders/counselors need to pay conscious attention to resolving these power and authority issues of the autonomy theme, not to covering them over through structured exercises. It is almost inevitable that this resolution comes down to the leader/counselor's skill for placing responsibility on group members for choosing activities, for interpreting power and authority dynamics in the group process, and for soliciting the consequent authentic counterdependent hostility that members experience toward the leader in the interest of autonomy in a self-confident and nondefensive way. These conflicts in the group process are not simply preliminary "cathartic" exercises. They are authentic expressions of the individual and collective wills of group members toward autonomy, closeness, and interdependence.

This review has perhaps overstated the case against the use of structured exercise in groups. Certainly, all groups need some structure (Bednar & Battershy, 1976; Churchill, 1959; Crews & Meknick, 1976; Gendlin & Beebe, 1968). The question is not "Group Counseling: To Structure or Not to Structure?" (Landreth, 1973). It is, as Landreth (1973) notes: How much structure is useful? Similarly, the use of exercises as part of this structure needs modulation in regard to their functions and those of the counselor. There is a middle ground—a way to balance the unstructured permitting of the group to flounder and mire unproductively and the highly structured licensing of more frenetic and leader-dependent activity.

Lieberman et al. (1973) came to the same "middle ground" conclusion in their research. The degree to which the leaders assumed an executive management function was related to outcome in a curvilinear fashion—too much and too little were negatively correlated with positive outcomes. Too much created a leader-centered, dependent group in which members decreased in autonomy and actual interpersonal skills; too little, as in a laissez-faire approach, resulted in a plodding, lifeless group in which more members dropped out. The highest-rated leader, on all rating scales, did use eleven structured exercises in the thirty hours of group meetings (pp. 51–54). However, none of these were preplanned or used to initiate any meetings and all were introduced as "experiments" in response to spontaneous group events and used with constant checking on how members wanted to use them: "Anything else you want to do with this?" "Anything more you want to say?" "Do you have any other ideas about how you might experiment more with this in the group, either now or later?"

Principles

This middle ground suggests that counselors can profit from some research-based principles as guidelines for the more conscious and disciplined use of structured experiences (Anderson, 1980b; for alternating guidelines, see Trotzer & Kassera, 1973; Zweben & Hammon,

1970). Five of these principles are summarized below and developed more fully in Chapter 9.

1. *Don't use structured exercises to enliven the group or its members emotionally.* The exercises used should be in tune with the current level of emotions in the group and help members to express their feelings through action. They should not be used to spark deeper emotional expression or to energize a listless meeting.

2. *Don't use structured exercises to accelerate "breakthrough."* The intent of effective structured exercises is for members or the group to experiment with behaviors which may more effectively meet their needs. They are not used to accelerate growth into "instant intimacy," "instant assertion," or any other bypass to the actual trials of developing skills useful inside and outside of the group.

3. *Use structured exercises to increase awareness of group process.* Rather than using structured exercises to control the group toward preconceived ends, they should serve as an experiment which increases the awareness of the relationship between behavior and needs. With this awareness, the members and the group can choose what they wish to do with the data and understanding generated from the exercise.

4. *Use structured exercises to increase autonomy and interdependence.* When the counselor uses exercises without preconceived ends and with expectation that members are responsible for what they do based on the awareness which results, he or she is contributing to their autonomy and interdependence.

5. *Help the group and its members to evaluate realistically the structured exercises that are used.* This principle relates to the tendency of group members to credit the experience or the counselor for the success of these structured exercises when used. The counselor needs to present to, and sometimes to remind, group members that the exercises were used as tools in their awareness on which they *chose* to act. The success comes from the responsibilities members took to use the opportunity and to act upon their awareness. This action makes the difference. And, in the final analysis, only they could do this for themselves.

Implications for Practice

The research reviewed in the last chapter and this present one unquestionably confirms that the counselor has some vital leadership functions in the group, but the members' growth does not evolve directly around the solitary sun of the counselor as leader. The evidence strongly indicates that the members' world in the group—their psychosocial interrelationships—is exceedingly significant in the process of change and growth. The medium for change is *through group process*. The counselor enables this change through functions and styles which provide *counseling through group process*.

Yet as significant to effective counseling as this evidence is, research suggests that very few leaders/counselors perceive the powerful effects upon interpersonal learning of the relationships between the member and the rest of the group (Lieberman et al., 1973; Schopler & Galinsky, 1981). Those least aware of the group's efficacy fashion a style and theory that emphasize direct leader functions of emotional stimulation and executive behaviors. As managers rather than providers, they obstruct rather than enable the natural evolving group process. They help very few and hurt many.

It is imperative that the counselor understand and utilize both direct and indirect functions in enabling group process in behalf of the group and its members. In direct functions, the counselor helps members through personal interaction with each individual in the group. In indirect functions, the counselor indirectly contributes to outcomes by helping to develop a group which is an effective agent of change. The counselor influences the growth of individual members by enabling the growth of group process.

Indirect Functions

The chief objective of the indirect functions is to help engineer the construction of an effective group. This "social engineering" comes from understanding what members bring to the group, the group's norms and evolving goals, and the group's structural and process variables as these are being experienced by members. The research of the normative structure of therapeutic groups reveals the important impact of group norms on outcomes and the relationship of these norms to the expectations of members and the leader/counselor. Original expectations are converted into group goals and norms. The counselor must make these expectations explicit in the beginning and throughout in the form of a workable contract with the group (Bednar et al., 1974; Estes & Henry, 1979).

The group at its best is a miniature mutual aid community. The roots of the word *community* are those found in the concept of "common." For any aggregate of people to become a group there must evolve a community that communicates commonness. There develop common goals, common norms, and a common bond, based upon common needs, a common ground, and a common purpose. The nature of the counselor's initial composition of the group, orientation to the group, and contract with the group is to clarify the mutual expectations of members and the counselor and to explicate the common goals of the group as implicit in these expectations (Doverspike, 1973; Hartford, 1972; Van Dyck, 1980). The agreement for these common goals and the procedures, roles, and norms for achieving them is the cornerstone of the contract with which the counselor provides a "blueprint" for the construction of a group that meets members' common and individual needs.

This contract draws heavily on the members' communication of their expectations and individual and common goals. The research suggests that it is difficult to impossible for counselors to reverse strong expectations which members have about their group goals and norms. Counselors can influence these norms most by strengthening existing expectations into decisive norms. Contracting begins the indirect function for influencing appropriate norms (Bednar et al., 1974). As members share their expectations prior to and during the first meeting of the group and the counselor shares his or her own expectations, goals and norms are being negotiated and established. All of these terms of the contract evolve from the common and shared purpose of the group. In renegotiating the contract during group process and in invoking it to spur members to work toward building the group as the effective agent for their individual changes (Estes & Henry, 1979), the counselor returns to seeking this common purpose and clarifying it. The questions for this indirect function become, "What are *we* here for? What are *we* doing together to achieve this purpose? How can *we* achieve it most effectively in our work together?"

To carry the indirect function effectively, the counselor must strike a balance between the group's interacting freely, moving along spontaneously, and its self-reflecting about how it is fulfilling its task. This illumination of process and challenge for work provides the major difference for the counseling group from the member's other small groups. Research also suggests that it provides the increased awareness and the cognitive insight from meaning attribution that is a most central dynamic for those who change most positively in a group experience (Lieberman et al., 1973; McLachlan, 1972). The counselor accents this balance of experience and reflection via assumption of indirect leadership functions in the group.

The counselor must also function indirectly to influence the structural and process variables which contribute to the group's and its members' growth. He or she must be aware of the particular roles that each person assumes and the meaning of these roles for each individual member and the group as a whole. The counselor's efforts to identify and correct problems in the psychosocial relationships among members in the group are crucial. This function is critical not only for the personal growth and the avoidance of negative outcomes for each member but for the whole group. If particular members of the group are not growing, the group's potential development is obstructed.

Therefore, the counselor needs to assume a phenomenological perspective. He or she must attempt to view the group experience from the position of each of the members. Behavior in the group must be read back to the experiential position of each member in developing an awareness and understanding of his or her needs; his or her perceived position, status, and role; and the meaning of these to the particular member.

The counselor can get a great deal of help for this awareness and contribute even more to the group process by having members do this themselves. He or she can obtain process and role feedback at frequent intervals throughout the group. However this feedback for increased awareness is garnered, the counselor should develop methods by which he or she may explicitly inquire into the perceptions of group structure and its psychosocial meaning for each member and the group as a whole (Ashkenas & Tandon, 1979). The counselor, then, from this position of awareness and through understanding the obstacles to group development, can help the group challenge these barriers to individual and group growth and strengthen the elements of interdependent mutual aid. By assuming these indirect functions, the counselor demonstrates high levels of caring and meaning attribution. When combined with moderate use of the more direct functions of emotional stimulation and executive directing, the counselor is well on the way to prevent any obstruction of the evolution of the group into a mutual aid social system.

Direct Functions

While group process is the major instrument for change, the research does demonstrate that the leader/counselor looms very large in the emotional life of the group. Even when counselors try to abdicate their direct leader functions, they will be seen as the "leader." Their words and actions will have power for good or ill for group members (Hurley & Pinchea, 1978). The counselor can best use this function through modeling emotional communication and caring (Truax, 1961); through making his or her expertise available to the group in procedural suggestions, interpretations, and sharing understandings (Larsen, 1980; Maier & Hoffman, 1960); and through providing corrective emotional experiences for members (Frank & Ascher, 1941).

The counselor models emotional contact and caring through the direct empathy expressed to each group member and the group as a whole. This requires a basic expressed respect for self-determination and choice and a deep appreciation for the fears of as well as the wishes for change. He or she accepts others where they are and recognizes that patience, time, and support are as essential as challenge to meaningful change. The counselor also discloses oneself as a person—albeit a person with a particular function in the group. He or she does not stay aloof or get trapped in the narcissistic needs to be the beloved and worshipped charismatic leader. The disclosures are more "selective authenticity." They are expressed because they are believed to be needed by particular members or by the group. They come out of this care. As some of the research suggests, we are most genuine in helping relationships with those we have come to care about (Carkhuff, 1969).

The counselor cannot directly function to provide expertise to the group unless he or she is an expert (Rosenbaum, 1969). This requires that the counselor have a central organizing conceptual framework about how groups operate to solve members' problems in living and about how one can influence this process in behalf of the group and its members. This knowledge is best when it is based on study, research, and experience—one's own plus (as in this chapter) others'. This knowledge helps the counselor function as a leader who respects and clarifies the hard work in group process and individual change and growth (Silbergeld et al., 1979). It also enables the counselor to make procedural suggestions and to attribute meaning through interpretations and through sharing his or her own concepts of individual and group process which can be trusted to help more than hurt.

This expertise is the fountain for the counselor's direct function of providing corrective emotional experiences (Scheidlinger, 1980a). The way the counselor elicits feeling expressions, responds to them, and reaches for responses from other members flows from an understanding of how feelings relate to awareness, choice, and behavior.

The counselor can provide a corrective emotional experience by help-ing members understand as well as express their feelings. This understanding includes some conceptual as well as experiential learning of how these particular feelings do relate to members' awareness, choice, and behavior and can lead to getting in touch with more creative and satisfying parts of themselves.

These direct functions, like the indirect ones, when carried out in this way, provide the core learning experience in a counseling group (or for that matter in any therapeutic group). The core is a here-and-now experience which increases awareness and understanding of the self and others. It is self-reflective. Members alternatively experi-ence and examine their experience. This examination, or "proces-sing," of the here and now as experienced provides members with increased awareness and a cognitive framework for understanding (Lieberman et al., 1973; McLachlan, 1972; Shapiro & Birk, 1967). The research does suggest most strongly that members must have such conceptual frameworks to enable them to transfer the here-and-now experiential learning in the group to their there-and-then out-side life and to continue experimenting with new types of behavior to promote their growth. Research on the stages of individual and group development, reviewed in the next chapter, provides an excellent framework for the conceptual understanding of the group process for *both* the counselor and members.

Conclusion

This review concludes, therefore, very similarly to the findings of Lieberman et al. (1973). Among their conclusions, we find

> A well-balanced intensive small group experience, then, with an accent on *reflection,* as well as experience and with a focus both on the present and on the future application of present experience, may be a potent vehicle for change. Most small groups will spontaneously evolve into a social unit which provides the affective aspects of the intensive group experience; *the leader's function is to prevent any potential obstruction of the evolution of the intensive experience, and in addition to be the spokes-man for tomorrow as he encourages group members to reflect on their experiences and to package them cognitively so that they can be trans-ported in the future* [p. 439; italics added].

Most of the leaders in their study were very skillful in doing what they intended to do to help. Yet several of the most skillful in this manner were especially obstructing of the group's development. They were ineffective and even harmful. For these leaders/counselors the level of skill was less the problem than their assumptions about how people change and about the necessary techniques to influence this change. The questionable and damaging effects of these leader/counselor's attempts to induce change is a failure not in skill but in theory and technology. Sharp skills not instructed by adequate theory and research for what promotes growth and prevents injury in groups can be powerful instruments for harm. Sound technique must flow from sound theory; that is, theory grounded in what we know from experience, study, and research (Rosenbaum, 1969; Scheidlinger, 1980a).

This research suggests that our methodological theory must provide principles and skills for helping groups to develop as the major medium for change. If our counseling groups are to be an agent for developing autonomy and interdependence and to serve as an antidote to alienation as the most prevalent social illness of our times, we must have a theory that instructs skills for achieving the members' potentials for mutual aid. With what we now know, this methodology is more effective if it provides skills for *counseling through group process.*

This methodology requires a conceptual understanding of the TACIT stages of group development. The theory and research of these stages—the remaining foundation of the TACIT skill model—conclude Part I in the next chapter.

4

Stages of Group Development

The major assumption of the TACIT model is that all interpersonal development evolves through inexorable stages represented by the sequential themes: Trust, Autonomy, Closeness, Interdependence, and Termination. While these stages of development represent most accurately the study of the evolution of small groups, there is evidence to support the hypothesis of the universality of TACIT development in interpersonal relationships (Anspacher & Anspacher, 1956; Carkhuff, 1969; Erikson, 1950; Moreno, 1974; Perls, 1969; Rogers, 1961; Yalom, 1980). These data increase the strength of the underlying assumption that the growth process in life comes from the balance of autonomy and interdependence in interpersonal relations. TACIT appears to mark the stages in life cycle and therapeutic growth in individual, family, and group process.

From the TACIT perspective, group process recapitulates individual developmental process. Individual members recreate their social worlds in microcosmic forms within the group. This participation combats their sense of interpersonal alienation through their accomplishment of the major tasks of developing their autonomy and interdependence. Autonomy and interdependence, then, become the major themes in group process. As the members work on these themes together, the group moves through stages of development in which members can meet these needs in themselves and become resources to meet them in others.

The need to belong and to establish one's identity with those one *trusts* produces dependent behavior. As initial trust needs are met to a satisfactory degree, the need for *autonomy* mobilizes the individual to feel out the limits of authority and control and can produce counterdependent behavior. With some resolution of the members' conflicts with autonomy, the need for *closeness* through affection and intimacy motivates people to risk more emotional contact with others. This contact increases needs to relate effectively with one another or to behave *interdependently* until *termination*. These basic needs, emotional issues, and behavior appear over and over again in the life of any group, but in looking at the development of the group over time, they tend to occur in sequence and can be used to characterize the stages of group development. Under the conditions proposed in the TACIT counseling model these stages of group development are more likely to occur.

This chapter is an overview of how autonomy and interdependence develop in individual and group process and how this development combats the alienation that troubled people bring to the counseling group. It presents theory and research supportive of the TACIT model of group development.

Concept of Development

Development is based on the belief, substantiated by much theory and research, that the individual is born into the world with inherent thrusts for growth. This thrust for growth guides our creative interaction with the environment in personally meaningful ways. In Maslow's (1970) model, for instance, the need for self-actualization, present from the first day in the life of the individual, is the predominant motivating need after the lower level needs are met. These lower level needs in hierarchical order are physiological, safety and security, love and belongingness, self-esteem or self-respect, and self-actualization. Individuals in the group can be conceived as manifesting behavior, in sequence, which attempts to meet these needs and to extend the environmental resources for further need-meeting toward self-actualization. The base of group process is the member's self-generative characteristics—the thrusts for growth—that ensure this development toward self-actualization. As members build a social system in the group that meets safety and security needs, they must, by their own growth thrusts, revise that system to meet their higher level needs of love, belongingness, self-respect, and self-actualization. The system must change, or grow, for them to grow.

All developmental theory includes this concept of development as a synthetic process which interweaves two antithetical tendencies of all living organisms: (1) to maintain continuity to conserve integrity, or survive; and (2) to elaborate discontinuity in order to develop, or grow. All process is an attempt to synthesize these polarities of survival and growth, maintenance and transformation. At every moment, we deal with the yin and the yang—that we are both living and dying, that we are both wishing for and fearing growth, that we are both separate from others in autonomy and united with them in interdependence. The rhythm of life, and of group process as a slice of life, is this flow from contact to withdrawal, from attraction to repulsion, from growth to survival. In those critical times of choice to give up the old and to move on to the new, to go with the growth thrusts in individual and group process, there are the moments of impasse in which the wishes for growth intensify the polarity with the fears of growth. Understanding these polarities in the tacit dimension of individual and group process permits us to facilitate the helping process through these impasses in which growth is wrought.

Counseling through group process can transcend or resolve the polarities that are so much a part of human personality and social living: security versus growth; autonomy versus interdependence; separation versus union; power versus intimacy; the Dionysian versus the Apollonian. As Jung (1926) notes in his concept of individuation and Maslow (1962) in his similar concept of self-actualization, these polarities are transcended through integration in the growth process. The optimal personality is *both* autonomous and interdependent, oriented toward harmony, relatedness, unity with other people and the world as well as clearly differentiated from others and striving to be fully one's self. This resolution of basic polarities happens on many levels in intensive small group experiences, such as counseling groups. We move from the trivia of social clichés on the surface of interaction to material at the heart of the self that is more deeply personal, more hidden, and seemingly more peculiar and socially unacceptable. Then, we reach a level where what seemed most wildly idiosyncratic and alienating proves to be most universal and uniting. It is precisely at this point, when the boundaries suddenly vanish, that we become aware of our utter inseparability from the group, from humankind itself, from all that is, and paradoxically, we experience simultaneously our uniqueness and wholeness as individual beings (Garland, 1981). In short, if we can return to the triangle of counseling group process presented in Chapter 1, the "I, " the "We," and the "It" melt into each other and yet retain their separate contribution to our self-actualization. This group process not only recapitulates but catapults individual growth and development. It reciprocates.

TACIT Development as Stages

The actual process of individual development is as unique as one's thumbprint. We come into the world with unique potentialities and each of us experiences an individualized interaction with our particular environment—so basic to the stunting or flowering of our potentials into actuals at every point in our development. And yet, just as people's thumbs may be more similar than their prints, when individual development is viewed overall, there are some common demarcated stages. These stages are the results of the evolution of particular themes and their recurrent crises for the individual.

These general themes for development are a result of what Erikson (1950) has called the "epigenetic principle." That is, each stage grows out of the events of previous stages. In Erikson's epigenetic pattern, which is directly incorporated into this model of counseling through group process, psychosocial development (growth in trust, autonomy, and so on) evolves through eight crises in human relationships (beginning with mistrust and shame and doubt) as related to eight stages of the life span (from infancy to old age). Crises here connote not threats or catastrophes but critical turning points in one life—a crucial period of increased vulnerability yet heightened potential (as reflected in the characters used in the printed Chinese word for "crisis": one for danger and one for opportunity). A basic psychosocial theme, or trend, meets a crisis during the corresponding stage (for example, basic trust versus mistrust in infancy). However, all of these themes of development are in principle present from the beginning and at all times. Then, as the person develops, he or she becomes ready to experience and to manage the critical conflicts within the specific cultural context and to incorporate the resolution of these normal crises into his or her personality as preparation for achieving the next stage of development.

The model of development presented in this book argues similarly that the epigenetic principle is the tacit dimension of individual and group development. "Tacit" means arising by operation of law. What is tacit is most often implied or indicated but not often directly expressed. Tacit also serves as a very useful acronym for the themes which mark the stages of this development; that is, TACIT for Trust, Autonomy, Closeness, Interdependence, and Termination. Again, these reflect the interpersonal themes in all human development. It is as one moves toward discovering and getting close to a separate self (an "I") in trust and autonomy that one can get connected with others in closeness and interdependence (the "We"), before death in the individual life cycle or termination in the cycle of group development (the "It"). In TACIT, the "acorn" develops the "roots" of trust and self-autonomy before growing into the strong and sturdy "oak tree" of close, interdependent, mutual aid relationship with others.

TACIT Development as Spiral

TACIT development entails both progress and regress. Werner (1964), a pioneer in the study of human developmental processes, clearly makes this point. Progression of any human developmental process—physical, mental, emotional, or social—moves toward higher levels of differentiation and hierarchical integration. That is, as one moves to self-actualization, one integrates prior psychosocial crises into one's current personality. In this view, pathology is a breaking down of this integration. The person is stunted in earlier, more primitive and less integrated systems of functioning. Some regression, however, is inevitable in all of development. Just as primitive systems do not simply disappear with progressive development but are hierarchically integrated into the more complex organization that emerges in the individual or group, so aspects of higher systems' functioning are preserved when change is regressive. Werner (1964) has described this inability after progress ever to return totally in regress to a prior state: "Just as any developmental stage preserves vestiges of the earlier stages from which it has emerged, so will any degeneration bear signs of the higher level from which it regressed" (p. 34). One cannot really go home again, either as an individual or as a member of a group.

Individual and group development, while mapped out in the TACIT model by signposts of particular themes and crises which reflect sequential stages, cannot be viewed as a simple step ladder. Because there is both progress and regress to recurrent themes as each new critical period is faced, development is best conceived of as a spiral. This spiral concept of development, as presented in Figure 4.1, therefore reflects certain realities of all process. First, the loops overlap and spring from each other, indicating developmental continuity between stages. Second, the loops form quantitatively and qualitatively separate and higher-level configurations, indicating development discontinuity. The continuity supports stability or

FIGURE 4.1. The spiral of TACIT development.

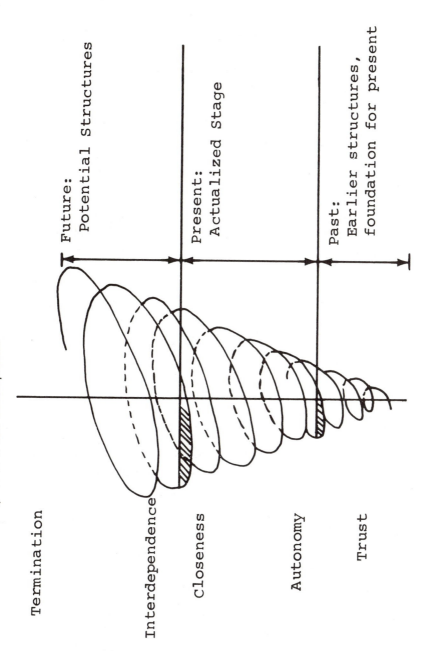

Future:
Potential Structures

Present:
Actualized Stage

Past:
Earlier structures,
foundation for present

Termination

Interdependence

Closeness

Autonomy

Trust

63

security. The discontinuity creates change or growth. Third, the loops demonstrate that the first step toward progress is regress. That is, progress includes regress, an equilibrium (or a "steady state") in the present stage, and enough disequilibrium (or "tension") to anticipate a future state.

Stages of Group Development

Use

The "wisdom of the organism" from the single cell and in the individual directs growth and development. The same is no less true for the group. Trust in group process comes from understanding its stages of development. This trust in development compels the counselor to understand how group process recapitulates and catapults individual process and to enable the reciprocal growth of each member and group as a whole.

Every group has its own unique membership. All members interact in a complex way with each other from the basis of their constituted social microcosm. Therefore, each group, like each individual, undergoes a highly individualized development. As each member manifests himself in this interpersonal microcosm, the complexity and richness of the interaction make obvious that the group process, over time, will be complex and certainly, to a degree, unpredictable. Nevertheless, all members are working out their existential human natures in a balance of individual autonomy and interdependence. As separate "I's" become a "We" in relation to the "It" of group counseling, TACIT themes evolve to influence a broadly similar group development. The TACIT development of the balanced "I-We" polarities is the base for members' wishes/fears—needs for trust, security, belonging, love, respect, and self-actualization and concomitant fears of hurt, rejection, engulfment, and so on—which members bring to early group experiences and which arise and direct their process together. TACIT group process becomes the medium for enabling individual member development. The counselor enables rather than obstructs this process from learning to trust and to flow with it and to help members break through the dams built from fears in order to free the flow of wishes and thrusts for growth. Then, the wisdom of the counselor parallels the wisdom of the group and its members.

Models

The thesis of this chapter and of this book is that group process recapitulates individual process in the stages of group development. Stages of group development have been studied extensively.* Only a few of these studies, however, use the recapitulation principle (Bennis, 1968; Hartman & Gibbard, 1974; Kellerman, 1979; Tucker, 1973). Only one, that of Tucker (1973), attempted some empirical research to support the hypothesis of recapitulation. He studied eight groups of a total of forty-four college students who met in a marathon counseling situation of two eight-hour sessions in two days. His findings do support recapitulation. The progression of individual members through autonomy and closeness to interdependence contributed to the stages of the group's development. This hypothesis was further supported by the finding that those individuals in the group who progressed most in their own development contributed most to the group's development, which also reflected movement through trust, autonomy, closeness, and interdependence, in that order. (Tucker's labels for these stages were Dependence, Autonomy, Positive Interpersonal Relations, and Differentiation or Positive Independence, as described in general behavioral characteristics so closely resembling the TACIT model of group development described below as to be indistinguishable from it.)

Also, the current models have some very different concepts of group development, even though their descriptions of stages so closely parallel each other and the model presented here. Some view this development as either cyclical, sequential, or spiral. Others refer to stages, phases, or trends.

The cyclical theorists view the process as one wherein history repeats itself. They see this as a recurring order of events in which there is a repeated sequence of major interactional themes (Bennis & Shephard, 1956; Bion, 1959; Hampden-Turner, 1966, for instance). In this model there is a discontinuous flow of themes which have been experienced in the past and encountered again in the future and must be resolved in one phase enough to move to the next.

---

*The author has tabled a chronological survey of well over 200 studies of stages of group development in experiential learning and growth groups; therapy and counseling groups; and naturalistic and problem-solving groups as these are placed in parallel to the TACIT themes in this current model. These tables were intended originally as an appendix to this book and are available from the author on request.

The sequential theorists view this flow as either discontinuous, wherein there is some overlap among stages, or continuous, and therefore with much overlap. Some view the sequential discontinuous flow as analogous to Erikson's (1950) life cycle, in which the resolution of prior crises or themes brings on new ones (for example, Tuckman's 1965 and 1978 poetic stages of forming, storming, norming, performing, and adjourning). In these models (the most developed, after Tuckman & Jensen, 1977, include Cohen & Smith, 1976; Garland, Jones, & Kolodny, 1973; Hartford, 1972; Klein, 1972; Lacoursiere, 1980), unresolved themes block or paralyze the flow of group process and stunt development into a specific state. The sequential, continuous theorists (Levine, 1979; Rogers, 1970; for example) visualize the flow as having the threads of themes which weave in and out of the pattern, while emerging as particular group themes in some sequence. Rogers (1970) describes this flow as a "varied tapestry, differing from group to group, yet with certain kinds of trends evident in most of these intensive encounters and with certain patterns tending to precede and others to follow" (p. 15).

The spiral model can be either sequential or "helical" (Banet, 1976). In this view the flow is regressive and progressive, spiraling in ever-deepening focus on the themes or issues (Banet, 1976; Bonney, 1969, 1974; Lungren, 1977). This model may view these themes as nonsequential trends rather than as phases (Banet, 1976), and certainly not as stages. In all models, however, there is the agreement of some evolution as defined in the dictionary as "an unfolding, a process of opening out what is contained or implied in something, a development." The dominant themes are present as seeds from the beginning and at all times in the process.

The second difference deals with whether this development is best viewed as stages, phases, or trends. Some (Cohen & Smith, 1976; Garland et al., 1973; Garland & Kolodny, 1981; Lacoursiere, 1980; Tuckman, 1965) use the term stages. Others (Bales & Strodtbeck, 1951; Braeten, 1974/75; Dunphy, 1968; Kaplan & Roman, 1963) view these signposts of change as phases, and still others (Cooper & Mangham, 1975; Heiniche & Bales, 1953) refer to trends. In general, "phase" suggests recurrence; "trend" connotes a central tendency; and "stage" depicts natural divisions of a changing process. Stage, particularly in a model of group development such as presented here—one that is seen as spiral and therefore discontinuous *and* continuous as well as cyclical in its recycling of unresolved themes—subsumes elements of both phases and trends. The basic premise, however, is that the group process does flow through inexorable stages that cannot be artificially manufactured or pushed. These stages relate to the individual development process. When the group returns to earlier themes in transitional or impasse "phases," it never faces the issues the same way as when first encountered. In a new state, discontinuous from the earlier one, the group confronts the continuous themes from a sequentially evolved "stage" that is different from prior ones. Therefore, the group is more adept at resolving the recurring crises. This ability to deal with both emerging and unresolved recurring themes, as in individual development, marks the group's level of maturity in its own process.

All group process, like individual development, is in many ways unique. No two groups, like no two people, are the same. Variations due to special group characteristics such as setting, composition, leader directiveness, and length of time also cause some alterations and uniqueness in the overall flow. A comparison of studies, however, indicates the remarkable fact that in this wide variety of groups, conceived by an equally wide variety of models, the stages of group development are much more similar than different.

This similarity comes from the existential given in all group life: autonomy and interdependence, or power and intimacy (Bennis & Shepard, 1956), or will & love (May, 1970). Our struggle to be true to the self and to unite with others is at the very core of our existence as human beings. Therefore, autonomy and interdependence themes are the areas in which we are most conflicted, most anxious, and most unaware. Our groups are the social structure and system we build to map a way to resolve these conflicts, the greatest sources of our wishes and fears, on the basis of where we are in our own individual development. These themes map overall group development and recur in order during aspects of regression. In the group, then, a particular stage of development is the existing balance of all of the forces impinging on events to deal with autonomy and interdependence, the "I" and the "We." As anxieties are increased when these conflicts arise, members use the power-dealing behavior of autonomy-seeking and structure to prevent closeness before moving to their human relations agenda. Only after the "I" needs are met more fully are the "We" needs sought and group process developed for closeness and interdependence. The following summary of the stages of development in counseling groups reflects this process (Anderson, 1979).

TACIT Model of Stages of Group Development

Trust

The major process theme in relation to the content theme in trust is that of involvement before choices of investment and commitment can be made. The search by members is for the potential of resources within the group to meet trust and security needs. The major questions to be answered by them before involvement are: "How is this going to benefit me? What does all this have to do with me?" These questions pepper discussions, often creating confusion about personal and group goals. At the same time, members are sizing up one another and the group through an arm's length exploration process. They search for a viable role for themselves, quite often predisposed toward those roles which seem to provide security from too much closeness and commitment, yet help them to influence (autonomy) the group system's actual goals and norms.

Although members are ostensibly together because of their interest in the common goal of the group and will ultimately build trust around their mutual commitment to this goal, the initial social forces are at work toward much investment of their energy in the establishment of initial trust through the search for approval, acceptance, respect, or domination, as these are found in group structure. They use approach/avoidance behavior to explore answers to the question of what membership entails: "What are the admission requirements, the price of the ticket to belong? How much must I give or reveal of my prized individuality? Should I involve myself for the gratification promised or remain lonely and left out? Will I feel more hurt if involved, and who may hurt me? Can my needs be met better through investment in another group?" At a near conscious level they seek answers to wish/fear questions such as these and maintain a constant, often subtle, vigilance for the types of behavior which the group expects and approves, as well as what this behavior implies about the system's goals and norms in relation to one's own needs. They explore the "I," the "We," and the "It."

While the group in the trust stage is often puzzled, testing, and hesitant, so too is it dependent. In counseling groups, members overtly and covertly look to "leaders" (especially the counselor) for structure and answers, as well as for approval and acceptance. There is the underlying hope that "If leaders, these powerful significant others, see me as belonging and O.K., then I am O.K. in this group." Much of the initial communication in the counseling group is directed toward the counselor. He or she is carefully studied for rewards, as members manifest behavior which has gained approval and acceptance from authorities in the past.

Through this interaction, members discover similarities and differences and begin to build the group norms for meeting security needs through consensus. This climate builds a base for closeness and cohesiveness, which is needed before members can risk their more authentic differences toward meeting their growth needs without severe rejection or judgment by other members, especially more powerful ones. It also creates the initial structure, characterized by the power and control of autonomy.

Autonomy

Once the preaffiliation trust concern is fairly resolved through the decision of most members to become involved with each other in the group, structural, or power and control, concerns emerge. The autonomy theme dominates. Commitment to the group increases both the wishes and the fears for more authentic human relations and the seeking for security and autonomy through the control inherent in structural positions, statuses, and roles. The group shifts from preoccupation with acceptance, approval, involvement, and definitions of accepted behavior to a preoccupation with dominance, control, and power.

The conflict characteristic of this stage is between members, or between members and the perceived leaders (such as the counselor). Each member is involved in establishing a preferred amount of autonomy, initiative, and power, and gradually a status and control hierarchy, a social pecking order, is established. The movement is from "I'm O.K. I belong here," to "I'm O.K. I *rank* here." The group begins to be stylized through the evolving structure. Communication patterns become established and forces are at work to freeze these patterns for member security in the mutually formed positions, statuses, roles, and norms. High-status members, who often particularly embody dominant norms in their behavior, tend to direct their comments to other high-status members, and low-status members participate through those with higher status. The trust at this point is not so much in other members and the self as people with common needs, purposes, and goals but a trust in a common predictable structure. The "We" is submerged in the "I-It" dynamics of seeking autonomy through power and control.

This phase can be most destructive for some members. Those whose place as low person on the totem pole reinforces already low self-esteem may drop out and be hurt before the group has an opportunity to resolve the hierarchical conflicts of this stage. Subgroups tend to come to the fore as important islands of safety wherein members can coalesce with others to guard their flanks. The scapegoats and isolates who cannot coalesce into subgroups may be particularly vulnerable and powerless to power clique rejections or attack, increasing their fears, loneliness, and isolation in human relations.

This struggle for control is part of the process of every group. It is always present to some degree, sometimes quiescent, sometimes smoldering, and sometimes in full conflagration.

Many counseling groups, ineffectively facilitated, may never move past this stage. In these, the counselor, too, has sought power and has entrenched this structure, either through creating the dependence on his or her directiveness or through overuse of structure in relation to the agenda of exercises (Anderson, 1980). Regardless, this stage usually does not dissolve without the group confronting a severe *impasse,* a phase of giving up the old with increased, somewhat immobilizing fears of the new. The counselor's skills are needed more in this stage and in the impasse than at any other time to help members confront the obstacles to their natural growth in group process. It is in challenging these structural obstacles to further development that exist in this stage that the counselor can most influence group process toward reciprocal growth for members and the group system. It is in dealing with the counselor's difference and his or her perceived place in this structure, for instance, that the group can find its own more authentic source of power to develop more equitably distributed resources for meeting more of the needs of all members. For instance, once the group discovers that the counselor functions as a specialized member with certain technical skills, and that his or her contribution can be evaluated for its value to group goal achievement, rather than accepted or rejected because of the structurally based authority behind it, the members are ready to discover the unique contributions all other members can make to the goals of the group and the meeting of their individual needs—the basis for closeness in the group.

Closeness

The third potential stage is the development of closeness and cohesiveness. Following the previous phase of much covert and often overt conflict, the group can gradually evolve into a cohesive unit. All members come into the group at this stage with some degree of equal importance to each other and to the group as a whole. There is an increase in morale and deeper commitment to the group's human relations agenda in the service of needs and goals. The mutual trust grows in each other as people and resources rather than as a trust in structural power and control. Spontaneous self-disclosures increase, particularly the sharing of feelings of closeness and here-and-now responses to the interaction. The group really becomes a group in the deepest sense of the concept as absent members for the first time are really missed and are of concern to others. The "We-It" now submerges the "I."

While a mutual aid system in the group is developing for intermember closeness and intimacy, there is some suppression of expression of conflict-producing feelings. Compared to the previous stage, group interaction seems to be sweetness and light, as the group basks in its glow of newly discovered unity. Eventually, however, this glow will pale and the group embrace will seem superficial and ritualistic unless authentic interdependent differences in the group are permitted to emerge. When fear of authentic feelings is resolved in the interests of interdependent mutual aid in member's interactions, the group has reached the maturity of interdependence—a state lasting for the remainder of the group's life with possible periodic and phase recurrences to each of the earlier stage dynamics.

Interdependence

The interdependence stage is marked by several dynamic balances of members' and group's needs. Autonomous and interdependent concerns of members are fused. Cohesion remains strong and is the anchor for dovetailing the here-and-now process and content concerns (the "I-We-It"). The processes in a mature counseling group involve "valid communication" in which the group as a whole and the individual members are expressively aware of what they are doing together. Members responsibly and spontaneously sense what self and others need to achieve their common tasks, and members are given what they need in proportion to their needs. This consciousness of mutual aid taps resources for individual, interpersonal, and group work through open feedback channels. Members' needs and the group system's goals are realized more fully, spontaneously, and creatively. Member differences are accepted, reached for, and used as resources in achieving the instrumental goals of the counseling group. This interdependence occurs until the group terminates, members transfer their increased identity, energy, and skills from the group to other social systems, or new members are taken in and create some recrudescence to the themes of earlier stages.

Termination

The last, or termination, stage can come at any time in the group's development. If the group separates following the interdependent stage, members emerge with a strong sense of competency in relation to the situations they face in life outside of the group. With this sense of competency wishes for meeting needs in human relations outweigh fears. Hopes are increased for more matching of their needs with resources to meet these needs in other life situations. These outcomes in the group are tinged with some regression to behavior more reflective of the earlier stages in the group. This behavior is based on some inevitable increased insecurities and is often a last attempt to deny separation through insinuation that members still need each other and the counselor.

If the group terminates during the earlier stages, the reverse is likely: feelings of inadequacy, fears stronger than wishes, increased mistrust in self and others, and less hope and faith about need-meeting potentialities. The feelings about separation are denied expression even more strongly, and increases in absences and dropouts are likely to occur.

This model of group development aids the understanding of events at any point in the group process and the current potentials for reciprocal growth in both members and the group as a whole. Group counseling entails facilitating members' interactions in such a way that the social system they are creating is moving from the trust and autonomy stages toward closeness and interdependence. The major task of the counselor becomes one of helping members to ameliorate the obstacles to this developmental group process and to facilitate the members' movement together toward interdependent mutual aid.

The helping process is one of actualizing the potential of members and their group process—to nurture the "acorn" into the "oak tree" it was meant to become.

Conclusion: Caveats and Promise

This chapter sketches a synthesis of TACIT stages from a number of theorists and researchers. Some caveats to such a synthesis as a guide to the counselor must be noted. First, the descriptions of group stages apply to the group as a whole, and while related to the TACIT development of individual members, not all members as individuals will progress through the stages or manifest the behaviors or reactions characteristic of each stage (Lacoursiere, 1980). Thus, while an individual's reaction to a particular stage may provide useful assessment and planning data (Bennis & Shepard, 1956; Occhetti & Ochetti, 1981; Yalom, 1975), the counselor must be careful not to impose expectations of behavior or to make unwarranted assumptions. For example, some individuals may remain relatively hostile and agressive throughout without severely retarding the group's development (Babad & Amir, 1978).

Second, the stages may not totally reflect a constellation of dominant behaviors as in the preceding descriptions. Several authors suggest that stages can be delineated only by increases or decreases in behaviors relative to other stages. For example, Babad and Amir (1978), testing Bennis and Shepard's (1956) theory of group development, found that the relative levels of various behaviors across meetings generally supported the hypothesis: avoidance or withdrawal (flight) and reliance on authority (dependency) occurred more during beginning meetings compared to later sessions, while warmth and intimacy (pairing) increased over time. They note, however, that a comparison of relative levels within each phase (e.g., dependency higher than fight in the Trust stage) did not confirm the theory. Therefore, attempting to identify phases by dominance or even presence or absence of a particular behavior alone may be misleading. It is the qualitative and quantitative *changes* in behavior which evolve from and demarcate these stages.

Third, not all groups enter later stages, and groups which do evolve through these developmental stages may proceed at differing rates (Garland et al., 1973; Lacoursiere, 1980; Levine, 1979; Sarri & Galinsky, 1974). Groups may never get beyond the Trust stage (Carrasquillo, Ing, Kuhn, Metzger, Schuburt, & Silveira, 1981; Hare,

1967) or may dissolve in conflict at the Autonomy stage (Beck, 1981; Peters & Beck, 1982). Similarly, the Trust stage duration relates to clarity or ambiguity of the task (Lacoursiere, 1980). Other factors which may affect whether a group develops as outlined and the speed with which it passes through stages include: (1) successful completion of the Trust stage through member involvement in the group and establishment of common goals (Bonney, 1969, 1974; Gazda, 1975; Sarri & Galinsky, 1974); (2) the degree to which group skills, structure, and norms necessary for a succeeding stage are acquired in preceding stage (Caple, 1978; Kellerman, 1979; Lacoursiere, 1980); (3) group composition factors such as ability of members to get along and their having skills for various group roles (Lacoursiere, 1980; Yalom, 1975); (4) individual characteristics such as age or developmental level of members (Carrasquillo et al., 1981; Garland et al., 1973; Garland & Kolodny, 1981); (5) group size—smaller groups of five to eight members are more likely to develop stages (Phillips, Gorman, & Bodenheimer, 1981); (6) the group leader's skill in facilitating development (Anderson, 1980b; Corey, 1981; Gazda, 1971; Lacoursiere, 1980); and (7) to a great extent, the leader's personal style (Angell & Desau, 1974; Lieberman et al., 1973; Weiner & Weinstock, 1979/80; Yalom, 1975). Also, erratic attendance and adding new members may delay group development (Northen, 1969; Phillips et al., 1981). Finally there are some differences in patterns of development between time-limited (weekly short sessions) and time-extended (one marathon session) groups (Tindall, 1979), between groups with experienced versus inexperienced members (Hill & Gruner, 1973), and between open and closed membership groups (Cohen & Smith, 1976; Copeland, 1980; Gazda, 1975; Hill, Lippitt, & Serkownek, 1979). With all these possibilities for variation in group development, it is not surprising that the actual research evidence about stages of development, while promising in support, is limited. In fact, most research arbitrarily defines the time parameters within which particular developments could be expected, not accounting for delayed or accelerated stage development. Given this, it is even more remarkable that these stages have been found with some consistency.

With these caveats (the difficulty of determining a particular stage, uneven development in the time dimension, and varying individual member reactions) this knowledge of group development is still of great use. It suggests what counselors can expect. For example, as Yalom (1975) notes, unprepared or inexperienced counselors can become defensive during attacks on the group leader and by their reactions hinder the group understanding that member rebellion is a typical reaction during autonomy. TACIT understanding assures a more appropriate counselor response. Similarly, he or she should not expect the group to do more than it is capable of at a particular stage—for example, extremely intimate disclosure or highly participative program activities during Trust (Northen, 1969; Yalom, 1975).

Group leaders as well as group members have different reactions to various phases (Henry, 1981; Hill et al., 1979; Winter, 1976). The counselor would do well to be aware of these reactions and not allow them to interfere with his or her interventions (such as anxiety about role or skill during Trust or ambivalence at Termination).

Finally, to the extent that stages can be determined for a particular group, the counselor can use skills as appropriate for the stage to help enable the group toward interdependent mutual aid. For example, the counselor could provide some structure and clarification through contracting during the Trust stage, enable appropriate norms and roles through the illuminating process in Autonomy and Closeness stages, and encourage group decision making and mutual aid in Interdependence and Termination stages. The next chapter presents an overview of TACIT functions and skills as based on this use of stages of group development in a group counseling methodology.

PART II
THE TACIT MODEL

5
Overview of TACIT Group Counseling Model

Almost all of the work to date on group development purports stages comparable to those of Chapter 4; few consider the function of the facilitator in relation to enabling the group's traverse through this process. The better designed empirical studies generally support the TACIT model without correlation to particular facilitator styles (Farrell, 1976; Heckel et al., 1971; Hill & Gruner, 1973; Knight, 1974; Lakin & Carson, 1964; Lungren, 1971, 1977; Lungren & Knight, 1978; Runkel, Holmes & Foster, 1971; Schutz, 1958; Thelen & Dickerman, 1949). Some of the more rigorous empirical studies have given more support for a recurrent phase rather than a sequential stage model of this process. This finding may, in fact, relate to the facilitator's obstruction of the TACIT process (Babad & Amir, 1978; Bennis, 1964; Dunphy, 1966, 1968; Near, 1978). This research and the other models of stages of group development derived from descriptive studies and conceptual reviews seem to assume that the facilitator does not matter much in this process. Lieberman et al. (1973) address this assumption explicitly in their research of therapeutic processes and outcomes. They note that most groups provide experiences in openness, closeness, a feeling of being a part of the group, a chance to find out others' usually hidden perceptions and feelings about themselves, an arena in which considerable emotional catharsis can occur, and a trusting atmosphere in which one may disclose usually hidden parts of oneself. This intensive group experience seems to develop as an integral part of the small group process; even members of unsuccessful groups reported this type of experience. They conclude (p. 157): "It takes a particularly potent and misguided leader, or a highly unpropitious norm-setting event to obstruct the development of the intensive group experience."

The flipside of this possibility of "a particularly potent and misguided leader" is the group counselor who has learned to facilitate rather than to obstruct this development. Such a helping process can instruct counseling through group process. Many of the models of group development do suggest particular tasks of the helper in a variety of groups (counseling, therapy, sensitivity training, and encounter) which influence the group's progress through the stages of group development. A compendium of these models suggests a basic stance toward the group and particular sequential counselor roles and skills in the pregroup phase, the TACIT stages, and the postgroup phase of this counseling. They inform the helping process presented in this text and summarized in an overview below.

Basic Stance and Functions

Stance

No better word describes the counselor's basic stance in the group than *enabler*. The enabler makes able, capacitates, empowers, benefits. The counselor empowers members through enabling the group process and each individual's potential. In enabling there is an element of facilitating which implies assisting in progress by easing and accelerating. However, facilitation does not mean expediting the process by pushing members through the stages. Facilitation comes from enabling members to use the power of their own choices and actions to progress—from *empowering*. The counselor's basic stance and actions must make the group able to accomplish its developmental process and its common content goals.

The counselor enables through basic respect and positive regard for each individual member and for the group as a whole and through knowledge and skills which facilitate members' awareness of their needs and evolving goals and the obstacles in their group process. In this text, the counseling model requires that the counselor have this expertise of process, how the content relates to this process (the "I-We-It" triangle as it exists at any time for the group), and what can be done to develop members' awareness of this process and to encourage their growth choices from this awareness. The counselor is not expected to be an expert in the particular content areas which serve as the common theme for the group—the life of the adolescent truant, the abusing parent, the prison inmate. In fact, the counselor in this model believes strongly that the experts in the particular life situations of members are the members themselves. The counselor expects to learn about these situations as members teach each other about them—not to teach members how to live in these situations. The counselor, however, can illuminate aspects of the life process which underlie these situations as these are reflected in microcosm in TACIT individual and group development.

The counselor, therefore, enables members to help each other through developing the group process. The tasks of this enabling are related to, but different from, the tasks of the members in the group. The helping process, then, is a *parallel process*. The parallel process implies that the tasks of the counselor and those of members are not only different but must be clearly distinguished from each other (Schwartz & Zalba, 1971). When one takes over the tasks of the other—as with the counselor who states the goals for the group—the typical result is confusion. The members have the task of establishing and commiting themselves to common goals in the counseling group designed to enable development through group process. The counselor's task is to confront members with what they are doing to determine goals and how they are working or not working together to accomplish *their* goals. The principle of parallel process clarifies the different yet interdependent tasks of the counselor and the group. Any obliteration of the differences between these two sets of processes, this division of labor, renders the work dysfunctional and the encounter itself manipulative, sentimental, and generally frustrating for all involved—members as well as counselor. The important work of counseling, and it is work, will not get done.

Functions

Lieberman et al. (1973) identify these tasks of the leader (counselor) in a variety of therapeutic growth groups. Their study found that growth group leaders, regardless of particular methodology, behave in particular ways. These aspects of leader styles cluster into four basic functions through which they enable the group's work. These are:

1. *Catalyzing:* This is the active catalyst role of stimulating interaction and emotional expression through such skills as reaching for feelings, challenging, confronting, suggesting, using program activities such as structured experiences, and

modeling. (Lieberman et al. label this "emotional stimulation.")

2. *Providing:* This is the provider role of relationship and climate-setting through such skills as support, affection, praise, protection, warmth, acceptance, genuineness, and concern. (They label this "caring.")
3. *Processing:* This is the processor role of expanding awareness of the meaning of the process through such skills as explaining, clarifying, interpreting, and providing a cognitive framework for change, or translating feelings and experiences into ideas. (They label this "meaning attribution.")
4. *Directing:* This is the director role through such skills as setting limits, roles, norms, and goals; managing time; pacing; stopping; interceding; and suggesting procedures. (They label this "executive function.")

Lieberman et al. (1973) discovered that these four leadership functions have a clear and striking relationship to outcomes. *Providing* and *processing* have a linear relationship to positive outcome: *the higher the providing* ("caring") *and the higher the processing* ("meaning attribution"), *the higher the positive outcome* (measured as changes in values and attitudes, self-concept, view of world, and view of others). The other two functions, *catalyzing* ("emotional stimulation") and *directing* ("executive function") have a curvilinear relationship to outcomes—that is, the rule of the golden mean: *too much or too little of these leader behaviors results in lower positive outcomes.* This finding suggests, for instance, that the counselor who does not serve at times as a catalyst will have unenergetic, devitalized groups; too much catalyzing (especially with insufficient focus via processing) results in a highly emotionally charged climate with the counselor pressing for more emotional interaction than the members can integrate (or "process" into their own experience). Too little directing—a laissez-faire style—results in a bewildered, floundering group; too much directing creates a highly structured, authoritarian group whose interactional process will be arrhythmic and not freely flowing and whose members fail to develop a sense of autonomy and interdependence.

Like the most successful leaders in this study, the effective counselor is one who functions moderately as catalyst and director and highly as provider and processor. Both providing and processing are critical. Neither alone appears sufficient to ensure success. Providing, or actively caring, establishes the climate and *support* for growth in the counseling group, but this change takes work. This work requires the *challenge* of processing and some catalyzing and directing. (Refer to Table 3.1, page 42.)

The TACIT Counseling Process

Trust

The general tasks and skills for group counseling through the TACIT developmental process relate to the four functions of catalyzing, providing, processing, and directing. In the first stage, the members' primary task is to develop trust. The counselor's parallel task is to enable a climate for this trust. This task requires some directing, catalyzing, and processing and a great deal of providing. Providing comes first from attending, observing, and active listening, and the use of empathy, warmth, and respect. (All skills mentioned in this section are elaborated later in the remaining chapters in Part II of the text. See Appendix for operational definitions and an example for measuring these skills.) In addition, providing comes from granting permission for both approach and avoidance through the use of reinforcements and satisfying members' needs, whether the need be information, tension release, friendliness, security, or whatever. Activities are noncompetitive, experiences nonfrustrating, and limits nonrigid. The counselor particularly needs to be fair and consistent, to validate all members, and to provide the hope that members can achieve their group and individual goals—simply by expecting and encouraging their work toward their goals.

Catalyzing comes from sharpening and clarifying each member's communication, especially the "I-We-It" elements. The counselor asks members to direct statements toward intended recipients in order to facilitate intermember dialogue and connections and to point out commonness. He or she also clarifies expectations, as these are implicit in comments, and elicits, accepts, and supports members' goals. In gently inviting trust, the counselor does not challenge the group for initiative and cooperation so early but supports each member's entry into the group by inviting participation and feeling expression and personally responding to each member.

Directing involves contracting. The contract begins with a clear statement of purpose, the counselor's stake in the process, general roles and procedures, and expectations of members' responsibilities.

The counselor also reaches for feedback regarding the contract, members' ideas about short-range and longer term goals, and the specific agenda for future work. The contract, then, is the verbal and nonverbal agreement among the group members and between the members and the counselor about the purpose of the experience, the nature of the content themes, and how they will work together to achieve these purposes (Kravetz & Rose, 1973). It is comparable to what in other skill models has been called "norming" and "task focusing" (Gill & Barry, 1982). In the model presented in this text this contract includes the determination of specific themes and the establishment of particular ground rules to direct the work.

Processing in this first stage entails calling attention to members' wishes and fears in beginnings, difficulties in exposing themselves and feeling free, and the elements of trust in what is being discussed. These skills are not used in a confronting and an "I-know-something-you-don't" manner as this will increase tension, lead to denial, or quite often be completely ignored in interaction while stored away in resentment and resistance. They are best used in terms of the naturalness and universality of these issues for beginning groups. At the same time, the counselor must not give the impression that this group is like all other groups and predictable— as it can never be. The processing includes some indication, and often is best put out as such, of the counselor's experience of these issues within the self, as he or she is excited and also a little anxious about this group experience and its unique as well as universal elements. The counselor also processes the feelings and unstated needs and goals behind communications by restating what he or she may have heard and observed about these, reaching for these, and checking these out. There-and-then content as it relates to here-and-now themes is particularly important to introduce. Finally, the counselor asks members to process what they are experiencing as commonness and difference and how they have proceeded to establish norms for their work together. This processing itself is vital as it helps to establish the norms for awareness and feedback of the here and now—the most powerful medium for what members will learn in the group.

Autonomy

In the second stage, the members' primary task is to develop autonomy. The counselor's parallel task is to enable a structure for the group in which members can assume responsibility for the work and discover the potential for interdependent mutual aid. This task requires a great deal of providing and processing and some catalyzing and directing. Providing here entails responding to feelings and content and being concrete. Support is given to members who are not a central part of the group by helping them state their experience of their position and to articulate the reasons for their choices (to be quiet, eccentric, critical, and so on). This support includes follow-up of dropouts and absentees.

Processing is probably more important at this stage than at any other, as the evolving group structure—those patterned positions, statuses, roles, and norms—can become entrenched as obstacles to people-to-people (rather than role-to-role) relationships. To a large degree, members will be unaware of this structure; therefore, the counselor must reach for processing from the group and add his or her own processing regarding the power and control or autonomy themes inherent in the current structure. This structure is processed in relation to the here-and-now needs it meets and obstructs, to the contract, and to how the current group structure and processes help or hurt particular members and the group as a whole meet needs and achieve goals. The here-and-now structure and process are related to there-and-then content and vice versa. The counselor particularly processes the autonomy and closeness issues underlying the conflicts which tend to emerge at this stage and the norms which have evolved for handling them, especially when these norms are defensively protective of conflict or influence conflict resolution in terms of win-lose positions. Similarly, the counselor helps the group process how it makes its innumerable decisions—both conscious and unaware ones.

The counselor as catalyst reaches for the expression of feelings, especially those which are in reaction to the structure. This eliciting and clarifying of feelings includes clarifying the members' beliefs behind these feelings and their current perceptions of the reality of the group as it relates to feelings and belief. There is also a reaching for both the consensual view of reality (that is, how all or most members view particular here-and-now events) and differences in these perceptions. To catalyze intermember interaction, the counselor calls for the group assuming its responsibility for the process, deflects dependency on him or her, redirects interactions toward the him- or herself to the members, and reaches for group responses to individual members (Breton, 1982). The counselor also encourages the expression of feelings, feedback, and evaluation of how they are working together toward goals. He or she also shares his or her own feelings, observations, and interpretations.

Most significant in catalyzing is the counselor's reaching for the anger toward him or her that is implicit in group interaction. Some disenchantment and anger toward the leader is a ubiquitous feature of all small face-to-face groups in the autonomy stage, but this is by no means a constant process across groups or in form or degree. The counselor's behavior may potentiate or mitigate both the experience and the expression of rebellion. Invoking greater negative responses are those counselors who are ambiguous or deliberately enigmatic, who are authoritative yet offer no structure or guidelines for members, and who overtly or covertly make unfulfillable promises early in the group. Suppressing the expression of hostility are those counselors who present themselves as anxious, uncertain, or frail, those who collude with members to avoid all confrontations, those who appear to need to be liked above all else, and those who remain so aloof and ambiguous that they give members nothing to attack. This suppression of vitalizing ambivalent feelings toward the counselor inhibits group development. It can lead to a counterproductive taboo which opposes the desired norms of interpersonal honesty, feeling expression, and freedom in relation to content and process themes. It can rob members of the experience of nonlethal aggression and anger. It can create (and often does) off-target displacement of resentment toward the counselor onto other members through such processes as scapegoating and encouraging and then destroying leadership attempts by other members. It is essential that the group feel free to confront the counselor, who must not only permit but, in the role of catalyst, encourage such confrontation. In discovering the counselor not as a role but as a *person* who carries out certain functions of possible benefit to the group, the members have taken a giant leap toward realizing that within the role-to-role interaction which has come with structure there is a subterranean gold mine of people-to-people events in the here and now of group process.

As director in this second stage, the counselor facilitates member autonomy and interdependence by clearly and consistently demonstrating that he or she does not intend to coerce or suppress members, or to reinforce coercion and suppression among members. The counselor actively indicates the importance of all members and avoids manipulating or exploiting them. Directing demands limiting and guiding members but not controlling them. The limits and guidelines come in demanding work, suggesting ways it may be accomplished, and protecting others from harm while there is the underlying freedom for the group to develop its collective will for interdependence or mutual aid. While there are conflicts among members and with the counselor for power and control over the group resources, the counselor needs to influence a group structure which promotes equal opportunity and freedom for all members.

In sum, in this autonomy stage, the counselor must not sanction the autocratic members even though their high level of participation helps to keep the group going. The counselor gives status and recognition to those who are denied them in the group; supports helpful "I-We-It" contributions and ignores others; teaches members, through modeling and feedback, to perform in ways that benefit the entire group; and consistently provides feedback on the power and control elements of group structure. Members then have the opportunity to be aware of their conflicts and exploitations, compare these actions with their contract and needs, and develop empathy for the needs and hurts of others. Again, the counselor actively solicits the less conscious hostilities bestowed on him or her as the "leader," and together with members, attempts to separate those reactions which are due him or her as a person and those projected onto his or her role and its symbol for members.

Closeness

In the third stage, when the members face the closeness theme, the counselor's parallel task is to encourage members to take the personal risks of self-disclosure and feedback that meet intimacy needs. Here the counselor serves primarily as a catalyst with higher use of providing and processing and some, but little, use of directing. Catalyzing involves modeling here-and-now self-disclosure and feedback interaction, encouraging intermember contact and self-explorations, reaching for feedback in interpersonal processes, reaching for the negatives underlying positive feelings, and reaching for growth needs. Providing requires personalizing meanings, problems, feelings, and goals and using genuineness and confrontation. It also requires providing opportunities for all members to come into the group with equal status as human beings. Processing entails detecting and challenging the obstacles which obscure the common ground, relating there-and-then content to here-and-now process, clarifying positive and negative feelings and intimacy issues (especially in intermember conflicts), and confronting how norms can be changed to better meet needs and achieve goals. Directing necessitates clarification of evolving purpose and renegotiating the contract.

All of these functions facilitate the more authentic autonomy and interdependence in the closeness stage through more explicit dealing with questions of direction and purpose. For instance, while the contract is directly renegotiated, the counselor encourages more genuine commitment to an "I-We-It" balance as a means to achieve the chosen and stated goals of members. Often, this includes encouraging more commitment to the agenda of interpersonal relationship needs within the group as well as to the content. The attempt is made to help members interact as people to people rather than as role to role, revealing their wishes and fears for closeness and asking for and accepting help. In short, they are held to their responsibility for themselves and others.

During the impasses that occur at the beginning of this stage, the counselor needs to help members express (verbally and nonverbally) the fears experienced as they sense that the environmental supports of group structure are giving way to the autonomous self-supports of authentic and close human relations. The counselor catalyzes this by expressing his or her own feelings; provides by accepting and personalizing these fears; processes by linking them to behavioral consequences through such questions as: "What are we doing?"; "Is this what we want?"; "What are we experiencing?"; "What will be the consequences for us of continuing to do what we are doing now?"; "How are we avoiding moving on?"; and "How can we best proceed from here?"; and directs by invoking the contract and suggesting particular procedures for resolving the impasse.

Interdependence

In the fourth stage—interdependence—the members' primary task is helping each other through mutual aid. The counselor's parallel task is enabling members to use the mutual aid system. All members now carry the functions earlier assumed by the counselor. The counselor (like all members) provides and processes and, less than other members, catalyzes and directs. Many of the models for these tasks in conjunction with group development suggest that the counselor participate like any other member or become a full-fledged member without a separate function (Bonney, 1969; Fiebert, 1968; Klein, 1972; Lakin, 1972; Levine, 1979). The fact that the counselor has some expertise and special resources for helping members in this stage, however, supports the continued use of parallel process. The counselor, here, does tend to eliminate use of catalyzing and directing, trusting the group for these, and in this sense is more an equal part of the membership circle. Nevertheless, the counselor's special knowledge of the dominant issues and dynamics of this stage of group development must be made available as resources for the group through providing and processing.

Through immediacy, genuineness, and self-disclosure, the counselor provides an invitation for members to operationalize their individual and group goals and develop special plans for achieving them. Much of the support is for the work that the group is doing. As this work gets done, the counselor illuminates the process, especially reminding the group of the reciprocal relation of here-now and there-then and their need to balance "I-We-It" needs as these evolve.

Direct providing and processing come from offering experimental activities, exercises, or techniques which may help the group and its members discover more concretely their specific needs and goals and their plans for how to meet these. These are offered and accepted freely as *possible* experiments to be used or not on the basis of their relevance to particular concerns of group members. They are not imposed on the basis of the counselor's authority, but suggested and explained in their functional relationship to the group's themes and needs. Their facilitation comes from their relevance and from the technical expertise of the counselor.

Termination

In the last, or termination, stage, the members must separate from the group and transfer their learning to their life situations outside of the group. The counselor's parallel process is enabling this separation and transfer. To accomplish this task the counselor will need to use high levels of all four functions: catalyzing, providing, processing, and directing. Catalyzing requires initiating the facing of termination by members and the inevitable ambivalences involved. Often the group avoids the difficult and unpleasant task of termination by ignoring or denying their concerns. The counselor must help them keep this task in focus, by repeatedly calling the members' attention to the impending termination. If avoidance is extreme—manifested, for instance, by an increased absence rate—the counselor must confront the group with their behavior.

Through providing one's own feelings about termination, the counselor supports the challenge of the reality of separation and the need to experience, own, and discuss it. In this discussion, the counselor provides for facing ambivalences by reaching for the negatives behind positives and the positives behind negatives.

In processing, the counselor responds to indirect cues for these ending feelings and dynamics—the absentees, the difficulty working, the regressions. He or she also encourages an evaluation of the experience—the "processing" of the overall group experience. This processing links the ending to there-and-then situations by encouraging the transferring of learning.

Directing entails making the limits of the group explicit by pointing out that the group will end and providing guidelines and perhaps exercises for this closing. Usually with a mature (interdependent, balanced "I-We-It") group, the best approach is a direct one. The members can be reminded that it is their group and that they must decide how to end it. It is important in this directing that the counselor not bury the group too early; otherwise the group is in for several ineffective and disillusioning "lame duck" meetings. The counselor through directing, processing, providing, and catalyzing holds the issue of separation and termination before the group and yet helps it keep working until the very last minute.

Within this helping process there is also a pregroup and postgroup phase which entails particular counselor skills. The pregroup phase includes composing the group, the intake interviews, orienting members toward the group, and preparing oneself as the counselor. The postgroup phase requires evaluation and follow-up procedures and skills. All of these phases and stages are covered separately in detail and with examples throughout Part II.

Summary

The following outline summarizes this overview of counseling through group process. The data on this outline serve as a thumbnail sketch for the processes covered in detail and through examples in the TACIT counseling model presented in the remainder of Part II. As noted, the counselor's functions flow from the basic enabling stance and the parallel tasks during the stages of group development. The most significant skills, then, are those which implement these functions. While all functions are used throughout to some degree, the primary functions carried respectively in TACIT are providing and directing in Trust; processing and providing in Autonomy; catalyzing and providing in Closeness; providing, processing, directing, and catalyzing through experimental activities and exercises in Interdependence; and directing and processing in Termination.

Outline Overview of Counseling through Group Process

(Pregroup Phase)
I. Trust Stage
  A. Process Themes
     1. Individual: *Involvement*—"Should I join?"
     2. Interpersonal: *Trust*—"Will I be hurt more if involved?" "Who might hurt me?" "Are my goals shared?"
     3. Group: *Security*—"Let's protect each other."
  B. "I"—Member Dynamics. Stereotypic behavior and perception of others; approach/avoidance; testing out; arm's length exploration; search for safe place (as in most recent groups); authority-oriented seeking for "O.K.ness"
  C. "We—Group Dynamics. Seeks commonness; downplays differences; dependent; "Tell us what you want"; puzzled, testing, hesitant; establishes protective norms; seeks structure in response to wishes/fears; provides security to begin work; checks out involvement of others
  D. "It"—Content Issues. Disguises underlying process; members particularly unaware of their feelings, especially fears; may express unrealistically high hopes for instant intimacy and deny common fears
  E. Specific Counselor Functions and Skills
     1. Task: enable climate for trust
     2. Functions and skills
        a. Providing: attending, observing, active listening, and empathy
        b. Directing: contracting
        c. Catalyzing: clarifying and elaborating
        d. Processing: sharing own feelings and reaching for feelings
II. Autonomy Stage
  A. Process Themes
     1. Individual: *Autonomy*—"Do I have enough power and control to get my needs met?"
     2. Interpersonal: *Belonginess* and *status* in the eyes of others—"Where am I and who's who?"
     3. Group: *Structure*—"Let's determine who controls resource allocation."
  B. "I"—Member Dynamics. Stylized behavior and perception

of others; control honesty to get position; seek status and roles to protect against overexposure and too much closeness; test how to get power; O.K.ness in rank
C. "We"—Group Dynamics. Seeks structure; entrenches communication patterns; win/lose conflict resolution and decision making; subgrouping, especially "dependents" and "counterdependents"; resents loose structure as fears authenticity; preoccupied with dominance, control, and power
D. "It"—Content Issues. Disguises battleground for "Who's running the show?"; irrational confrontations of leadership in there and then and here and now; verbal pressure on silent members, scapegoats, and isolates; determined by high-status members, especially conscious decision making
E. Specific Counselor Functions and Skills
1. Task: enable functional, nonrigid structure
2. Functions and skills
a. Processing: illuminating, relating here-now to there-then, reaching behind conflicts and decisions
b. Providing: personalizing, supporting
c. Catalyzing: reaching for feelings and perceptions, redirecting interactions
d. Directing: demanding work, invoking the contract

(Impasse Phase)
III. Closeness Stage
A. Process Themes
1. Individual: *Disclosure*—"I want and fear to be known."
2. Interpersonal: *Closeness*—"I want others to understand me and be close to me."
3. Group: *Cohesiveness*—"We are together."
B. "I"—Member Dynamics. Investment in group; desires more closeness and feeling expression; perceives here and now; feels warmth and potential acceptance; O.K.ness in belonging
C. "We"—Group Dynamics. Seeks interpersonal concerns for agenda; reformulates and recommits to purpose and goals; builds on warmth; misses absent members; concerned about everyone being "in"
D. "It"—Content Issues. Expresses personal feelings; may include jealousies; addresses norms about closeness (not status); disclosures can be deep and high in risk; trust in group reflected in content (not in structure)
E. Specific Counselor Functions and Skills

1. Task: enable self-disclosure and feedback
2. Functions and skills
    a. Catalyzing: encouraging intermember feedback, reaching for empathic contact, confrontation
    b. Providing: modeling self-disclosure and feedback, sharing own feelings
    c. Processing: clarifying purpose, illuminating process, detecting and challenging obstacles to work (especially impasses)
    d. Directing: renegotiating the contract

IV. Interdependence Stage
   A. Process Themes
      1. Individual: *Self-actualization*—"I want to grow."
      2. Interpersonal: *Interdependence*—"I'm O.K.; You're O.K."
      3. Group: *Reality*—"We are all different yet we are all similar."
   B. "I"—Member Dynamics. Spontaneous and creative behavior; perceives self and others in here and now and relates to there and then; experiences real concern for others; expresses own difference and seeks differences in others
   C. "We"—Group Dynamics. Seeks mutual aid; members given what they need in proportion to intensity of needs; valid communication (knows what they are doing); uses feedback
   D. "It"—Content Issues. Expresses purpose in behavior more and in content less; much "I" and "We" in the "It"; reflects cohesion and conscious choice; communication specific, direct, and clear
   E. Specific Counselor Functions and Skills
      1. Task: enable use of mutual aid
      2. Functions and skills. Providing/processing/catalyzing/directing: offering experimental activities

V. Termination Stage (Depends on stage reached before)
   A. Process Themes
      1. Individual: *Competence*—"I am captain of my own ship" or "I can't."
      2. Interpersonal: *Hope*—"We can grow together" or "We can't."
      3. Group: *Accomplishment*—"We did it" or "We didn't."
   B. "I"—Member Dynamics. High hopes or high fears in experiencing some regression and in relating to world outside of the group

    C. "We"—Group Dynamics. Holds on; faces reality of ending with sense of accomplishment *or* absentees, dropouts, disillusionment

    D. "It"—Content Issues. Reflects wishes/fears; mourning; moving on; *or* regrets

    E. Specific Counselor Functions and Skills

        1. Task: enable separation and transfer

        2. Functions and skills

            a. Directing: initiating termination, holding out ending, closing

            b. Processing: focusing on ending, evaluating, and following up

            c. Providing: sharing own feelings

            d. Catalyzing: reaching for feelings and evaluation

(Postgroup Phase)

6
Trust

The Trust stage of the TACIT model begins before the counseling group formally meets. In this pregroup phase, the "group" is a concept in the mind of the counselor and a vague expectation for members. This pregroup phase affects greatly what happens when the members actually see each other together face to face for the first time. Then, the trust theme predominates.

Therefore, the principles and skills for composing and convening the group come before the first meeting. This chapter presents this phase before considering the early meetings. Throughout Part II, beginning in this chapter, two separate groups are used for detailed examples of the TACIT model in action. The first is a group of preadolescents in a school served by two college students. It is based on the recordings of one of these students. The second is an example of my own work with adolescents in a community setting. Critical incidents from this group are presented at the end of each chapter in this part. This chapter concentrates on this counseling process in the first stage of TACIT group development. It considers member, group, and counseling process in relation to the development of initial trust.

Trust in the Pregroup Phase

There are three separate aspects of the pregroup phase (Berne, 1963; Hartford, 1972). These are the private, the public, and the convening. The private refers to the idea of the group formed in the mind of the counselor. The public is the announcement and explanation of the group to others. The convening includes the activities which go into setting up the first meeting. The common threads of this pregroup tapestry are the principles and skills for group composition, the theme-setting, and pregroup preparation.

Group Composition

Group composition is a recognized vital element in successful groups (Bertcher & Maple, 1977; Melnick & Woods, 1976; Slavson, 1955; Yalom, 1975). There is, however, comparatively little knowledge about how to compose groups effectively. The work that has been done focuses primarily on the homogeneity (similarities) and heterogeneity (differences) of members. No consensus of these variables evolves from this work. Some research suggests that homogeneity in relation to the task orientation of members is most important for predicting a cohesive group (Ahumada et al., 1974; Copeland, 1980; Harrison, 1965; Harrison & Lubin, 1965; Reddy, 1972; Taylor, 1980; Yalom, 1975; Yalom, Houts, Zimerberg, & Rand, 1967). Others suggest a principle of "complementary heterogeneity" wherein members are interpersonally compatible with at least some other members in relation to particular criteria (need for affection, control, inclusion; extraversion or intraversion; and so on; Rose, 1973; Schutz, 1958a; Slavson, 1955). In general, the researchers agree that composition must support cohesiveness and provide enough homogeneity for the support of "sameness" (or in the same boat) and some heterogeneity for the challenge of "difference" (or some people rowing, some looking out for land, and so on). In addition, all tend to agree that too much difference is destructive for cohesiveness (Pollock, 1971; Woods & Melnick, 1979). None draws a distinct line between what is an appropriate level of homogeneity and heterogeneity.

The most developed model for group composition is Bertcher and Maple's (1977). They suggest that the composition balance homogeneity in descriptive attributes and heterogeneity in behavioral attributes. Descriptive attributes refer to age, sex, educational level, and such other statuses as married, single, probationers, students, and so on. Behavioral attributes refer to such traits as talkativeness, intraversion, dominance, clowning, and so on. In the domain of behavior, they propose that the range of rating on any one characteristic for all group members (for instance, conformity) not be too great. In other words, they support the rule of the golden mean in heterogeneity of behavioral attributes: too much or too little difference in important behavioral characteristics of members prior to joining the group can greatly obstruct either cohesion or productivity.

Initial trust in the group does depend on some sense of similarity for members. More so than particular descriptive and behavioral attributes, this trust evolves from a sense of similarity about goals.

The initial member question is not whether other members will be exactly like me. Rather, it is whether the other members want the same thing from the group as I do—whether they share my goals. Members explore this question by assessing how the group does or does not work together and what the group is working on from the very first interaction.

Therefore, the skills for the pregroup phase call for the counselor's abilities to communicate the purpose of the group to prospective members, to connect this purpose to the counselor's stake and each member's needs, and to "tune in" to the member's early fears and expectations about the group. An important principle for composition is that members share a *common* theme that reflects *common* developmental needs and *common* goals (Crandall, 1978; Woods & Melnick, 1979). Forming the group around a common stated theme that can be clearly and directly communicated to prospective members abets this composition. It supports initial trust and cohesiveness and challenges the group to work toward accomplishment of goals. One other important principle for group composition is "pairing"—that is, trying to assure that each individual has at least one other person compatible in relevant characteristics in the group.

The current weak state of knowledge about group composition does not provide predictive confidence for an effective group (Schopler & Galinsky, 1981) and, therefore, does not justify a great deal of counselor time and effort spent on composing the group. More useful is the knowledge we have that members' expectations translate into group goals and norms. The counselor can clarify these expectations, influence those that are not definitive, and suggest some specific ways the group might work together. Any plans for group composition should quickly advance from the private phase of the counselor's expectations and goals to the public phase of involving prospective members and others in forming and convening the group.

Use of Theme

Within the principle of pairing for composing the group, the setting of a theme that suggests common needs, purposes, and goals for prospective members is especially useful and provides the structure for TACIT process. Theme-setting concerns the selection of a theme and its precise wording. Themes must be based on a professional assessment of the needs of prospective members and are initially set by the counselor. This procedure assures a common ground of theme interest for members before joining the group. In the case of members required to join the group, it provides the common framework in which to begin, whether the beginning is marked with a high interest level or with common resistances. The assessment can relate themes to (1) *common life situations,* such as "Managing on an AFDC Budget" or "Parenting Day Care Children"; (2) to *common problems,* such as "Overcoming Unemployment" or "Staying in School"; or (3) to *common developmental tasks,* such as "Working Successfully with Others in School and Play" or "Keeping Myself Productive After Retirement." The basic assumption of theme choice is consistent with the rationale of the approach; if it is true that the theme has an important effect on the kinds of concerns members can bring up for discussion, then the extent to which the theme fits the circumstances and needs of members is extremely important.

Once the theme is selected there still remains the problem of its precise wording. Words, as overall themes, can have an important effect on members' expectations. There are two specific guidelines for theme-wording: (1) Themes should be worded positively rather than negatively. For instance, "Getting Along Better with My Spouse" is better wording than "Problems Between Husbands and Wives." (2) The use of the pronoun "I" and the "-ing" form of verbs helps themes to become more personal and more energizing. For example, "Being Myself at Midlife" is more enlivened than "The Problems of Midlife Crises."

Most often the initial theme is followed by a series of subthemes for each meeting. In fact, an early meeting often includes the subtheme of "Setting Subthemes" or "Choosing Future Themes." Ideally, a subtheme reflects a partialized focus on the overall theme, is broad enough to permit varying member reactions, and yet is explicit enough to evoke meaningful associations and feelings within that member.

Preparation

The preparation in the private phase expedites the public phase when it includes plans which can be communicated to the prospective members in individual contacts prior to the final counseling group composition and initial group meeting. The suggested procedure for these plans is as follows (Bertcher & Maple, 1977):

1. What are the common needs (or "problems") that could be addressed by the group?

2. What are my goals for the group? (These would certainly be renegotiated with members once the group begins to meet.)
3. What is the theme for this group?
4. Based on these preliminary goals and the theme, what are some of the critical attributes needed by group members, both descriptive (age, sex, education, statuses, etc.) and behavioral (abilities and experience)?
5. What are your plans regarding:
   A. *Support:* What do you have to do to create optimum conditions within your setting, or agency, for this group? With whom do you have to clear this idea, etc.?
   B. *Size:* How large do you want it to be? (The TACIT theme-centered group is best with seven to ten members, but it could range from five to fifteen members.) How can you ensure a pool of prospective members to get sufficient numbers?
   C. *Environment:* Where will you meet? What needs to be done to make the meeting place conducive to the group's work, etc.?
   D. *Time:* When will you start? How long will the group experience last? (The TACIT theme-centered group is best with eight to fifteen meetings.) How often will you meet? At what time of day, etc.?
   E. *Choice:* What will be the degree and nature of choice about joining the group? Will this be an open group (takes on new members after the group gets started) or a closed group (does not bring in new members once the group begins and supports TACIT development more)?
6. How will you obtain information about the critical attributes for each potential member? How much and what kind of information will you need from referral sources, your own group or individual interviews with potential members, holding an orientation group session, and/or using members' self-reports on particular questionnaires or instruments?
7. How will you compare and select potential members by using particular descriptive and balanced behavioral attributes and/or by determining common needs, expectations, and goals as related to the selected theme?
8. How will you notify potential members that they have, or have not, been selected?

As these procedures are planned and implemented, the counselor has begun to prepare members for the group. The overall theme for the group clarifies the common ground and implies group goals. Members can begin to relate their needs and expectations to these goals and the theme. Throughout this process of engaging members in the group, the counselor must "tune in" to what potential members are experiencing in their wishes and fears for joining such a group. While preparing members, the counselor needs to prepare oneself.

"Tuning in" is the counselor's skill for preparatory empathy (Schwartz, 1976). The counselor anticipates the potential feelings and concerns of prospective group members. This attempt to guess accurately what might be going on for these prospective members while they are considering joining the group prepares the counselor for reaching for indirect communications and for responding to these directly (Shulman, 1979). When we alert ourselves to what might be the wishes and fears of these particular prospective members, we can help them express and clarify them in our contacts related to forming the group. For instance, the counselor tunes in to the mistrusts and fears of parents who abuse their children as potential members of a counseling group with the theme "Being More Effective Parents." When these parents ask the counselor what will happen with the information they share in the group, the counselor who has tuned in can respond directly to their fears of official retaliation by noting them and by clarifying the principle of confidentiality as it is appropriate to this group. Basically, tuning in requires answering the question: What would I be experiencing in feelings and concerns if I were this person in this situation considering joining a group around this theme?

Example

Now let us look at these principles and skills of the pregroup phase in one of the counseling groups which is used throughout the chapters in Part II: group counseling using the TACIT model in a project with fifth-graders in the school. The counselors are students in a college course for the purpose of learning to work with groups and which I taught.

The pregroup (private) phase began when I decided that the best way to learn to work with groups effectively was to work with one. At the same time a teacher in an elementary school in my community consulted me regarding particular problems in her fifth-grade classroom group. The school represented the microcosm of a mixed racial and lower socioeconomic part of the community. Several of the kids in her classroom were resistant to learning activities and especially disruptive. They prevented the learning of others. As we discussed this behavior in relation to developmental needs, we grew excited about the possibility of a group service program for all of the youngsters in both of the fifth-grade classes in this school. I clarified these needs as I understood them and developed a preliminary program for providing counseling groups to meet these needs through the students in my class. In conjunction with both of the fifth-grade teachers, the elementary guidance counselor assigned to the building, and the principal of the school, I drafted a proposal which got approval from the Director of Pupil Personnel Services and the Superintendent of Schools. Following are excerpts from this proposal:

> The counselor's function in the public schools is one of mediating between the need of the child to use the school and the need of the school to serve the child. One of the barriers to establishing this common ground between the child and the school is the child's stage of psychosocial development in relation to the classroom environmental demands. Quite often the child's normal developmental tasks do not match with the school system's task demands. Enabling students to accomplish primary developmental tasks can free them to use skills more effective for classroom learning.
>
> The groups are established to help members accomplish peer-related developmental tasks. The specific objectives are related to the primary developmental tasks of preadolescents (age 9–13).
>
> The point of departure for many programs with this age-group is the developmental theory of Erik Erikson (1950). Erikson views the most important psychosocial developmental task of preadolescence as industry, if accomplished, and the development of inferiority if social supports for industry skills are not forthcoming. The base for industry is the resolution of the earlier development of basic trust, autonomy, and initiative versus mistrust, shame and doubt, and guilt. These earlier tasks are primarily accomplished in relationship with adults in which the child experiences an orderly, predictable relationship, a sense of self-control without a loss of self-esteem, and a sense of direction for the child's own behavior.
>
> The peer group is the major medium for learning industry without restricting feelings of inferiority. Socially, this stage is most decisive. The child needs to learn that industry requires cooperation with others (division of labor) and feeling a special sense of worth for what one produces with others. This interdependent work is based on mutual trust, self-control (autonomy), and initiative.
>
> The intricate relationship of work to self-esteem at this stage of development often leads the child to look toward school as a chore rather

than a delight. The excitement stemming from new learnings and friendships needs concerted attention. Otherwise, many children begin marking time in school. Additionally, peer group norms take on primary significance. If the definition of success in the peer group counters the classroom norms, children may work hard (industry) on those tasks which defeat accomplishment of school work.

Some form of systematic program devoted to helping the child understand self and others can serve as a deterrent to the crushing of the child's interest in school at this stage of development. A TACIT theme-centered group program takes this important, perhaps most important, requirement for successful social functioning out of the realm of chance and into the mainstream of the school experience.

The purpose of group work with these students is the development of interpersonal and group membership skills which could enhance self-esteem. In this sense the group experience is developmental and structured in such a way that members can accomplish peer-related preadolescent developmental tasks. The intent is to have direct bearing on interpersonal and learning satisfactions in the existing classroom group and to provide for the learning of important preventative skills to ensure better use of the group-based learning experiences in the classroom and outside. Specific objectives are: (1) developing members' ability to relate to peers without giving in to antisocial peer group pressure; (2) developing the ability to cooperate with others toward accomplishment of group projects; (3) developing the ability to find a satisfactory place of belonging in reference to peer activities; and (4) developing a sense of self as worthwhile and competent.

The chosen theme, based on the common developmental tasks and the above objectives, is "Getting Along with Others in Groups." Relevant subthemes are "Letting Others Know Me," "Getting to Know Others," "Resolving Interpersonal Conflicts," and "Completing Group Projects Successfully." These subthemes in this order relate to both overall theme relevance and the sequential TACIT process "themes" associated with the stages of group development. Same-sex groups are composed from two fifth-grade classrooms in one school, as based on developmental needs and to increase homogeneity. Members from each classroom are mixed in composing the individual groups to ensure maximal heterogeneity within the commonality of developmental task. Each group meets for ten meetings weekly with two advanced student co-workers.

The seven treatment groups are composed of five to six members. The counselor pairs are matched for complementary knowledge and experience in working with preadolescents and in using program activities. All groups meet in the school building for one hour per week for ten consecutive weeks on Tuesday mornings.

All group members are pre- and post-tested through two instruments. A Behavior Checklist is designed in conjunction with the teachers to rate behavior change both in the classroom and in the group.

This checklist is marked by the teacher for each youngster, based on classroom observation, both before the first group meeting and at the conclusion of the group meetings. The same checklist is marked by the student group workers at the end of the third, sixth, and ninth meetings. This checklist serves also to indicate behavioral attributes used for composing the groups.

The second instrument is a sociometric which requires group members to rank each other on three criteria: (1) ability to cooperate in the group; (2) confidence in self; and (3) caring about the group. These are administered at the end of the third and the last meeting to measure increased accuracy in interpersonal perception (empathy) and to note particular self-concept changes during the experience.

The next step in this project was helping the student-counselors tune in to the prospective members in order to orient them to the groups. Classroom time was taken for them to review their knowledge of preadolescents. Then, they were asked to return in fantasy to a day in their lives when they were fifth-graders. The discussion of the fantasy sensitized the student-counselors to such themes as the importance of their esteem as seen through the eyes of their peers, their need for close friendships, and their wishes and fears for closer relationship with adults—especially with parents and teachers. Next, they rehearsed explaining the groups to the fifth-graders in their own classroom, anticipating feelings and concerns, and encouraging the kids to join the group and get their parents' permission slips signed to permit this participation.

The actual orientation session held by the student-counselors with the fifth-graders closely approximated this "tuning in" experience. The preadolescents were excited about the groups, wondered about some of the specific activities they would experience as related to the theme, and had several questions about how the groups would be composed. The student-counselors responded to these indirect clues by directly noting the fears that they may be in groups with some kids that they thought could not understand them and that they may be required to do some things they would not really want to do. They responded to these fears with some assurance that the children would be in groups with at least some other kids who seemed similar to them, that the group together would plan the activities, and that no one would be required to participate in any activity if he or she did not really want to. The Parents' Permission Slips were given out and returned unanimously the next day. Then, a second orientation meeting was held wherein members discovered who would be in their particular group and who would be their student-counselors. The groups were ready to begin.

Trust in the Early Meetings

Individual Process

When the group actually begins, the Trust process theme is reflected in members' orientation to each other ("I-We") and the content theme ("I-It"). On some level of awareness, each person coming into the group has three sets of questions for which he or she tentatively explores answers. The first set is questions about *me* (the "I"):

> "How should I present myself here?"
> "What do I want and what do I have to do to get it?"
> "Can I be who I am and belong to this group?"
> "What's safe to disclose and express about myself here?"
> "Will I be so different and not understood that I will feel left out, alienated, alone?"

Another set of questions relates to others (the "We"):

> "Is there anyone else here like me?"
> "Will I get understanding and support from anyone here?"
> "How are they going to feel about me and what are they going to think about me?"
> "What do they want from me and from this group?"
> "Do we share common goals and can we work together toward these goals?"

The third set of questions relates to the counselor and the process (the "It"):

> "What are we going to be doing here?"
> "What are the rules or expectations here?"
> "What am I going to be required to expose about myself, or to discover about myself that I don't want to know or want others to know about me?"
> "How will I be treated—judged? rejected? bullied?—or accepted and cared for?"
> "What is the counselor's stake in this process?"
> "What kind of person is he or she?"

Group Process

The members explore answers to their questions about self, others, and the counselor from the time they first sit face to face in the group. This exploration seeks some assurance of a climate for basic trust on which to choose to involve (not yet invest or commit) themselves in the group. They approach and avoid participation in a cautious seeking for potential goals. They size up each other and the counselor through an arm's length exploration process. They search for a place and a viable role for themselves in the group. This place and role enables them to feel secure, to experience an initial sense of belonging, and to feel important to the group, provides security, protects members from early exposure, yet gives them influence over the evolving group goals and norms.

Initial trust comes from their perception of group structure. As if they had entered a dark room for the first time and could not find the light switch, their fears are intensified until they feel their way around the structure of the room as related to expectations of where the furniture may be placed and where they may find some light. So it is in the group. They search for a structure which is familiar in terms of positions, statuses, roles, norms, and aspects of approval, respect, and domination.

This puzzled, testing, hesitant search is especially dependent. Members expect the counselor to provide answers to their fearful and unstated questions and to direct them to a position and role for initial trust. They particularly look to the counselor as the leader to validate themselves. There is the underlying hope that "If this leader, this significant other, sees me as belonging and O.K., then I am O.K. in this group." Much of the initial communication is directed toward the counselor as leader. He or she is carefully, constantly, and subtly studied for expectations and rewards. Members manifest behavior which gained approval from authorities in the past. Therefore, they do not connect with what other members have expressed and do not synchronize interaction.

As members are encouraged to interact with each other around the theme rather than with the counselor (to connect the "I," the "We," and the "It"), they discover similarities and differences. As they follow the ground rules, they build group norms for meeting trust needs through early security and consensus and a vague sense that their goals are shared—are "group goals." This climate, as it increases trust, builds a base for cohesiveness. The opportunity for risk of more authentic participation and the disclosure of differences increases. The structure evolves through which members can feel safe and can begin to trust that others might understand and care about them. The group, as a group, begins.

Counseling Process

During the Trust stage the primary task of the counselor is to enable a climate in which members get answers to the trust questions they are silently asking. The counselor must carry out fully the providing (or caring) function and moderately assume the directing, catalyzing, and processing functions. The skills for translating these functions into counselor activities involve the following: attending, observing, contracting, active listening or empathy, clarifying, and elaborating.

Skills

Attending.   The counselor attends physically, contextually, and personally (Carkhuff, 1980). Attending physically means getting one's body ready to tune in to the members and to communicate interest. We need to posture ourselves to face members as squarely as possible, to lean toward them, and to maintain face-to-face eye contact with all members if possible. This is as important as we greet and communicate with individual members before the group begins as it is once we sit with the group in a circle. Attending contextually refers to arranging the counseling environment to communicate our interest and support for group members. This skill suggests that chairs be placed in a circle, which can facilitate the members' communication of interest and attentiveness to each other. Also, the chairs, if possible, should be of the same height to communicate equality and partnership rather than authority and power. Finally, attending personally may involve meeting immediate physical needs of group members as well as the posture (squaring, eyeing, and leaning) which indicates warmth, respect, interest, and attentiveness. Physical needs may include concern about each members' hunger and comfort as well as needs for solitude or activity at times. Depending on the times of group meetings and the "tuning in" preparation, the counselor may attend to physical needs by offering snacks and drinks at the group meeting.

Observing.   Observing includes noting the nonverbal communication of members. This communication can give messages about members' energy level and feelings. The messages in groups come from body postures, facial expressions, appearances, spacing in relation to the group and other members, and seating patterns. These clues may be our most basic evidence to understanding where other members are throughout the group experience. They especially help us to know them in the very first meetings when there may be incongruences between what members communicate verbally and nonverbally. High energy and interest are communicated by strong attending postures of group members (squaring, eyeing, and leaning forward). Members react quite often to other members with their posture and with facial expressions more readily than through words in the early meetings. Reaching for the direct expression of these indirect cues can enable members to begin to relate to each other and invite more contact from individuals in the group. ("Jack, you were very interested and frowning as you were listening to Jill talk. I sensed some strong reactions in you to what she was saying. If I'm on target, could you share those with Jill and us?")

Contracting. Contracting involves three basic skills (Schwartz, 1971; Shulman, 1979). These are clarifying purpose, clarifying roles and responsibilities, and reaching for members' feedback (their perception of their individual and collective expectations, goals, and stakes in the process). In the TACIT theme-centered approach, the purpose of the group must be stated simply, directly, and without jargon. It should openly reflect the stake of the setting and the counseling and the possible stake of the members in the group process. In counseling the fifth-graders in groups, the student-counselors could not clarify the purpose adequately through such jargon as: "We are here for you to experience the stages of group development so that you can move through trust, autonomy, closeness, and interdependence in order to increase your self-actualization and achieve more in your school classroom." Some of the kids would likely be scared that they would be getting a vocabulary test and caught in not understanding. Or they would likely ask, "What in the world do you mean?" Rather, the student-counselors began the contracting by clarifying purpose somewhat as follows:

> My name is Trudy Sell and this is Joy Seavers. We are student-counselors. Your teachers asked us to help you learn to get along with each other better in groups. That is the theme for our group: "Getting Along Better in Groups." We believe we can help you talk about things and do things together in this group for you to learn to get more for yourselves and give more to others in other groups, such as your

classroom. We know you are wondering what this group will be like and would like to answer any questions you have about what we have said.

Such a simple statement of purpose and theme calls forth a more direct discussion of the member's feelings and concerns regarding trust. They do not have to use subtle messages and interaction to discover why the counselor is there. The counselor does need to anticipate the likely questions about how the counselor might help. This concern, stated directly or indirectly, requires some attention to clarifying roles and responsibilities in contracting (Kravetz & Rose, 1974). In the TACIT approach, the counselor can introduce the ideas of the need to balance "I-We-It" interaction and the ground rules, especially the "Be Your Own Chairperson" rule. He or she can also indicate that each member's responsibility is to associate as much as possible to the theme, to select appropriate subthemes for each session, to get to know what the theme means to the member himself and to other members, and to take responsibility for helping each other accomplish individual and group goals. The contract establishes the concept of parallel processes in the group process; that is, it specifies the task of the counselor as enabler as related to the purpose of the group within the setting and the counselor's stake in group process and the separate tasks of the members as they relate as individuals ("I's") to each other ("We") around the theme ("It"). As Schwartz (1971) has noted:

> The convergence of these two sets of tasks—those of the clients and those of the agency—creates the terms of the *contract* that is made between the . . . group and the agency. This contract, openly reflecting both stakes, provides the frame of reference for the work that follows, and for understanding when the work is in process, when it is being evaded, and when it is finished [p. 8].

Contracting is negotiating. Both members and the counselor are involved in the clarification of purpose, theme, and tasks. Therefore, reaching for member feedback is essential. Members are asked for their reaction to the stated purpose, theme, and tasks and their suggestions on how to proceed. This negotiation itself contributes to initial trust by indicating that the counselor is concerned about the individuals in this particular group and wishes to be accountable to them.

The contract permits group members, at least in theory, to hold the counselor accountable for his or her actions. Even though members may often feel powerless (and frequently may be) to confront the counselor about upholding the terms of the contract, its use shows respect and encourages shared responsibility and partnership in the work together. Contracts, in this sense, can reduce group members' dependency upon the counselor. They are not expected to enter into relationships with each other and the counselor simply on the basis of the blind trust that their interests will be capably served.

This reaching for feedback in negotiating the contract is especially important in groups of involuntary members. These are groups in which members may be coerced to join—as in prisons, for parolees, with abusing parents, with those who are truant or "act out" in the schools, and so on. The "tuning in" anticipates member resistance, anger, and high levels of mistrust in beginning these groups. The members' discovery of counselor's stake in their interest and their opportunity to influence the contract are vital dynamics to lessen this mistrust and to communicate respect for the choices they do have—their own level of investment and participation in the group.

The initial contract is then lived. The counselor in the TACIT model does not provide a wide range of activities to spark interaction. He or she helps members get started on discussing the theme and uses skills of active listening, empathy, clarifying, and elaborating to help members ("I's") focus interaction with each other ("We") around the theme ("It"). He or she provides by balancing the "I-We-It" through the functions of catalyzing and processing member-to-member connections and with directing only when members need to be reminded of the terms of their contract.

The best procedure for living the contract and carrying out these functions moderately to help the group get started is the "triple silence" (Cohn, 1972). In the triple silence members are asked to get into contact with: (1) the theme ("It"); (2) their own individual here-and-now feelings about being in the group ("I"); and (3) the other members in the group ("We"). For example, the student-counselors with the fifth-graders asked them to shut their eyes and to become aware of their feelings about themselves in groups in which they have been members—perhaps their classroom, perhaps on the playground, perhaps with their families, and so on. This invites a connection between the "I" and the "It." Then they were told to open their eyes, to look around at the others in this group, and to become aware physically and emotionally of their reactions. This can link the "I" and the "We." Finally, the "I-We-It" connection was encouraged by the following directions: "Close your eyes again and please remain silent. In your imagination, picture a member of this group who you might like to be more like in groups. Now in your imagination tell him or her why you would like to be more like him or her and imagine his or her response."

Then the counselor introduces, or reintroduces, some of the important ground rules and invites participation and interaction. One way of extending this invitation is for the counselor to communicate:

> Let's now talk about whatever you want to—the theme, my suggestions to you, your thoughts, experiences, or feelings—whatever you want to talk about. Please be your own leader (chairperson) and try to get what you want from the group and to give what you want to give. I will do the same as my own leader (chairperson) and try to understand and help others understand what you are saying, what you want, and what you are experiencing here. Please interrupt when you are bored, distracted, angry, or experiencing anything which prevents your participation.

An important element of contracting in the TACIT model is the establishing of ground rules for suggested ways of proceeding to interact in behalf of group goals. This skill has been called "norming" in other models (Gill & Barry, 1982), as the ground rules present potential norms for members to use in pursuing their interactional concerns (Cohn, 1972; Greenwald, 1972; Levitsky & Perls, 1970; Shaffer & Galinsky, 1974; Zinker, 1970). With the exception of the "Be Your Own Chairperson" rule which is stated in the introductory procedures, these guidelines are usually introduced when they are most appropriate. For example, the "Speak One at a Time" rule would probably not be mentioned at the beginning of the group but would be introduced only at a point where several members were speaking at once, or where two or more members were making side comments to each other secondary to the main group interaction. These rules are presented as procedures or possible group norms to be kept in mind while pursuing interactional concerns. If followed as much as possible, they can facilitate the "I-We-It" balanced TACIT process. Seven of these potential rules are as follows:

1. *Be your own chairperson.* That is, you are responsible for choosing what you want to talk about, share, and do in the group. Take initiative. Try not to merely react to others and to wait to be contacted by others. Reach out, and contact others. Try to be yourself, to share yourself, and respond to others genuinely. This includes choosing your own goal(s) for these meetings.

2. *Speak to individuals.* As a general rule, speak to individual members rather than to the group as a whole. This helps to establish and develop relations with individual members. You can be more direct, concrete, and specific in your interactions and get closer to each other.

3. *Speak as "I."* As much as possible use the pronoun "I" rather than such general pronouns as "we," "you," "they," or such abstract and depersonalizing substitutes as "one," "people," etc., when speaking to the group. Strangely enough, the pronouns you use can make a difference is getting to know and getting closer to others.

4. *"Own" our interaction.* Part of taking initiative is "owning" the interactions of others. In the group, when two members speak to each other, it is not just a private interaction. All members "own" the interaction and need to contribute their own thoughts and feelings. Your tendency will probably be not to own the interactions of others because you do not want to "interrupt." Being tactless is one thing; spontaneous involvement and feedback, motivated by care, is another.

5. *Deal with the here and now.* Try to establish some here-and-now immediacy. When you talk about things that are happening or have happened in the past outside the group (the "there and then"), try to relate what you are saying to these members in this group and how you see these affecting you. This does not mean that you should never deal with the there and then, but try to do so in order to further the task of establishing and developing relationships within the group.

6. *Disturbances come first.* None of you can be fully involved in our group process as long as you are acutely bothered by something, experiencing emotional interference, or wanting to withdraw. There will be times when each of us will experience blocks to our involvement. At these times it is important that we try to share these disturbances with the group or reach for this sharing if we sense it in others.

7. *Speak one at a time.* Interaction can best proceed when we avoid whispered side conversations, do not all talk at once, and prevent the confusion of trying to listen to more than one speaker at a time. If we use this practical guideline of speaking one at a time, we can avoid much of this confusion and concentrate our energies on those individuals who are talking.

The ground rules are designed to enhance the learning of the autonomy ("be your own chairperson"; "disturbances come first"; "speak as I") and interdependence ("own interaction"; "speak to individuals"; "deal with here and now") which together constitute the assumption of responsibility within the group. The "speak one at a time" ground rule is the most practical and is designed to avoid the confusion of several members speaking all at the same time and to teach members how to listen to each other within the group.

Some contracting techniques are useful to help the group to focus upon the theme of the meeting and to use the ground rules. For example, in relation to "be your own chairperson," the counselor might wonder aloud if a silent member is getting from and giving to the group as much as he or she would like. The counselor might even encourage the silent member to take a few moments, while the group waits, to develop in fantasy his or her own "wishes" as to what he or she would ideally like to see happen within the remainder of the meeting—either in relation to him or herself, to others, or to the theme. The counselor might then, once the silent member has had the fantasy, encourage the member to try to make it occur in reality. The ultimate choice of whether or not the silent member verbally participates belongs to him or her (autonomy). The member may, of course, as a result of the counselor's encouragement, begin to participate more fully (interdependence).

The counselor, through the "disturbance" rule, encourages each member to let the group know when he or she is too distracted or preoccupied to partake fully in the theme-relevant group discussion. However, this kind of self-chairpersonship, which is difficult at best, may be especially burdensome at those moments when a member is upset. Therefore, it is especially important for the counselor to be aware of the signs of disturbance in any member and to encourage the member to express concerns to the group. It may often be sufficient for a member to simply talk about the feeling, especially if the member then receives some understanding and/or support. At other times, especially later in group process, some structured experiments might be more appropriate. For example, the member who feels overwhelmed by a fear of rejection in the group might be encouraged to go around to each member and begin his or her statement with "I want you to like me for my . . ." which the member then completes differently in each instance. In using this rule, the counselor attempts to limit the expression of each disturbance to the here-and-now context as much as possible. Its purpose is not to resolve severe personal disturbances but to help the member experience and "own" the distress to a point where the member can return his or her attention to the group's work.

Another useful technique for operationalizing the "disturbances come first" rule is the "shuttling" procedure. When members or the entire group seem to be avoiding or resisting the work at hand, they are asked to shuttle between here-and-now contact of the group experience and there-and-then withdrawal in fantasy. For example, the counselor may ask all members to go in fantasy to a place where they feel better than they do in the here and now and to get in touch with that experience. Then they are asked to return silently to the here and now of the group and to get in touch with their feelings about being "here" versus being "there." Next, they are instructed to return again to the more comfortable place, shuttle again back to the here and now, and to discover what is "there" that is missing "here" for them. A third shuttle to there and then and here and now can be suggested, along with instructions that they try to bring more of what they experience in the "then and there" to the "here and now." In other words, they are encouraged to try to "be their own chairperson" and attempt to make the group more a resource for meeting the contact and/or withdrawal needs discovered in the fantasy shuttling.

A useful way of encouraging group members to discover that they are often other's best resources when the "own our interactions" is to "stop-action" and ask each member to share what he thinks is going on between two members, or between the counselor and a member, in a particular interaction. Another technique for introducing this ground rule is to ask the members of the interaction to choose two to three other members who were not actively involved and check out what they were experiencing during a particular interactional episode. The goal is the opportunity for more active and responsible interaction from all members.

The "speak one at a time" ground rule is, in a sense, the most practical of the seven. It constitutes an attempt on the part of the counselor to prevent the confusion of several members speaking simultaneously. All those wishing to speak could be encouraged to decide among themselves who will talk, or the counselor could ask each of them to say quickly what he or she wants to say, like the snapshot technique mentioned earlier.

This rule is also invoked when there is only one member speaking as part of the formal group interaction and when subgroups have whispered separate conversations to this main speaker. The counselor can encourage such subgroup members to make their statements, one at a time, to the group at large, since they reflect responses to the group process, or disturbance, and as such are an invaluable part of the group process. In other words, in this approach the content of these whispers can never be totally irrelevant to the group interaction. This request is never given as admonishment for the purpose of embarrassment. It is always asked in the spirit of concern for the members' interaction in relation to self-chairpersonship, speak as I, disturbances come first, and owning the interaction rules.

Many of these procedures for contracting were used in the fifth-grade groups. In these groups, the "triple silence" and introductory procedures got members started in living their terms of the contract. Then the counselors used more fully the active listening, empathy, clarifying, and elaborating skills.

Active Listening and Empathy.   Active listening is responding to members with what one hears. Because the counselor in the TACIT approach wants members to respond actively and with empathy to each other, he or she does not use the skill of active listening after every member's comment (as it is often used in individual counseling). Rather, the counselor uses active listening under two special conditions. The first is the situation in which a member has risked communication in the group and no other members respond; the second is when responses by other members to a particular communication do not fit with the understanding the counselor got from the message.

Active listening requires responses at three levels—often in sequence (Carkhuff, 1980). All three levels attempt to communicate understanding. Together they constitute the skill of empathy. Empathy involves suspending personal judgments and as the American Indians expressed it: "Walking a mile in the other's moccasins." Through empathy, the counselor tries to crawl inside the skin of members, to see the world through their eyes, and to understand what they are experiencing. Much research has identified the empathy skill as a central one in all successful counseling (Carkhuff, 1969; Rogers, 1961; Shulman, 1979; Truax, 1968a). Empathy is expressed through active listening at the levels of content, feelings, and the relation of feelings to content.

In responding to content, the counselor shares the degree of empathic understanding of a message by paraphrasing in his or her own words the words heard from a particular member. Basically the counselor responds with something like "You're saying _____" or "In other words _____." If this content is accurately reflected to the member, he or she should experience that the counselor hears what the member has said. At that level, the member feels attended to, listened to, and understood.

Responding to feelings requires reaching for the emotional part of the message, sharing the counselor's "hearing" of the nonverbal feelings expressed in the way the message was delivered, and sharing how the counselor understands the other would be feeling in the situation. These feelings include those that are directly expressed in the words and those which the counselor has picked up from indirect expressions or from the empathic "guessing" about what they are. The members feel particularly understood when the counselor (or other group members) can reflect their feelings at a level deeper than their own awareness (Anderson, 1978; Carkhuff, 1969).

The third or deepest level of active listening and empathy is responses which connect feelings and content. These responses deepen the meaning and understanding for the member who communicated and for the understanding of other members. Feelings are always in reference to content. They exist for certain reasons. When feelings are complemented with content in our responses, the person can feel uniquely understood. Feelings tend to be universal in group experiences (Anderson, 1980a). The individualized aspect of feelings is the specific content for the person who is experiencing them. We all experience love, pain, anger, joy, and fear. But we do not love or fear the same realities. Responding to feelings and content means putting the members' feelings into words and relating these feelings to the content of the message: "You feel unsure of this group because you don't believe others here can understand you." "You feel excited about what Jill said because you also have experienced the fears she is expressing." And so on.

Clarifying. Clarifying skills entails helping members communicate accurately to increase the potential of their being understood and helping them direct this communication to the intended recipient. Active listening in itself is clarifying. As the counselor feeds back the message about content, feelings, and the relation of content to feelings, members are able to assess how their intended messages are being received, at least by the counselor, and can alter communication to express the message more accurately. This process clarifies.

Clarifying skills can also contribute enormously to the group's building of initial trust around common goals and themes and other similarities. The counselor can especially listen to what members are expressing indirectly about their expectations, wants, and/or goals for themselves and the group. This listening permits these to surface for clarification of their commonness with others in the group and their relation to the group's stated purpose, theme, and contract.

Clarifying also involves using the ground rules to help members speak for themselves, speak to individuals, speak as I, and place disturbances first. In addition to responding to content, feelings, their relationship, and the goals implicit in the communication—"You feel _____ because _____, and you want to _____ in this group"—clarifying requires questioning. The counselor needs to ask: "What is the statement behind your question?"; "What are you saying about what you hope happens for you or others in this group?"; "What is going on for you right now?"; "Are you directing that message to anyone in particular in this group? (If so, who?)" This last question is an especially important use of questions for clarifying early in the group. It encourages members to make contact with each other as a prerequisite for developing trust and initiating the TACIT group process.

Finally, a special use of clarifying in the early group process is reaching inside silences. Silences are always meaningful. They are an important form of communication. The counselor who asks for the meaning of a silence he or she does not understand or who shares his or her own understanding of the meaning of a particular silence and checks whether this understanding is accurate is clarifying both for him or herself and for other members what the silence means.

Elaborating. Elaborating skills are closely related to clarifying. The difference is that they are designed to move members farther in expressing understood concerns rather than to further the counselor's and members' understanding per se. The elaborating skills include moving from the general to the specific, containment, focused listening, and questioning. In moving from the general to the specific, the counselor reaches for the feelings behind content, seeks the relation of a member's there-and-then concern to here-and-now group process, and tries to get details of specific content and feelings. Containment means actively not acting. That is, we choose to hold back responses to permit a member to elaborate on communications without premature interruption or closure and to permit openings for other members to respond. Focused listening is "honing in" to the important aspects of messages to encourage elaboration of these. Particularly focused upon are the here-and-now components of a communication—the content, feelings, and goals related to the person's experience in this group at this time. Questioning in the elaboration process involves requests for more information on particular aspects of vaguely stated content, feelings, and/or goals.

Dynamic Balancing

These Trust skills, as well as all of the TACIT skills, dynamically balance the group. Dynamic balancing refers to the counselor's activity in ensuring that the group process does not remain overly focused on any one part of the "I-We-It" triangle. The skill lies in detecting those decisive points at which the group is becoming stuck and is therefore most ready for a shift of some kind, for instance, from "I" to "We."

Certain techniques are helpful in making these transitions. For instance, the snapshot go-around technique can be used to help the group know where each of its members is at any one time. In this device, the counselor creates a "stop-action" situation by snapping his or her fingers and saying: "Please try to pinpoint just where you were at the moment I snapped my fingers and stopped the action. Now go around, each in turn starting from my left, and give a brief statement of what your inner experience was at that point" (Shaffer & Galinsky, 1974). It is important that this exercise be handled in a disciplined way; each member is to be as brief as possible, and each person should proceed in order without spontaneous interaction. In other words, even though one member's experience may have involved negative comments about another (or the counselor), the other (or the counselor) is not given a chance to reply until a formal "go-around" has taken place. This is a relatively easy way to introduce a "We" focus and is designed to promote a greater sense of group cohesion, one of the most important variables in any group process related to successful outcomes for members (Yalom, 1975, pp. 45–69). Dyadic interactions can be intensified by having the two members experiencing conflict and tension line up facing each other at opposite ends of the room, walk toward each other in the center, and nonverbally respond to each other; or be asked to role-play each other and continue their dialogue; or be asked to express *both* their resentments and appreciations; or be asked to repeat *in their own words* what they heard the other saying to the satisfaction of the other that this message was the intended one before making one's own response to the other. In these situations, the "We" focus will be intensified, though now its scope will be reduced to two people instead of the entire group. If the formal theme relates to interpersonal relations, these techniques will simultaneously strengthen the "It" point of the triangle.

A particularly useful technique for helping the group focus on the "We" dynamics of the evolving structure of the group is the following: The counselor moves to the center of the group and says, "I stand for the group at this moment. I want each of you to nonverbally place yourself in the room in relation to me as the group where you are presently experiencing your position in this group. Move around freely until you find a spot that best reflects this current experience of your place in the group. We will stop when everyone seems to have settled on a place." At the conclusion of this exercise members are asked to hold their places and through the "go-around" technique, to state how their physical place reflects their current experience of their position in the group.

In relation to the "It," the counselor strives to keep the theme in clear, not perpetual, focus throughout the group process. The theme gets optimum not maximum attention. A continual theme focus produces oversaturation and fatigue. Just as the natural rhythm of the perceiver is such that one cannot keep a stimulus "figure" for too long without it becoming "ground" (Passons, 1972; Stevens, 1971), group members can better attend to a theme if it is occasionally allowed to recede into the background. Spontaneous interactions unrelated to the theme, statements of disturbance, humor, and laughter, brief "snapshots" in which each member states whatever he or she was experiencing at a particular moment regardless of whether or not it is theme-relevant—all have a place in the group. The counselor's task is to return the group to the theme—sometimes subtly, sometimes obviously—but only when this is not done by the spontaneous behavior of the members themselves.

Expertise in the thematic area on the part of the counselor is useful, but it is not absolutely necessary. It is rare in counseling groups, where the theme centers on members' common problems or life situations, for the counselor to have as great an understanding of the content theme as members. The focus is primarily upon members' give and take at their own level around their common goal—the theme. The counselor needs to come to meetings with some plans for the theme discussion, but the best principle is to "overplan and underuse" (Tropp, 1972). The preference is the group's own proposals to approach the specific theme which was agreed upon between the group and the counselor at the end of the prior meeting. The "It" is theirs. The counselor's plans are based on thinking through the possibilities of common meanings of the theme for the group and how these might be explored. This planning can enhance the understanding of leads which come from the group and the offering of procedural suggestions if the group does not have any of its own. The decisions on focus and procedures are based on open agreement between the counselor and the group and related to the purpose and the time structure. Meetings are not aimless and eternal. The counselor needs to assure that time is not wasted. In a very real sense, every moment is precious.

Principles for the First Meeting

These introductory procedures and counseling skills can be summarized in certain principles which provide structure for the first meeting of the TACIT theme-centered group (Shulman, 1979). These are:

1. The counselor needs to introduce members to each other.
2. The counselor needs to make a brief, simple opening statement of the theme, which tries to clarify the agency's or setting's stake in providing the counseling group as well as potential subthemes (issues and concerns) that members might feel as urgent.
3. The counselor needs to obtain feedback from the group members on their sense of fit between their ideas of their needs and the counselor's and agency's or settings's view (the contract).
4. The counselor needs to clarify his or her function, tasks, and roles as explicated in the TACIT methodology.
5. The counselor must deal directly with any specific disturbances or obstacles to the group getting started (such as their stereotypes about group counseling, other members, or the counselor as an authority figure; or in the case of an involuntary group, their anger).
6. The counselor needs to encourage intermember interaction rather than discussion only between the counselor and individual group members, through introducing ground rules.
7. The counselor needs to develop a supportive culture in the group in which members feel safe and begin to have their needs for trust met.

8. The counselor needs to help group members develop a tentative agenda of subthemes for future work.
9. The counselor needs to clarify the mutual expectations of the agency or setting, the counselor, and group members (for example: the counselor's role, regular attendance, meeting starting on time, and ground rules). These expectations, rules, and regulations concerning structure are part of the working contract.
10. The counselor needs to gain some consensus from group members on specific next steps, such as central subthemes and concerns and the subtheme with which they wish to begin the next meeting.
11. The counselor needs to encourage honest feedback and evaluation of the effectiveness of the group.

These principles, procedures, and skills are designed to enable trust in TACIT group development. Now let us turn to examining these in action in an example of TACIT theme-centered group counseling.

Example

The following example demonstrates the use of the understanding of these counseling principles, procedures, and skills. It follows the earlier information on the counseling group project with fifth-grade preadolescents in school.

The counselors with this group are Trudy, the recorder, and Joy.* The members are six boys who meet with the counselors in one of the two empty classrooms. They are Chris, Darren, Jeff, Mike, Randy, and Ricky. The overriding theme is "Getting Along Better with Others in Groups."

In the following recordings we see the wishes/fears of the Trust stage in action. One worker, Joy, is ill and misses the first meeting. All members are present. Trudy begins by sharing her observations and feelings.

(I can point to the exact place at which our group process began. Its beginning was at the moment we walked down the hall into the classroom. Immediately, Darren and Chris argued over who was to lead the group [to the mystery of where we were actually going to go].

*Ms. Trudy Sell. The other worker was Ms. Joy Seavers.

Randy followed Darren, and Chris wanted to lead also. Mike walked beside me, smiling, and Ricky followed close behind. Jeff took special caution to be in the back of the group as we walked toward the room. As I am looking back on that beginning experience, I am surprised to see that the individual personalities in this first meeting very much reflected what I have just illustrated.)

Meeting 1

The group is fairly aggressive as a whole. Their fears, anxiousness, and confusions were masqueraded in their behavior. Except for Jeff, no one displayed initial phases of silence or uneasiness. They didn't wait for me to begin the experience. Darren immediately sat down at the teacher's desk. Chris stretched himself out across two desks and everyone else talked at once, except Jeff. I suggested that we move into a circle. Everyone plopped down onto the floor, responding: Darren moved the teacher's chair into the circle. I asked him to sit down with the group and he refused. Different members tried to get him to join us, but without success. Chris jumped to his feet, moved behind the chair and dumped Darren to the floor. I hadn't even introduced myself yet. I picked up the teacher's chair, put it into place, and walked back to the group. Everyone was sitting in the circle. The episode was over, Chris had helped me, and Darren seemed content with where he was now sitting. I decided to leave it as it was.

I introduced myself and the members began to ask me many questions about my classes, my car, etc. I spoke of my brothers and they picked up right away on telling the group of their brothers and sisters. Darren spoke fast and very loudly when telling the others about his older brother's sex class. I happened to glance at Jeff and he started to talk about his sisters. I sensed that he felt he had to because everyone else did. He seemed uninterested in what he was saying. When Jeff finally began to feel more comfortable, Chris interrupted him, then Darren interrupted Chris, saying he was "tired of this stuff." I said that we would talk about something else when Jeff was finished speaking. I pointed out the fact that everyone else got to talk without interruptions. I moved back to Jeff, but anything that he wanted to say was gone now. He was quiet again.

I was surprised at the way the group actually "helped" me move from one issue to the next. As I was just ready to discuss the theme, Chris asked, "What are we going to do here anyway?" Darren answered, mimicking someone's interpretation of the theme: "We're here to get along with everyone else." I ignored the sarcasm in his voice and asked the group what it meant to them. Everyone except Jeff and Ricky offered a meaning for the theme. They were all speaking at once. Ricky and Jeff eventually started also. I decided to hold on to the confusion for a few moments in order to see if it bothered anyone else. They became louder and louder until I finally yelled, "Wait a minute." Mike backed me up, yelling, "Talk one at at a time." We then established our first ground rule, just as Mike had put it. Everyone agreed and if it happened again, it was an accident. They remembered the rule and became aware of when it was violated. I then used the "triple silence." Afterwards the discussion led to their suggestion that they play a game.

The group then decided to play a game with a nurf football which was already in the room. As we played, I could see Jeff becoming more uncomfortable. Ricky loved the game and was a very good sport. Darren fought hard for attention and wanted everyone to throw the ball to him. He and Randy got into a fistfight over a dropped ball. I had to break it up, and said, "Is this any way to get along with others?" Darren said, "Yes," and Randy was silent. I handled the situation through the reactions that I saw. They both seemed very embarrassed and stood beside each other with no hostile feelings being evident. I decided that it was momentary anger—it was felt, expressed, and over. I didn't want to just end the games with that episode, so I made up another one with the nurf ball. Unplanned, but successful, this game proved to be a security activity and helped to rid Randy and Darren of their embarrassment.

One person stood in the middle, threw the ball in the air, and called someone's name; that person then ran to catch it. The game was very noncompetitive, and it really seemed to unite the group (partially because it was an outlet for uneasiness caused by the fight, and also because it gave them the opportunity to relate to others, feeling secure when someone chose them to get the ball). It worked fine because there was absolutely no favoritism. The choosing was very well balanced, and I noticed the members working to "include" Jeff. He responded. He started clapping, laughing, and really getting into the game.

At the end of the meeting we talked about the next meeting. Chris was curious about Joy and wondered if she would be like me. I told him that she wouldn't, because we are two different people. We had a brief discussion of how people are different. I tried to make them realize that Joy would not be just like me, but that we were alike in certain ways. I explained that she was looking forward to being with us but she couldn't because she didn't feel well. (I had explained this before, but they asked again.) I said that Joy was part of our group even though they didn't meet her in the first meeting.

Meeting 2

The continuance of Trust and the beginning of Autonomy took place in the second meeting:

I introduced Joy to the group and they readily introduced themselves to her. Joy had brought a blanket for us to sit on. Everyone except Chris and Darren seemed to like the idea. Chris and Darren sat on desks, refusing to sit down with the group. We asked them to tell Joy about our first meeting since she wasn't there. Everyone started telling her about the games we played and how much fun they were. Darren was very quick about telling her how he fell over a few desks. He assumed the same role as in the previous meeting. Joy asked them what else they did, and I was disappointed because it was almost as if they couldn't remember anything but the games. I had to direct them to remembering our discussions of the theme, of our ground rule of "speak as I," and the general purpose of the group. I even reminded them of the snack.

We introduced the subtheme of "Cooperating in Groups." Next was a conversation about physical fighting which really brought certain attitudes of members to the surface. I asked Darren if most of his punching around and hitting was for real or just for fun. He said that most of it was fun, but he likes to fight for real. Darren said he likes fights because he likes to see people bleed. I asked him why and he said he just likes it; no reason. I asked him if he likes people to hurt *him* and of course he said *no*. Then I said, "How do you feel when someone hurts you?" He said that he feels like hitting them back. I am sure that Darren knew exactly what I was trying to do but he couldn't break through the barrier of the presence of his peer group watching him and listening. I felt a definite need to have him start accepting responsibility for himself, so I tried to share my feeling with him. I explained what it felt like inside when someone hurt me. He just looked around, saying nothing, and feeling uncomfortable. He was afraid to get that close so I didn't push it.

Another prevailing issue in this meeting was the struggle for power and control. This seemed to be reflected in the decision-making process. The group became tired of sitting around. "All talk and no action," as Randy put it. We proceeded to decide what we would do as an activity, but many conflicts arose. Chris and Darren wanted to go outside and play football. *They* wanted to do this, and that's what the *group* would do! Chris went over to get the football and Darren jumped up, ready to go. Joy and I asked if everyone wanted to play football but not everyone did. Chris was a little upset and Darren was angry. We told them we had to decide as a group. I was surprised that Chris suggested something else. He said that we would play records. I asked if anyone else wanted to do this and Jeff raised his hand, saying nothing. Everyone else said playing records would be fine so Chris turned on the record player. Darren was upset, so we decided to play a few records, then go play football.

Chris stood at the front of the room with a make-believe microphone, singing with the music. Everyone ignored him, except myself. I stood there and watched him. I told him that he had a good voice. I felt that Chris needed recognition at times. There have been different instances when I have noted feelings of inadequacy from him. He is thirteen years old, as opposed to the others who are ten years old. One time the group told me about this and he didn't like it because they explained his older age by telling me how many grades he had flunked. I noticed that he is more mature in certain ways and I think that Joy and I should bring this maturity to the surface. Of all the members, he is the one whom I see as having a definite need for outwardly expressing how he feels. He seems to be close to understanding the reason for our project, and some individual focusing on him will help the group. For example, when Chris really wanted to play football but realized that not everyone else did, he was concerned about the confusion. Everyone seemed to like the records and he was pleased. Even Darren temporarily forgot his anger at not being the decision maker and others sat around, watching and listening to the music. They didn't want to dance, but they said that they liked watching us. Jeff was moving to the music until he noticed that I saw him. He stopped, looking very embarrassed. Then he got up and started to walk around.

Jeff is very afraid to become close to the group or anyone in it. It seems like he is holding so much back. He acts very nervous most of the time and I can feel his uneasiness. I've been trying to help him by deliberately directing small questions or just statements toward him. He never looks directly at me and usually his hands are moving as he does talk. He hasn't developed very much trust in the group. Only last week when we played football did I notice him responding to the group.

We never did make the football game. More records were played than was planned and we only had ten minutes remaining for our meeting. It didn't seem to bother anyone but Darren and Chris. Chris felt that we should still go out. Darren became furious and started blaming everything on Jeff. He was stomping on the floor and screaming about how it wasn't fair because we had decided to go out previously. It was difficult for me to understand what was going on because Jeff hadn't said anything. He only raised his hand to show that he would like to play records. Darren kept saying that it was all that "stupid Jeff's" fault that we played records too long. I confronted Darren by asking him why he didn't interrupt the dancing if he wanted to go out so badly. He simply would not admit that it was fun playing records and he forgot about football because of this. He just blamed it on Jeff again. Jeff was very upset, but didn't say anything to defend himself.

Ricky suggested that we decide on what we would do next week in the remaining minutes. Everyone agreed. Jeff was relieved that the conflict was over, and Darren stomped over to a desk to sit down with arms folded. We all decided to play football as soon as we got there next week. I asked Darren if he agreed and he just nodded his head. No one was really excited about the next meeting though. It wasn't a good way for the meeting to end at all, but the time was up. Everyone said good-bye and we left. I glanced back into the room. Darren looked back at me and made sure I saw him pouting. He was still in the seat that he had gone to after the conflict.

In this meeting, group members were fearing a closeness that the group could provide them. The counselors had been trying to enhance autonomy through providing an atmosphere where trust can be developed. Also the members were given every chance to be involved in decision making. This very process of making decisions leads to the struggles for power and control.

Summary

The Trust stage of the TACIT approach involves a pregroup phase and the early meetings. The pregroup phase requires moving from the private concept of the counselor to the public announcement of the group and the plans for convening it. Group composition and pregroup preparation are two important elements of this planning. The theme is chosen, potential members recruited and selected, and other plans for the first meeting are finalized. Then the group begins.

The first meeting is significant for creating a climate of trust to meet members' needs. The counselor needs to carry out fully the providing function and moderately the functions of directing, catalyzing, and processing. These functions are carried out by the skills of attending, observing, active listening or empathy, clarifying, and elaborating. The first meeting follows principles designed to structure the group for members' trust, autonomy, and initial interaction. These include clarification of the purpose in the theme and of the parallel tasks of the counselor and group members. Introductory procedures, proposed ground rules, and the counselor's responses manifest this stated contract and contribute to the establishment of initial trust.

The understanding of the Trust stage of TACIT group development and the principles and skills for the TACIT approach direct the counselor's activities in the first few meetings. These activities are demonstrated in a group with fifth-grade preadolescents in school. The group gets started, finds some initial trust in shared group goals and structure, and moves toward the process of the Autonomy stage.

Critical Incidents

Each chapter in Part II concludes with some critical incidents from another TACIT group, this one involving adolescents. These critical incidents are presented for the purpose of reviewing and summarizing some of the skills presented and to permit the reader to interact with the material by considering what you would do in response to these examples. A "critical incident" describes an event in the group which represents a significant point of choice for group members and the counselor. Critical incidents have been used to demonstrate stages of group development (Cohen & Smith, 1976), to assess leadership styles (Wile, 1972), and to study comparative methodologies for group counseling (Churchill, 1974; Corey, 1981).

The critical incidents in Part II follow the format suggested by Cohen and Smith (1976), with some adaptation. Each incident includes the stated meeting subtheme, a statement of the group context of the incident, and the event preceding the choice point. At the choice point you are asked to give your preferred response as the counselor and your rationale for this response. Finally, I present the response suggested by the TACIT model and a brief statement of its rationale.

The group consists of ten adolescents, five young men and five young women, all of whom were referred because of symptoms of school truancy. All, too, had some history of drug or alcohol abuse, and in a number of behavioral characteristics manifested much isolation and alienation from teachers, peers, and families. They decided to join the group with the theme of "Helping Each Other Stay in School," for fifteen meetings after a joint referral from the local school system and the public children and youth services agency. They were active clients in the latter as a result of their truancy, which was considered a "status offense" in their state juvenile justice system. I worked with the group as a demonstration of the use of the TACIT model in providing counseling services to such consumers.

The male members of the group are: Steve, a sixteen-year-old black; Gomez, a fifteen-year-old Puerto Rican; Tom and Jerry, both fifteen years old and white; and Mark a fourteen-year-old black. The female members of the group are Cheryl and Chris, fifteen years old and black; Judy, a sixteen-year-old and white; and Sandra and Jane, both fifteen years old and white.

Critical Incident 1

Subtheme. Getting Acquainted

Context of Incident. This is the first meeting. The initial group climate is a mixture of awkwardness and anxiety. Members seem unsure of their direction and unfamiliar with one another. After the initial "triple silence," some particularly anxious members make a few statements to the group with little response. One group member, Steve, who appears somewhat more aggressive, has apparently decided to initiate some action. He begins to speak in a loud, demanding tone.

Choice Point
Steve: "Hey, this is a waste of time! Let's get going. I think we should go around and each tell something about ourselves. You know, introduce ourselves and tell why we're here."
Gomez: "O.K. You start."

The group picks up on this idea and continues until everyone is finished. Now, it is your turn. Everyone is watching you closely and expectantly.
What would you do at this point? What is your rationale for this response?

TACIT Response.   The counselor initiates work on the group theme via contracting skills. These skills involve introducing self, sharing some of self, clarifying purpose and theme, clarifying roles and responsibilities, and reaching for feedback: "I am _____ and I am here to help you to learn to help each other to stay in school. Because I see this as a mutual aid group, one in which you help each other, I want to get to know you and help you get to know each other. I see my role as helping you to listen to, respond to, and help one another. In relation to the purpose of this group, I wonder how far this go-around has taken us in beginning to know each other. My guess is that it helped us break the ice and provide a way to fill in our time to relieve some of our fears. I think we may discover some more about each other toward the theme 'Helping Each Other Stay in School,' if we can share more of your individual goals for the group. That is, what do you want for yourself from being in this group? What do you think of what I have just said and of my suggestion?"

Rationale.   On the surface, this incident is a simple suggestion to put names and faces together in getting to know each other. It is an "ice breaker." At another level, the event reflects the group's reaction to their need for structure, their increased anxieties, and some feelings of dependency (their wanting to hear from you). They need, too, some encouragement to work and some trust that they can, with some initial guidance, do this work themselves. The response clarifies the group purpose and theme to provide some direction for the work, initiates a processing norm for the group (by referring to fears underlying interaction), and clarifies the counselor's role directly and indirectly by providing some guidelines for proceeding and by reaching for feedback.

Critical Incident 2

Subtheme.   Developing Trust

Context of Incident.   This event occurred in the second meeting, during the early part of the group's life. The members were still in an exploratory, fearful, wandering phase. They tended to avoid dealing with strongly expressed needs of individual members. One member who was quite anxious made a request of the group. This request was ignored and the group started off in a new direction, discussing an altogether different topic.

Choice Point

Jerry: "Let's discuss things in the group that keep us from knowing each other. I'd like to see us start by telling what we dislike most about each other."

There follows a moment of awkward silence, then the group starts off on another topic as if Jerry's statement had not been made. *What would you do at this point? What is your rationale for this response?*

TACIT Response. The counselor uses the active listening skill to respond to Jerry and contracting skills to suggest the "disturbance first" ground rule and to reach with empathy for the group's goals: "I need to interrupt. I am having trouble following this discussion because I am still with Jerry's comments. Therefore, before I can continue I need to hold myself to the 'disturbances come first' ground rule. I believe we left Jerry hanging. Jerry, I sensed your feelings of mistrust of where you stand with others in this group because you don't know them. My guess is that this is an issue for others but we might be afraid to discuss this. I wonder if the group wants to continue without responding to Jerry. What were you experiencing when Jerry was talking and what do you want to do about this?"

Rationale. The surface issue seems to be a legitimate request on the part of one member which was subsequently ignored by the others. The request was for personal and threatening information, however, increasing mistrusts and fears. Other important underlying issues are the group's responsibility toward individual members and the norms governing topics for discussion. Finally, the theme of the group and the contract calls for members' learning to deal with the needs of individual members, process itself (by being aware of what it is doing and how it affects members), and make more conscious decisions. Active listening responds to Jerry's feelings and content. Clarifying ground rules, goals, and norms for the group can help the group attend to the "I-We" interaction behind the "It."

Critical Incident 3

Subtheme. Developing Trust

Context of Incident. This incident also occurred in the second meeting. The discussion of the subtheme "Developing Trust" included several pessimistic statements by various group members regarding the lack of trust in the group, along with statements of the difficulty in trusting others. A generally gloomy prediction of the group's future came from Chris, who had been vacillating between being dependent and counterdependent thus far in the group meetings and who had made several attempts to lead the group.

Choice Point

Chris: "So what I guess I'm saying is I think we have an impossible task here. I don't think I'm going to trust anyone in this group completely in fifteen weeks. It just ... I don't know ... can't be done."

Following her statement, other group members nod their heads pessimistically. There follows a long period of silence.

What would you do at this point? What is your rationale for this response?

TACIT Response.   The counselor uses active listening skills to respond to Chris' feelings and content and reaches for wishes behind fears in Chris' ambivalence through elaborating: "You and others are discouraged about what we can accomplish in this group and yet you do seem to want something to happen for you. What do you think may help you to trust other members more than you do now?"

Rationale.   The counselor uses active listening to respond to *both* Chris and others. This is a group issue, yet the counselor avoids intense processing or overinterpretations in the Trust stage. The response is meant to establish a more supportive and free atmosphere, yet to create a climate for work. The noting of the naturalness of wish/fear ambivalences for Chris and other members invites her and others to express the wish side and to consider concrete solutions for resolving the surface and underlying trust issues.

7
Autonomy

The Autonomy stage of the TACIT model evolves as initial trust is established and most members have decided to involve themselves in the group. Then members seek autonomy in using the group's resources. This autonomy shifts members' preoccupation with acceptance, approval, and involvement to concern with dominance, power, and control. The group becomes a more potent instrument to help or to hurt. Unfortunately, too many groups do not resolve the power and control conflicts of the Autonomy stage. They entrench themselves in this structure. They hurt powerless members and limit the potential of growth for powerful ones. Too often, the counselor is a major obstruction to the group's development beyond this stage toward Closeness and Interdependence. At no point in the group's development are the counselor's function and skills more vital to individual and group growth than during this Autonomy stage.

In fact, many members entering counseling groups have little real hope for their wishes for authentic closeness and mutual aid to be fulfilled. They expect the group to be similar to others in which they found their satisfaction in positions and roles which confirmed some of their identity even though they might have experienced the frustration of increased alienation and feelings of not being understood. Our family groups, classrooms, work groups, and even friendship groups may serve more as a battleground for conflicts over power and control than experiences in closeness and interdependent mutual aid. We expect competition for positions, statuses, and powerful roles. We doubt, while we wish for, the possibility of cooperation toward mutual goals and having others be as concerned about our own needs as theirs. We learn to win or to lose, and we develop behavioral patterns in groups to increase our winning at the expense of others' losing. Counseling groups, to make a difference, must be an experience in mutual aid. They must enable members to regain faith in people and to risk moving beyond the competition for group resources to meet one's own needs at the expense of others.

Autonomy Conflicts

Almost all of the work done on the stages of group development view the Autonomy stage in such terms as "frustration," "conflict," "counterdependency," "control," "fight," "negative autonomy," "competitiveness," "disillusionment," "anger," "rivalry," "storming," "power bid," "rebellion," "authority-orientation," "resistance," "structure," "aggression," and "dissatisfaction." These all imply an early crisis in the group. Much of this work signals the catastrophic side of this. It often is experienced as such by members and the group "leader." Bennis and Shephard (1956), for instance, noted this stage as based upon an "authority crisis" wherein members wrestle with the leader for control of the group yet really want to be dependent on the leader for directing the group. They propose that it is only when members can overthrow the leader in rebellion that they can resolve their ambivalences about authority and can use the leader's resources for resolving the "intimacy crisis" which evolves.

Crisis, however, as the Chinese characters for their printed word of this concept reflects, involves both danger and opportunity. The Autonomy crisis is more pronounced perhaps in those groups in which members sense a potential for more authentic interaction and whose members have decided to join to fulfill these wishes. At the same time, they develop a structure from their fears that these wishes might be fulfilled. We both want and fear closeness, self-disclosure, being understood, growth, and interdependent mutual aid. While the fears influence the structure, the conflicts, and the crises of the Autonomy stage, the wishes remain and provide the opportunity—with help—for its resolution. The crisis itself reflects the growth of closeness and interdependence. If there is fighting in this evolving structure, there is also the potential for loving in the group.

The most detailed models of stages of group development indicate that the resolution of power and control dynamics leads to group cohesiveness, harmony, affection, warmth, and the revision toward a more equitable and less hierarchical structure (Bennis & Shepard, 1956; Cohen & Smith, 1976; Garland, Jones, & Kolodny, 1973; Gibbard & Hartman, 1973; Hill, 1976; Lacoursiere, 1980; Sarri & Galinsky, 1964; Schutz, 1958; Tuckman, 1965). Models which focus on the counselor's function and role in this development view this stage as an opportunity to resolve the negative autonomy of rebellion and to develop the positive autonomy by members' assuming responsibility. Members need to understand the evolving group structure and process and to choose to revise these more in line with wishes and less as defenses for fears. Movement is from "I won't" to "I want" and "I hope we want this, too." The suggested functions and skills of the counselor range from processing group structure (Bonney, 1969; Garland et al., 1973; Kepner, 1980; Klein, 1972; Lacoursiere, 1980; Levine, 1979; Northen, 1969; Yalom, 1975) to modeling the empathy which can help members recognize the hurts of others, compare these with their contract and needs, and manifest their wishes more than their fears in their choices in the group (Carkhuff, 1980; Corey & Corey, 1977; Culbert, 1970; Klein, 1972; Rogers, 1970; Saretsky, 1977; Trotzer, 1977). The principles and skills for the enabling functions of Autonomy spring from the understanding of these wishes and fears of members and how these are reflected in group process and dynamics.

Individual Process

The members in Autonomy have three sets of questions related to the "I," the "We," and the "It." The first set concerns the "I":

> "Where do I stand and rank in this group?"
> "Do I have enough power and control to get my needs met?"
> "How can I get more status and power in this group?"
> "Will I lose some of my position, status, and power if I am honest about my feelings?"

The second set involves the "We:"

> "Who's who in this group?"
> "How do others get power in the group and how will they use it?"
> "Would others care about me if I did not assume the position and roles they expect from me?"
> "Who ranks ahead of or below me in this group?"
> "Will the most powerful members continue to control this group for meeting their own needs at the expense of others?"

The third set relates to the "It," especially the counselor and the process of this particular group:

> "What is the appropriate behavior (norms) of this group?"
> "What is expected of us?"
> "How does the counselor give status to some members and deny it to others?"

"What would happen if we challenged the counselor's power?"
"In our decisions, what does the counselor really want and
    approve of without telling us?"

These questions pepper interaction. The "It" is often disguised
and is safe content that serves more as the battleground for forming
"I-We" relationships than as authentic focus on the theme. Individuals censor much of their responses through their perception of
what the powerful others may want to hear and their seeking for
more powerful positions in which to control group resources. Or they
take the roles of victim, scapegoat, or silent member—thereby demanding some attention by those who seem to be running the group.
Some are not so entrenched in this structure, appear more committed
to the group goals than to their own place in group structure, and
tend to settle for more moderate status during the early Autonomy
stage. These members are called "independents" by Bennis and
Shephard (1956) as different from the "dependents" who seek direction from others and the "counterdependents" who express their
dependency by aggressively fighting those with power and authority.
Often the independents are primary members for initiating the
movement from negative autonomy toward positive autonomy during this stage. Nevertheless, members' communications at this stage
include many attempts to command a particular relationship with
the group and the counselor as well as to report information with
relevance to the stated theme.

Members are especially aware of how decisions are made. While
they find it difficult to reflect this awareness when asked, they are in
constance vigilance for who most influences particular decisions
(both formal and informal ones) and who benefits most from such
decisions. The informal decisions are occurring all the time. Who
selects topics; who initiates them; who changes them? The formal
decisions occur when members are conscious as a group that they are
making them. Effective groups, which can revise structure to move
through this stage, consciously process their decisions and make the
informal decisions formal ones.

Group Process

As members move together from Trust to Autonomy, power and
control concerns dominate. The group develops a hierarchical structure of positions, statuses, roles, and norms for permitting certain

members to control the allocation of group resources such as time, attention, status, and emotional contact. Members compete for these resources, and conflicts evolve.

The conflict here is between members or between the members and the counselor as the perceived leader. Each member negotiates a preferred amount of autonomy, initiative, and power. Gradually a status and control hierarchy, a social pecking order, is established. The movement is from "I'm O.K. I belong here" to "I'm O.K. I *rank* here."

This structure stylizes the group. Communication patterns are established and forces are at work to freeze these patterns in the mutually formed positions, statuses, roles, and norms. High-status members, who often embody dominant norms in their behavior, tend to interact more exclusively with other high-status members. Low-status members participate through those with higher status. Trust at this point is not so much in other members with common needs and goals who share a common theme. Rather, trust is in a common, predictable structure. Members trust what they can control more than who they can contact.

This stage hurts some members. Those low on the totem pole may be reinforced in their low self-esteem. They may drop out and be hurt before the group has a chance to resolve the hierarchical conflicts of this stage. Subgroups develop as important islands of safety where the members can ally with others to guard their flanks. Subgroups also serve as support for power in influencing group decisions. The scapegoats and isolates who cannot coalesce into subgroups are particularly vulnerable to power cliques. They may be rejected or attacked in a manner which increases their fears, loneliness, and isolation in human relations. If their hopes for acceptance and understanding were high, they may lose most (if not all) of their faith in themselves and others. The group could increase rather than ameliorate their feelings of alienation.

This struggle for control is part of the process of all groups which take on significance for members. In the counseling group, it is always present to some degree. Sometimes it smolders. Sometimes it is quiescent. Sometimes it conflagrates fully. The counselor contributes greatly to TACIT development by challenging these structural obstacles. As the group deals with the counselor's place in this structure, it can discover its own authentic source of power in its potential for mutual aid and caring. It can develop its resources to meet the needs of *all* members.

The emergence of ambivalence and hostility toward the counselor is inevitable as the group confronts the authority theme of Autonomy. Members project dependencies upon the counselor as an omnipotent source of satisfying their needs. Simultaneously, their autonomy needs are seeking a climate free from domination and supportive of interdependence. The counselor refuses to feed the hunger of the omnipotent mystique, holds out faith that members can assume responsibility to find their own direction, and expects only that they confront the obstacles to goal achievement as explicit in their contract and theme. This confrontation includes the counselor as an obstacle as well. Then the counselor can influence a group structure that promotes equal opportunity and freedom for all members. For instance, if members can express their ambivalence and hostility toward the counselor, rather than off-target behavior directed toward the control of each other, they can get in touch with their own power to meet needs—both their own and others'.

When members discover that the counselor functions as a special member because of technical expertise and skills, they can evaluate the counselor's contribution for its value to their goal achievement. They can accept or reject the counselor's activities on the basis of what helps, not on the early autonomy basis of the authority symbol the counselor represents. At this point members are ready to discover the contributions they and all other members can make to the goals of the group and to TACIT development. They can open up the structure for the equality, cohesiveness, and beginning interdependency of the Closeness stage.

Counseling Process

The task of members and the group is to develop a structure supportive of needs and goals rather than a hierarchy for power and control. The counselor's parallel task is to enable this functional, nonrigid structure. Therefore, the counselor uses the functions of providing and processing to a great extent and those of catalyzing and directing to a moderate extent. These functions relate directly to the findings of Lieberman et al. (1973) about effective leaders. Their finding may be explained now as follows: those leaders who helped the group resolve Autonomy stage themes were those with the highest changers and fewest casualties. As you may recall, these were leaders who used high levels of caring (providing) and meaning attribution (processing) and moderate levels of emotional stimulation (catalyzing) and executive function (directing). These functions, carried out as such, prevent the destructive processes of this stage and enable members to confront obstacles to TACIT group development.

The providing skills are those which personalize the feelings and content of this stage as this supports all members. The processing skills entail illuminating power and control dynamics, sharing feelings, relating here-and-now interaction ("I-We") to there-and-then themes ("It"), and reaching behind conflicts and decisions. The catalyzing skills include reaching for feelings and perceptions. The directing skills are demanding work and invoking the contract.

Skills

Personalizing. Personalizing responses to feelings and contact takes place on four levels (Carkhuff, 1980). These are personalizing: (1) meaning, (2) problem, (3) feelings, and (4) goals. In Autonomy, the counselor personalizes the meaning of the members' particular situation in the group to them by responses to their communication and behavior: "You feel left out, because you did not get to participate much today"; "You feel afraid because you believe some members of this group will challenge what you have to say"; "You feel selfish because you believe you have been monopolizing the discussion." By personalizing the meaning of particular member's communications in relation to issues of power and control, members may at least feel understood by the counselor and increase their awareness of how their power-seeking restricts the possibility of their growth needs being met. Here, the counselor does not respond to all communications. He or she personalizes when other members do not respond, or do not seem to understand the Autonomy message, and when the counselor perceives dominant themes related to the current group structure in what a particular member expresses: "One thing you experience personally in relation to your current place in the group keeps coming up over and over. . . ."

Personalizing the problem is a most critical task in helping members and the group as a whole to resolve power and control themes. It confronts the negative autonomy of dependency and control and calls forth the positive autonomy of responsibility.

Personalizing the problem is confrontative (Carkhuff, 1969). In responding to personalized meaning, the counselor helps members discover the impact of the group situation on the member. Personalizing the problem asks members to take responsibility for their situation in the group by becoming aware of how they contribute to the situation. This response entails feeding back how or what the member (or members) does or does not do which leads to the situation: "You feel left out because *you can't* take the opportunities you've had to participate in this group"; "You feel afraid because *you haven't* risked expressing yourself to see if other members of this group would agree with you or not"; "You feel upset because *you weren't* checking to see if other members felt left out by your talking"; "You (the group) are having trouble getting started and are looking at me as if I will direct and *you* really *haven't* expressed this to check it out with me"; "On the one hand, you have agreed to the subtheme for today and on the other hand, you have really not considered it. I wonder if we need to discuss a new subtheme or if there are other disturbances going on for you today." This personalizing of the problem provides opportunities for deeper awareness and understanding and for more responsible and need-meeting choice.

The next step in helping members and/or the group understand where they are in the evolving structure in relation to where they want to be is personalizing the feeling. In this response, we help the members experience how they feel about themselves in the particular meaning and problem of Autonomy themes. It includes responding to disappointments and doubts: "You feel disappointed because you can't act immediately on your opportunities to participate/check out other's reactions to you/give others a chance to talk, and so on"; "You (the group) feel doubtful that you can make your own decisions because you have been depending on me too much."

Finally, the counselor can personalize goals. Personalizing the goal helps members (or the group) understand where they are in relation to where they want to be. This response is the flipside of personalizing the problem. It gets to the wishes so often indirectly expressed in feelings of disappointment, disgust, or doubt: "You feel disappointed because you can't act immediately on your opportunities to participate/check out others' reactions to you/give others a chance to talk, and so on, *and* you want to be able to"; "You (the group) are doubtful that you can make your own decisions because you have been depending on me to make them and you now want to make them based on what you want rather than on your guess about what I want." This personalizing of meaning, problem, feelings, and goals provides the basic support, if accurate, for members. They feel understood yet challenged to develop toward their fuller potential. These responses can reflect the caring that attends to others and intends what is best for them.

Illuminating. Illuminating skills are related to personalizing but are designed for members to increase awareness and to attribute meaning to their group events. Yalom (1975) refers to this skill as "activation" and "process illumination" of the here and now. The focus is on the group examining itself, studying its own interactions, and integrating its experience into some conceptual understanding of what it is doing. Members look at their own process with the counselor's help. They illuminate what they are doing, how they are doing it, and why they are doing it in terms of what it means about aspects of their needs, their goals, and their relationships with each other. The illuminating skill for helping the group "process" itself may be the most significant of all for enabling members to resolve the power and control structure of the Autonomy stage.

This illuminating skill requires that the counselor move the group to the here and now and establish the norm that the group discuss itself in the here and now—that it relates the "It" to its own "I-We": its positions, statuses, roles, norms, wishes and fears, needs, obstacles, goals, and the effects of these on its ability to achieve the stated goals explicit in the theme and contract.

Illumination of process requires that the counselor: (1) recognize process, (2) surface group tensions, (3) attend to his or her own feelings, (4) provide activities which help group members assume a process orientation, and (5) facilitate members' acceptance of process illumination (Yalom, 1975). Recognition of process begins with a theoretical model of group process. The counselor who understands TACIT process and dynamics is in a position to make meaning of the data observed and experienced in the group. Particular data to observe are the nonverbal: Who sits where? Who looks at whom when speaking? Do some members look at the counselor while addressing comments to other members? If so, they may be particularly dependent on counselor approval and conflicted about authority and therefore have difficulty resolving power and control issues. Do members pull their chairs away from the center of the group while professing interest in the group? Does a particular member move from sitting close to the counselor in one meeting to sitting across from him or her in the next as a first flicker of expressing resentment toward the perceived "leader"? Who is absent and how do these absences relate to group events? This nonverbal behavior frequently expresses elements of individual and group process of which members are not yet aware. These observed nonverbal communications can be used to illuminate process when they are shared or responded to by the counselor or other members.

What is not communicated, or is omitted, may reflect process as much as what is done or said. For instance, the group that never confronts or questions the counselor may be particularly conflicted about their autonomy. The avoidance of such topics as power, money, status, sex, or death may also reflect process. Positions, statuses, and roles can particularly come to the fore when they are shifting because one or two high-status members are absent.

The content itself can often be a disguised and an unaware trial balloon of here-and-now process communication. I remember how suspicion and mistrust of any leadership during the Autonomy stage could be reached for behind discussions of President Nixon during the Watergate investigations. Often talk about people who could not be trusted, authorities who were unjust, and confidentialities that were violated is a reflection of the experience of these issues, or the fears of them, in the group.

The counselor can surface group tensions by anticipating them and noting them in the group. The struggle for dominance in Autonomy creates much tension. As members jockey for positon in the pecking order, members fear they will lose while others win. Even as the hierarchy is established and tends to be agreed upon, conflicts and tensions will flare up. The wishes and fears of individual members become wishes and fears of the group and create the tension manifested in such behavior as encouraging group leaders and then shooting them down through taking potshots at them, seeking evaluations from the counselor yet resenting any interpretation which appears judgmental, and pushing for honesty yet disapproving of any expression of authentic anger. In all of these situations, the behavior on one side, the wishes, increase the fears on the other side. Tension increases. Identifying this tension and helping members stay with their feelings and become aware of what they are experiencing and doing helps members face the polarities of their wishes and fears. The opportunity for integration of these in the choices to proceed may enable resolution.

The counselor's own feelings often are the most important clues to recognizing and understanding process. The counselor's feelings are a microscope for viewing slices of the group process. The counselor who feels confused may mirror the group's confused attempts to make him or her feel powerless and helpless. So, too, might be the counselor who feels shut out. Often during the conflicts of Autonomy the counselor is put on the spot by the group in its dependency-seeking demanding that he or she must direct the process to be helpful, or must disclose much more than any other member. The feeling of being put on the spot can be used, if expressed, to illuminate the underlying process of expecting the counselor to resolve the tensions of power and control conflicts rather than looking at how the group can resolve these itself.

Activities which help members assume a process orientation are those which help influence norms for the group's stopping, looking, and listening to where it is. They periodically tug members out of the here and now and invite them to consider conceptually the meaning of the transactions which have just occurred. The counselor switches on a self-reflective beacon. For example, the counselor can interrupt the group at an appropriate interval and say, "We are about halfway through our meeting today and I wonder how everyone feels about our meeting this far." He or she may share observations and reach for meaning: "I'm not sure what is going on in this meeting, but I am aware of some obvious communications. Bob has been very silent and staring at the floor, Joan moved her chair back several places while Jack and Jill were debating why we are having trouble getting started today. Joe has been glaring at me as if he is angry while this is going on. What ideas do you all have about what's going on here today?" Also, the counselor may share observations, feelings, and his or her ideas about what these may mean in terms of group process: "I noticed so many of you looking at me while Jack and Jill were fighting and I felt put on the spot—as if I were to rescue you from the tension their fight created for you and the group. I believe these fights will be inevitable in the group and you are now afraid to respond to them. Perhaps you are afraid to take sides in which you might win or lose—or to permit the group to develop a norm which supports honest confrontation. What do you think?"

Nonverbal activities are especially useful for helping members assume a process orientation. Members during Autonomy are often more able to show than to talk about the structural elements of group process. They can experience these together more strongly by acting them out. The counselor can ask members to place themselves in relation to the center of the room and to other members in a manner which reflects their perception of their place in the group. Or ask them to form a single line that reflects their ranking of themselves and others in the group. Or ask them to use themselves physically to "sculpture" the group as they see it. Or suggest that subgroups who are involved in conflict have a "showdown" where they line up facing each other and silently walk toward each other and express themselves to each other nonverbally. All of these activities illuminate process when they are "processed"—that is, they are discussed verbally for the analysis of meaning of the data derived from the "experiment."

The counselor needs to facilitate members' acceptance of process-illuminating comments. The principles of effective feedback, used by the counselor and by members, help make the illumination palatable. This includes the avoidance of pejorative labels in interpretive remarks. Instead of "You are a manipulator," it is far more acceptable to the other (and far more true!) to say, "When you told me that you couldn't trust me because I haven't gotten angry yet, I felt manipulated. I believe you were trying to see if I would get angry because you wanted me to. Are you aware of this?" Especially in the conflict of Autonomy, members might hurl important feedback to one another and the group in ways that the truth may be lost in the defensiveness of labels, exaggeration, or nontruths. The counselor needs to help tone down the noise of these interactions to enable members to hear the tones which may resonate some accurate awareness: "Jack, you have shut out everything Jill has said about her anger at your monopolizing this meeting. Yet you have tried to corner her in her responsibility to initiate discussion, to be her own chairperson. You prevent yourself from getting anything different here. Will you try something? Ask yourself if there is *anything* in what Jill is saying that is true for you. What parts strike an inner chord of your awareness? Could you forget for a moment the things that are *untrue* and stay with those that are *true* for you?" Then later: "Jill, I'd like to ask you to do the same." Or, to the group, the counselor may similarly say, "You really jumped on Joy for saying she felt most of you were acting phony in the group, that you were not honest and too polite. You accused her of being the one who was phony by not participating. Could you hold back your anger at Joy for a moment and consider if any of what she said may hit home? Because you reacted so strongly, I suspect this is a very meaningful issue for more than just Joy in this group. Does this strike a chord with any of you?"

Through this feedback, through questions, through the activities which help members process, through attention to the counselor's own feelings, through surfacing tensions, and through recognizing process, the counselor illuminates the here and now. The other side of illumination is focusing members' attention and awareness to the here and now. This focus is the purpose of the next skill—relating here-and-now interaction to there-and-then themes.

Relating Here-Now and Then-There.   The skill of relating the here and now to the there and then and vice versa is the ability to connect the "I" and the "We" to the "It." Especially during Autonomy, when members are assuming roles in the group familiar to those they tend to take outside, this skill is important. The problems members experience in structure and the difficulty they have admitting power and status needs are reflected in the content. This content often avoids here-and-now concerns in disguised attention to more abstract there-and-then themes. As the counselor relates these there-and-then themes to the here-and-now group process, members can increase their potential for learning. This skill does not suggest a rigid norm that requires all content to be reflective of the here and now. Research suggests that effective groups have open boundaries in their norms for appropriate content, which is in the control of group members rather than the counselor (Lieberman et al., 1973). However, the connection of the "I" and the "We" of the group structure and process to the "It" of there-and-then content is inevitable in counseling groups. The counselor's task is to help members experience and become aware of these inevitable relationships.

First, the counselor must "think here-and-now" (Yalom, 1975). This task permits the counselor to shepherd the flock of group members into an ever-tightening circle by heading off errant, superfluous historical or outside material as strays and guide members back into the present circle. Whenever an issue is raised in the group, the counselor considers, "How can I relate this to the group's theme and its process? How can I make it come to life in the here and now?" These questions alert the counselor to possibilities for helping members make contact by focusing from outside to inside, from the abstract to the specific, from the general to the personal.

The member who describes a hostile confrontation of a power and control conflict with a roommate or friends can be asked, "If you were angry like that with anyone in our group, who would it be?" or, "With whom in this group do you believe you might get into the same type of struggle?" If the member shares that one of his or her problems is that he or she stereotypes others, the counselor can bring this to the here and now by the questions, "Can you describe the ways you've stereotyped some of us in the group?" and, "Who do you feel has stereotyped you in this group?" If a member describes his or her there-and-then problem as being easily led, the counselor can increase the here-and-now theme by asking who in the group could influence him or her the most and who the least. Those concerned about being humiliated can be asked who in the group they imagine might ridicule them. The here-and-now contact and learning can then be deepened by reaching for the responses of other members:

"How do you feel about these stereotypes?"; "Can you imagine your-self ridiculing him (or her)?" Toward this contact the simple techni-ques of asking members to speak as I, to look at one another, and to speak directly to the intended recipient of a message can be enor-mously useful.

Resistance to this here-and-now interaction can be anticipated. Often these skills both steer members into more intense, real, and fearful here-and-now interaction and simultaneously interrupt the content flow in the group. Members may resent these interruptions. The counselor must attend to these resentments as they, too, are part of the here and now. The group's flow and the counselor's concern for work in the here and now needs to be expressed: "Jack, I had two reactions as you were talking. First, I was delighted you feel comfort-able enough now in the group to participate. Second, I felt that it is hard for the group to respond to what you're saying because it's so very general and far removed from you personally. I'm interested in what's been going on inside you in this group over the last several weeks. While you've been silent, I sensed that you were very much aware about what we've been doing. Can you share some of these feelings and observations with us?"

Resistance also calls for counselor responses that focus on posi-tive interaction and on the safety and distance of "ifs" to lessen the perceived threat of here-and-now content. Such questions as "Who do you feel closest to in the group?" or, "Who in the group is most like you (or most understands you)?" accentuate the positive connections. Use of the subjunctive "if" mood in such questions as *If you were* angry at someone in this group for dominating you, who *might* this be?" and, "*If you could* participate more like another person in this group, who *might* you wish to participate like?" provides some safety and dis-tance in here-and-now interaction during the Autonomy stage.

If members during this stage resist risking personal disclosures (and they often do), they can be encouraged, at least, to risk disclo-sures about their disclosures (what Yalom, 1975, calls "metadisclo-sures"). For example, a member who has been silent and who has shared some general there-and-then content might be asked, "What was it like for you to talk in this group just now?" Others can be asked, "What's been the hardest thing for you to share so far?" or, "When we ask you questions about yourself, how do you feel? How do we know when we might be pushing you too much or when you really want us to push you?" or, "How do you rate the risk you just took as you are experiencing it inside—low, medium, high, or very high?"

Silences are particularly rich sources of data for here-and-now awareness of the group's process. These riches can be tapped by noting: "Much seems to be going on for us in this silence. There is valuable information for us here if we could only excavate it. I wonder if each of us could tell the group some of the thoughts we had during the silence that we thought of sharing but did not say." Often, this skill is best preceded by the counselor's own sharing: "I've been feeling antsy during this silence, wanting to break it, not wanting to waste time, but also feeling irritated because I seem to be the one always doing this work for the group. I wonder what you were experiencing during this silence."

The group can be encouraged to evaluate its own process in relation to individual member's needs and goals in the here and now. Such comments as asking the group to imagine that the remaining thirty minutes of the group have passed, that they are on their way home, and asking them to share their disappointments about the meeting today can encourage this processing. Members can be asked to stop action and reflect upon what has been the most productive (and/or least productive) part of the meeting so far. Whenever the counselor can shift the group's attention and awareness from the there and then to the here and now, he or she performs an important service to the group. If the group succeeds in focusing upon itself, the result will likely be a more cohesive, interactional atmosphere which maximizes TACIT development and counseling outcomes.

Implicit in this skill is the assumption that the counselor knows the most propitious direction for the group at a specific moment. The interpretation does not have to be perfectly precise and accurate, however; the timing does not have to be impeccable. Even incorrect or poorly timed comments relating the there and then to the here and now can serve as a spotlight for focus on the current drama of group structure and process and illuminate the meaning of group events for members. The broad principles which provide helpful direction to the counselor are those derived from an understanding of TACIT group development. In Autonomy these suggest that the group's awareness of its own structure as implicit in all group events is a prerequisite for preventing the entrenched structural obstacles that prevent members' needs from being met in their lives outside of the counseling group. This very processing and attention to the subterranean data of the here and now makes the basic difference between this experience and others in groups. It increases the potential for the development of Closeness and Interdependence in TACIT group process.

Reaching Behind Conflicts and Decisions.   A special use of the "pro-cessing" skill during Autonomy is reaching behind conflicts and decisions. Most important is the counselor's helping the group to understand some of the inevitable impersonal elements of conflicts and how decisions are made (Cowger, 1979). Members entrenched in these structural dynamics manifest more selfish power-and-status-seeking behavior, which is not considerate of others. Therefore, some members are hurt and resentful while others carry on business as usual without empathetic awareness of having hurt others in their interaction. Some of these hurts and resentments can be deflected and powerful members can develop more sensitivity to their impact on others by understanding the impersonal and stereotypic dynamics of conflicts and decisions and by understanding that real people with real feelings were experiencing these group events personally.

The skill of reaching behind conflicts and decisions requires that the counselor tune in to the personal reactions to these more imper-sonal interactions. For instance, the counselor can illuminate these issues in his or her own experience: "Jack, you made several assump-tions about what I am thinking and feeling in this group without bothering to check these out with me, to get to know me. I am uncomfortable about your stereotype of me as manipulating this group because I have not told you how to resolve this conflict. You don't really know me. I was sitting here feeling that Jill must be hurt by your anger at her as the manipulator you described—as I have felt with your anger at me. I would like to know more about how you see me in this group other than your label as manipulator. I will let Jill speak for herself but she may also want more specific feedback from you."

The counselor also needs to draw feedback from the group on what each is experiencing, especially during moments of conflict and decisions. These include such questions as: "I sense a tension in the group as a result of the conflict we just experienced. What is going on for you who are feeling tense?" or, "We just made a decision to change the topic and move away from the anger that Jack expressed toward Jill without really being aware that we made such a decision. How did we make it and what do you feel about this?" The counselor particularly can reach behind the conflicts and decisions by eliciting the hurts which members may be expressing nonverbally: "Jane, you looked as if you were going to cry while we were discussing our subtheme for next week. Are you willing to share with us what is going on for you? I would really like to know."

Finally, a useful technique in reaching behind conflicts in a way that increases intermember awareness and empathy is the "listening game." In this activity the counselor asks combatants if they are willing to try something while they are interacting with each other. If they are, the counselor suggests that they continue their interaction with one additional "rule." They must state in their own words what they heard the other (or others) say and the other (or others) must agree that they were heard accurately before the restater makes his or her own comments. This "game" often defuses the structural elements of conflict—the struggles for power or dominance or the win/lose—and brings the conflict to the real and more resolvable level of person-to-person (rather than position-to-position or role-to-role) encounter. As this encounter continues, the group can be asked to suggest potential solutions to the conflict with only one "rule" for the suggestion: It must be a solution in which no one loses and both combatants win.

Similarly, counselors can enable the group to make more effective decisions by reaching behind the way Autonomy decisions are made in a manner that "counts" certain members "in" and powerful and other members "out" and powerless (Larsen, 1980). This requires that the counselor adopt a style of decision making which supports the norms of shared power and influence among members so that every member "counts." When members discover that they all "count" and that their needs rather than who has the power is the major issue in decision making, they have taken a giant step toward resolving the power and control dynamics of TACIT development.

The counselor who helps members explore their "I count, you don't count" decision making can introduce members to a model of "decision-by-consensus." The research shows this norm as most helpful (Hall & Watson, 1970). In consensus the norms support decisions made on the basis of "I count; you count." In short, the group is encouraged to move beyond win/lose decisions to "no-lose decisions." The counselor can show the difference by reaching behind decisions to see whether they were based on assessed needs of all members or on preconceived solutions by a few. As alternatives are proposed, evaluated, and ranked, the counselor can ask which solution from among those generated meets the needs of all members, or how those selected can be modified to meet all members' needs. Again, the counselor builds a base for reaching behind decisions toward establishing consensus, equality, and mutual aid norms from his or her own influence on decision making: "You've decided to work on the subtheme of Resolving Conflicts today and now we're off the topic. I think it would be helpful to stop for a moment and discuss where we are as a group and how we would like to commit the rest of our time. What do you think about this?" The counselor can also reach behind the consensual decisions for the positive experience and feelings: "The experience we just had is an example of 'decision by consensus.' What did you observe about this process and how do you feel about it?" One of the greatest gauges of movement through Autonomy toward the more equal opportunity structure of Closeness is the group's ability to resolve conflicts in a no-lose manner and to make decisions on an "I count; you count" basis. Reaching behind conflicts and decisions illuminates the obstacles to this process and spurs members to challenge these in behalf of their needs for more close, authentic, and interdependent encounters.

Reaching for Feelings and Perceptions. Many of the aforementioned processing skills do catalyze members toward emotional contact in the here and now. However, the more moderate use of the catalyzing function during Autonomy includes some specific skills. One of these is reaching for feelings and perceptions. Reaching for feelings and perceptions includes checking for underlying ambivalence, supporting communication in taboo areas, reaching for individual communication in the group, and reaching for the group response to the individual (Shulman, 1979). All of these skills are designed to catalyze intermember contact and awareness during Autonomy.

One of the dangers in group counseling is that a member or members may choose to go along with the counselor or the group through artificial consensus or submission. Meanwhile, they may feel very ambivalent about a particular issue, decision, or seemingly agreed-upon procedure. In this situation it is vital for the counselor to catalyze honesty by checking for underlying ambivalence: "You all seem to be agreeing with this decision, but I wonder if some of you don't feel quite so excited and positive about it. Do any of you really differ with this?" Similarly, members who express negative feelings about a particular event most often are resisting facing some of their positive feelings. While members often fear conflict during Autonomy, they also sense some excitement about the possibility of spontaneity and honesty in the group and may resist facing this side of their experience. The counselor who says, "You have expressed your anger and concerns about this conflict we have experienced, but I wonder if you also may see some positives in this. Who is aware of some possible feelings you have on the other side of this conflict?" In general it is a useful principle throughout the group process to reach for opposites in feelings and perceptions. When members evaluate the group or a particular segment with nothing but positives, it pays to reach for the negatives. Likewise, negative evaluations should follow with reaching for the positives.

Members who are involved in conflict are making some connection to each other. While they may seem to be attacking each other, the fact remains that in the underlying process they have taken on significance to each other (Cowger, 1979). Therefore, they become a source for learning more about the self, perhaps even taking back disowned parts of one's self projected onto the other(s) toward further integration. Members who attack those who have assumed leadership positions and roles can be helped to get in touch with their own power and leadership needs. This task requires the counselor to reach for the appreciations which accompany resentments: "Jack, you have told Jill what you resent about her influence on this group. Can you now tell her what you appreciate about her participation?" Realistic choices for the individual members, for interaction between and among members and for the group as a whole, can evolve only from experiencing, being aware of, and "owning" ambivalences.

Support for members in taboo areas means reaching for feelings in relation to themes that are constrained because usual social norms define these issues as unacceptable. One of our most powerful taboos, and one that restricts awareness and entrenches structure during Autonomy, relates to feelings toward authority. Parents, teachers, employers, and other authority figures tend to discourage feedback on the nature of our relationship to them. We learn very early in childhood that honest expression of our resentment toward those in authority is fraught with danger. People in authority have the power to hurt us, to make us feel "bad," and to restrict us from meeting our needs. At worst, we tend to please them by withholding our feelings about them. At best, we may hint at our feelings and reactions. Often, the expression of positive feelings toward authority is as difficult. Because we fear that if we express the appreciations we may slip into sharing resentments, we hold on to all these feelings. Our peer group also tends to teach us that expressing positive feelings and reactions to those in authority is "brown-nosing," "apple-polishing," and demeaning. This socialized taboo creates a formidable obstacle in the working relationship between the counselor and the group when this authority theme is so much in the forefront of members' attention during the Autonomy stage.

The counselor must catalyze a culture in which the norms resocialize members to confront the authority theme. He or she does so by reaching for their feelings, again both positive and negative, behind the indirect cues reflecting authority issues. The counselor, when catalyzing the authority feelings and perceptions, must be comfortable with his or her own imperfections. This security can help members begin to see the counselor as a person, rather than as a symbol—a very significant step in members beginning to see themselves and others as imperfect, yet O.K., people rather than as symbols and stereotypes of positions, roles, and statuses. Surely when the counselor reaches for authority-oriented feelings and perceptions or for feedback on his or her own meaning to members in the here and now, the counselor will be readily reminded of his or her imperfections. The counselor will have made mistakes and members will have stored these mistakes vividly in their memories. Even most skilled counselors will discover that they missed some members' communications or lost track of their function, or made a judgmental statement that implied lack of empathy for some of the real struggles members were experiencing. Members will share these reactions and feelings toward the counselor's mistakes and his or her inevitable imperfections readily when given half a chance. This expression of negatives in relation to the taboo of authority and the experience of understanding by the counselor can provide a significant "corrective emotional experience" for members, free the group to confront frankly other taboo areas in their process (such as "sibling rivalry" for the counselor's attention), and, for the counselor who especially needs to be liked, the sharing of positive feelings toward the counselor as both an "authority" and a person for members.

The counselor deals with the authority theme and supports members in taboo areas by reaching for their feelings and perceptions. When members talk about the there-and-then themes of a strict parent, a crooked cop, a teacher they don't respect, and so on, the counselor can activate the here and now by asking: "I wonder if some of that message was directed toward me as an authority figure for you in this group? How do you see me in this way and what feelings does this stimulate in you toward me?" Members who are habitually late or who particularly differ with all counselor responses can be confronted with the potential meaning of this behavior in relation to the authority theme: "I get the impression from your lateness (or from how much you differ with me no matter what I say) that you have some particular feelings about your relationship to me in this group. How do you perceive me and what are your feelings toward me?" The group as a whole often reflects its ambivalences about authority by asking for direction from the counselor and then furiously resisting any suggestions the counselor makes. Here, the counselor can catalyze a culture with norms that permit confronting authority by opening this issue up for the group by stating his or her own feelings as a person and encouraging the members to share theirs. Fór instance, the counselor can say, "I really feel in a bind. On the one hand, you are looking to me to direct the group at this point, to be the chairperson; on the other hand, when I have offered suggestions on how to proceed, you have seemed to resent this direction. I think I can be most helpful to you now, and you to me, if we can take time to talk about what's going on for you in relation to your perceptions and feelings about me and my role in the group." This catalyzing has recently been proposed as a major function in helping members take the risks necessary for coping effectively with stress in group process (Breton, 1982).

In checking for underlying ambivalences and supporting communication in taboo areas, it is important for the counselor to reach for individual communication in the group and for group responses to the individual. The counselor is wise to concentrate efforts in the early phase of each meeting on helping individual members present their concerns to the group. Each session during the Autonomy stage tends to begin as a slow form of feeling out the group. Members endeavor to determine who is attempting to capture the group's attention for their own themes and how these themes may represent the theme of the group's concern. Often individual member's concerns reflect the group's major process (if not content) theme for the meeting. The counselor needs to consider: "What are we working on this session? How does this member's concern relate to the group's concern now? What are the themes in this interaction?"

The counselor here starts where the group and individual members are. He or she does not rush in with an agenda simply because group members' communications seem unclear. Likewise, the counselor does not assume that simply because the group had agreed to deal with a specific subtheme at the end of the previous meeting, this subtheme will be the topic for the current session. Even if members begin by addressing the subtheme, the counselor would do well to monitor the discussion in the early part of the meeting to sense whether the interaction confirms the selected subtheme or suggests that members are going through the motions of a group session.

Members are always working on something. Even though the content and interaction may not seem directed toward the group's purpose and stated theme, it is always purposeful. Even disturbances to the theme-centered work reflect some present orientation to the group process. Often, they especially mirror this current process.

Hence, there is the ground rule that "disturbances come first." When the counselor tunes in to early discussion with the questions of, "How does this connect to our theme and our work?" and, "What is troubling this particular member?", he or she has increased the opportunity for helping the individual member relate a concern to the group. The group can attend to its own here-and-now concerns when the counselor catalyzes the expression of the individual by reaching for this communication to the group: "Joan you want something from us today. I wonder what this is and how you see this group helping you with this."

The other side of this skill is reaching for the group's response to the individual. The counselor then catalyzes response and empathy from other members: "Do you understand what John is saying—what his concern is, and what he wants from us? Will you respond to this?" The need for this empathic group response is greatest when strong emotions are expressed. Often, however, during Autonomy, strong emotions tend to scare members into nonresponse. When this occurs the counselor may feel upset and angry. He or she may be shocked, discouraged, and surprised that group members appear not to be listening, that their eyes glaze over as if they are lost in their own thoughts, or that they quickly change the subject or rebuff the member who has bared such intense feeling. The counselor must move from this natural reaction to an understanding of the situation, especially in its TACIT process dimension. The group's response most likely is a signal, not that members are disinterested in the theme of the communication, but that the theme is having a powerful impact on them. Part of this impact is the intensifying of their fears of authentic interaction, closeness, and responsibility toward others at the same time they wish for this relationship. The counselor can best reach for the group's response by noting the avoidance of response, the naturalness of the fears, and redirecting attention to the individual's communication. For instance, the counselor can say, "John just took a big risk with us by baring some of this pain with us. I believe we left him hanging by shifting the topic suddenly and diverting our attention to his needs. I sense what he said had a powerful impact on you but you weren't sure how to respond to him or were afraid to stay with him. I wonder if we can take a few moments and stop and in silence become aware of what reactions his pain stimulated in us. Then perhaps we can return to John and share our responses with him. Is that O.K. with you, John?" This response helps to challenge the obstacles to mutual aid which are inherent in the Autonomy stage and reaches for the group's empathy in relation to the individual's current theme.

Demanding Work. The directing function largely entails demanding work and invoking the contract. This section examines the first of these skills—the counselor's ability to demand work from the group. In the group, the counselor demands work by holding the group to focus, challenging the illusion of work, reaching for work when obstacles threaten, and focusing the group on problem-solving mutual aid (Schwartz, 1971; Shulman, 1979).

Schwartz (1971) describes the demand for work skill in these terms:

> The [counselor] also represents what might be called the *demand for work,* in which role he tries to enforce not only the substantive aspects of the contract—what we are here for—but the conditions of work as well. This demand is, in fact, the only one the [counselor] makes—not for certain perceived results, or approved attitudes, or learned behaviors, but for the work itself. That is, he is continually challenging the client to address himself resolutely and with energy to what he came to do [p. 11].

The counselor particularly demands work when he or she monitors when the group is working and when it is not and what the group is working on. Resistances to work are expected and, if experienced, can be the basis of choices for the group about what they are willing and able to work on. Particularly useful is holding the group to focus.

As the group deals with a specific subtheme, associations and other related concerns and issues may result in a form of rambling. The group, especially during Autonomy, finds great difficulty in concentrating on one theme at a time. The counselor needs to return the group to the subtheme when members do not do this themselves. The intent is to consider the theme with maximum, not optimum, attention. Often, the movement from one concern to another is an evasion of work. The group does not stay with one theme for fear the concern is very real for the group and members may have to deal with their associated feelings. When the worker confronts this rambling and holds the group to focus by reminding it of its selected theme for the meeting, the group gets the message that the counselor, at least, means to discuss the tougher feelings and concerns.

One of the greatest threats to the effective counseling group is the ability of the group to create an illusion of work. Groups can often fall into a pattern of high participation around talk that is surface, abstract, general, there and then, and safe. This becomes an illusion when the counselor permits this interaction to substitute for the pain of struggle and growth which marks any TACIT development.

Schwartz (1971) comments on this illusion as follows:

> Not only must the [counselor] be able to help people talk but he must
> help them talk to each other; the talk must be purposeful, related to the
> contract that holds them together; it must have feeling in it, for without
> affect there is no investment; and it must be about real things, not a
> charade, or a false consensus, or a game designed to produce the illusion
> of work without raising anything in the process [p. 12].

The skill of challenging the illusion to work involves detecting the
pattern of illusion over a period of time and confronting the group
with the reality of evasion.

Challenging the illusion of work is one way of reaching for work
when obstacles threaten. It requires the support of underlying
empathy for the difficulty in moving on, mixed with the challenge of
the reality of the group's purpose, theme, and contract. The counselor
notes: "I know it is hard to risk how we really feel about each other
today, especially after the tension of last's week's conflict, but I
wonder if you really want to spend the whole hour talking about
yesterday's World Series game?" A useful principle for reaching for
work even when obstacles threaten is the movement from the general
to the specific. Work is often avoided when members fear or resist the
risks inherent in group process by expressing their concerns in general, abstract terms. Individual members can be encouraged to be
more specific and concrete in elaborating these general themes,
or the general concerns of one member can be made more specific
for the group by asking other members whether they feel the same
way.

The connecting of individual problems, expressed as specifically
as possible, with group concerns seeks the common ground which
supports work. The counselor focuses the group on problem-solving
mutual aid when he or she recognizes the common problems among
members, or helps the group discover them, in a way that can translate into a common theme to which members can commit their
efforts. The group is more ready to confront resistances and to work
when they do feel the support of "being in the same boat" and when
there is some potential for empathic understanding from members
toward increased mutual aid. The counselor can focus on this potential by reaching for it when it appears to exist in the group. This
mutual aid can be particularly related to the demand for work when
confronting resistances in the Autonomy stage: "I sense that most of
you are having trouble working on our theme today. Do any of you
have any ideas about how we can help each other get past this
resistance and get on to our work?" In other words, mutual aid can
begin in the group's problem solving when the counselor makes the

problem of individual members and the group as a whole the *group's problem*—including the problems of the obstacles and resistances to work.

Invoking the Contract. The second major skill of the moderately used directing function during the Autonomy stage is invoking the contract. The contract serves as the commitment to purpose and work. The counselor can use the contract terms as the model for exploring the group interaction, including his or her own role, and for encouraging members to make choices about their group structure and process. The counselor invokes the contract when he or she asks: "Is this what we agreed to do together?"; "Are we working on our stated group goals?"; "Can we try to use the ground rules which we agreed upon in our contract?" These questions and others remind members of the purpose of the group, the ways they have decided to proceed, and how members may be swerving off the course they have set for themselves.

If there is much digression from the terms of the contract, the counselor may need to raise the question of its relevance and re-negotiate its terms with members. However, in Autonomy this re-negotiation may be premature: group issues in power and control and resistance to work toward authentic themes may make any contract terms difficult to follow. In the Closeness stage which follows, this renegotiation is more appropriate. The counselor can better help members to consider what it takes to uphold their initial contract than to attempt to renegotiate it so quickly. Often, the group decisions for interaction, when they are compared against the contract, can initiate members to more attention to their wishes for closeness and to the hurts and frustrations of others. They can, then, recommit themselves to the work required. The counselor, too, must consistently invoke the contract with him- or herself. The best guidelines for what the counselor chooses to do in the group are those which are consistent with what was agreed upon by members in the initial contract. When this contract is important to the counselor as reflected in his or her living it, it becomes more real and meaningful for members.

Principles for the Autonomy Stage

The Autonomy stage can last for several weeks or several months of group meetings, depending upon the nature of members, the group, and the counselor. Members who are particularly mistrustful of authority and involved in power and control may spend much of their process in Autonomy. These would include teenage gang members, prisoners, and probationers, among others. Open-ended groups may create longstanding Autonomy themes. I once consulted with a counselor who had an open-ended group of fathers whose sons were involved in therapy for "emotional disturbances." This group had had forty meetings over a full year with three fathers there from the beginning and three to four others joining and leaving the group after it had begun. It was not until the forty-second meeting, when a new member who entered the group initiated discussion about the group's structure and the members' rivalry for the counselor's attention and then cried in desperation of his needs for help that this group resolved enough of the Autonomy themes to begin interaction reflecting the Closeness stage. Too many groups, because of the lack of the counselor's knowledge and skills, never get through the Autonomy stage. They begin and end with the counselor's strong structure and direction of the process and provide the illusion of work so that members' status needs are met in sibling rivalry for the counselor's attention and approval. The most effective counseling groups can resolve Autonomy issues and conflicts early in their process. The following principles integrate the skills which the counselor can use to enable this early resolution as much as possible through the TACIT theme-centered approach:

1. The counselor needs to begin each meeting where the members are and be especially attuned to what individuals are working on and how this work relates to the current group process themes.

2. The counselor needs to monitor the evolving group structure and its reflection in group process events.

3. The counselor needs to activate a here-and-now focus in the group and to illuminate the here-and-now process through the systems of feedback in the group.

4. The counselor needs to help the group confront the authority theme with empathy for its taboo, with its reality for the group's process, and with support for members' abilities to take responsibility for themselves.

5. The counselor needs to increase the group's awareness of its norms for the expression of feelings, problem solving, conflict resolution, and decision making.

6. The counselor needs to use subthemes to relate there-and-then to here-and-now concerns and to hold members to focus and work.

7. The counselor needs to encourage the group to evaluate its work in relation to its contract and to the needs and goals of members.
8. The counselor needs to assure that the Autonomy crisis is not relieved in illusion by his or her structuring the group and directing the interactions.
9. The counselor needs to trust the process; that is, the counselor needs to understand that the way around the Autonomy stage is *through* it and that members, when aware of their process and free to do so, will choose what is best for the group and themselves—structure based in all members' needs and promoting equal opportunity, spontaneity, closeness, and empathy.

Example

These principles are reflected in the counselor's use of self in the following example. The example demonstrates the Autonomy crisis and its beginning resolution.

This example continues the counseling with fifth-grade preadolescents in groups that was begun in the last chapter. In this record, we find the Autonomy issues emerging directly in the third meeting. They are resolved through this meeting and the next three. The four meetings follow and include the counselor's observations, thoughts, and feelings in parentheses.

Preadolescents: Meeting 3

We played kickball instead of football at the beginning of the meeting. The changed decision was made quickly and smoothly. Joy wasn't feeling well, so she didn't take sides. She rolled the ball for both teams. The teams weren't really chosen, they just fell together. Everyone got along much better in this game than in the previous ones. There wasn't any fighting. It turned out to be a lot of fun, and the losing team (which I was on) didn't even mind the loss. Before we went out, Joy and I set the time limit of twenty-five minutes. They were upset when the time was up, but they were curious about what they needed the pencils for. (Their teacher had them bring pencils for the survey.)

(I noticed that the members have now realized that we are a group because they show me in various ways that they are involved with one another. The "I-It" concern has fairly been resolved and the fears of intimacy which were very evident in Meeting 2 have brought the need for structure to most members. I saw this in today's meeting through members attempting to "fit" somewhere. The need for trust in different members is not as important now. Those trusts have mostly been established. The trust they are searching for now is in the group somewhere.)

The project of writing feelings about the group on a piece of paper proved to be very successful in providing Joy and me with insights of individuals that weren't previously expressed. But more important, this project gave individual members the opportunity to think about their position in the group. I was surprised that no one objected to this. They seemed to enjoy it after they got started, and they didn't even bother each other.

I really noticed the "peer court" being in session in this meeting. The members are very much aware of each other because of their need for position. A major process theme is the need for various members to dominate. Darren, wanting to lead the group, was the person who organized the decision of playing kickball instead of football. He asked for a show of hands in making the decision. "Unanimous," he stated. Ricky, who previously sat back to let others rid themselves of anxieties, needs to dominate in the sense of concentrating on the theme. He is emerging as a person who really wants the group to get along.

Through this exercise, I used the skill of "helping group members with interpretations of their roles." It seemed to initiate some thought about their place in the group; something that can't be accomplished fully when playing kickball or football.

Because of the need to understand their own roles and position in the group, I had them perform the exercise where the members place themselves somewhere in the room, according to the closeness that they feel. Chris wanted to know if he could leave the room. We said "no" but if he felt that far away to place himself at the edge of the room. He did so. Randy sat under a desk at the other end of the room. Jeff walked over to the window, gazing outside. Darren, Ricky, and Mike sat close to Joy and me.

This was such a good way to end the meeting. The way they placed themselves was very representative of what I have been perceiving. We asked why they positioned themselves in those ways. The three boys in the middle said they liked the group and felt good about it. Randy didn't know why he was under the desk, and Chris said that he felt far away. Jeff said that he just wanted to look out the window and feel the air come through the register. We asked them to think about the exercises that we did.

We had a few minutes to plan the next meeting. They wanted physical exercise, but were not as intent on it as last week. I see some better understanding of purpose. Ricky suggested that we talk about the group again, after we played a game. Everyone seemed to agree.

(I think an important consideration in the next meeting would be to concentrate on resolution of hierarchical conflicts. It would be particularly harmful to certain group members if their low self-esteem was simply ignored.)

(I can now see some group process coming into play and this has really helped my own feelings about the group. I feel that I've been providing members with various things that meet their needs. Some of them need an atmosphere with security, some need friendship, and all of them have the need to release tension in various ways.)

Meeting 4

As we walked into the room today, everyone except Jeff and Ricky was in a single pile on the floor, wrestling. We stood there watching them for quite some time. They were just having fun with each other and I wanted to hold on to that togetherness for a while. Jeff and Ricky were enjoying watching them. I could tell that neither of them felt excluded.

Darren noticed us watching them and began to get the group together. He told everyone to "knock it off" because Joy and I were "waiting." Gradually the boys got off the pile and moved toward the spot where we usually form our circle.

The cold, bitter weather today seemed to rule out decisions of going outside to play a game. There was a bit of reluctance to accept the fact, as various members opened the window telling Joy and me how "warm" the air was. But as the cold air swept through the room, the window was closed and any decision for an outside game seemed to filter out.

We immediately introduced the idea of the exercise that we had planned with the blindfolds. Chris seemed a bit uneasy with this and he brought up the idea of football. Everyone else was curious about this exercise, deciding that they wanted to do it. Chris said that it would be all right.

Joy and I put the blindfolds on everyone and a lot of them started wandering around, exploring the room. I got up and led them back to the circle. We explained that everyone had to be quiet as we passed the objects around. Each person was supposed to explore the object, then pass it to his right. After one object went around the circle, we asked each person to take turns saying what they felt. No one was to say the name of the object while describing it. They each took a lot of time touching the soap, tea bag, and Band-Aid. Everyone followed the rules of the game. They were giggling and really getting into the game. I noticed them moving closer to each other. The fact that each boy was in the same situation, not being able to see, only relying on touch, seemed to provide something common for the group.

When the blindfolds came off, Ricky went to get his glasses and Chris and Jeff started playing with the balls. The fact that Jeff got up to interact with Chris was very significant in indicating Jeff's conception of himself in relation to the group. He seemed very sure of himself as he threw the ball to Chris to catch. (It was distracting to the group, but in my thoughts, Jeff's new sense of "belonging" outweighed the need for them to join the group.) After a few minutes passed, we asked them to come back to the group. They both responded; Chris bringing the ball with him.

(I have developed an effective form of confrontation with Chris that is nonverbal. Somehow we have established a very good eye contact, and many times I only have to look at him to get a response. The ball in the group circle bothered me. I'm not quite sure how it happened; I didn't say a word when Chris looked at me. He felt my distaste with the object, looked at the ball, then me again, and threw it to the side. He returned my smile.)

Joy and I then explained that there was something important that we wanted to talk to them about. With that, different members began running around the room. Mike and Darren stood on their hands. Jeff turned somersaults. Joy raised her voice saying "this is exactly what we want to talk to you about." Darren came in immediately, telling everyone to get "organized."

(Darren has emerged as a leader for the group. In previous meetings, he struggled for this position through displaying aggressiveness and overt behavior. Through those techniques, he did not achieve that position. Different members were bothered by his actions and resented them at times. I feel that I helped Darren deal with his need by using the skills of "stepping down strong signals." I never reinforced those actions and never showed any approval of them. I also knew that complete disapproval would not help him either. The need to lead is definitely present. I felt that in helping him realize this need, I could also see whether the need would result in destructive domination of the group. It has not. Darren has found his position, is very comfortable with it, and does not use it to dominate in any sense. What is equally as important is the fact that most of the members are also comfortable with his position. Darren's strong signals are for the most part fully understood by Darren and because of this, they are received without distortion by other members.)

The group followed Darren to the circle and Joy began to tell them that we become frustrated when everyone runs about, ignoring our needs to get together and discuss the progression of the group. The group members became silent as we both used the skill of "sharing our feelings." At the end of this self-disclosure, I asked if everyone understood what we were saying. Darren began, truly empathizing with our feelings. Randy quietly said, "He's taking up for them." Not everyone heard him, so I asked him to tell the group what he said. He didn't want to, but with some urging from me, he finally did, laughing. I asked Darren if that was true and he said "no," that his statement came from what he was thinking. Confronting Randy (who always sits near me), I asked him why he felt that way. He said he didn't want to be in the group and the only reason he was is because he didn't want to be left alone in the room when every one else went to their groups.

(I really didn't see Randy's statements as real. He projects too much enjoyment of the group, many times, for me to see any significance in his words. Instead I feel that Randy is experiencing ambivalence and possible hostility toward me. He really needs my approval and undivided attention. I have been catching little "flirting" facial expressions, in his search for my approval of him. When I don't acknowledge them, he seems to get upset. He is showing some hostility toward me because I show no favoritism. I feel that some jealousy came out as he saw that Darren is beginning to feel what I have been stressing all along. I am showing him that I do not intend to display the favoritism he wants. During further meetings, I plan to leave myself "open" for any hostility that Randy may feel. Suppressing this expression would only suppress his individual growth. I want to show Randy that I refuse to allow dependency upon me. I will make him aware of his exploitations so that he has the opportunity to develop autonomy and interdependence. I believe that the Trust stage and the Autonomy stage are overlapping at this point. The members have decided to become involved with each other. But at the same time, "fears of intimacy" are still present. As we talked about the group [the first real discussion we've had] different members would quietly offer expression of how they feel. They weren't comfortable with those feelings to the point of fully and loudly verbalizing them. When we asked them to repeat what they had said, they would not. There is still resistance of self-disclosure in certain members, especially Randy and Jeff. During today's meeting, though, I saw Jeff opening up a lot more. He is beginning to be less afraid of the more dominating members, realizing that he has a position in the group also.)

The members now realize that at the end of the group session we should plan for the next meeting. I was happy that they needed no direction with this at the end of the meeting. They are beginning to see the purpose of our meetings more clearly. Their focus on next week did not lean toward an outside activity. Instead, they were thinking of something that we could all do together inside. Chris became bored, put a record on the record player, and started dancing. I incorporated his own interest into something that would be good for not only him, but for the group. I said, "That sounds good Chris. We can all listen to the music as we plan the next meeting." He came back to help us with the planning.

We all decided to have a party next week in keeping with our "Getting Closer" subtheme. Everyone decided what he could bring. I got a piece of paper and wrote everyone's name down and what he would bring. Everyone moved very close together as we planned the party. Chris said that he had a dollar saved and would spend that on the party. He said that he really wanted to do that.

As the meeting ended, everyone was excited about next week. Joy and I left and Jeff followed, telling us to have a nice week.

(Because the opportunity to be one unit will exist next week as we have the party, I want to focus on that. I want to reinforce the emerging feeling that "I am important; I am a part of the whole.")

Meeting 5

When we arrived at the room, I noted the excitement about the party. Everyone had special concern in showing Joy and me that they had not forgotten to bring the food. Joy and I had forgotten the blanket, though, but it didn't bother anyone. As a group, we pushed desks together making a long table. Everyone helped to organize the food, each boy walking around, giving everyone a portion of what he had brought. I sat down beside Jeff, who shies away from me a lot. He had brought cookies and they happened to be my favorite kind, so I told him. He seemed happy about that and he told me to let him know when I wanted more.

(Jeff is gradually reaching out, if only in small ways. I think its very important at this point to direct him toward self-expression. The need is definitely there. Either he doesn't recognize this need, or he is having trouble understanding it. I have been using the skill of "reaching for feelings" with Jeff. He is struggling to accomplish his task, even though he may not understand what that task is. While the group is talking about something and Jeff is not responding, I have been directing questions to him. [For example, Darren was talking about preparing the drinks that he had brought. We discussed how it felt to do things for the group. Jeff offered nothing, so I asked him what he thought about that.] In the initial moments of this confrontation [and many other instances of this], Jeff seems thrown off-balance and even confused with a very simple question. At times, I find it hard to believe that he really is that confused. So at the same time that I "reach for" feelings, I "wait for" them. Jeff becomes uncomfortable with the silence knowing that I will not go away, and usually responds in some way. It's only in the past two meetings that I have been using these skills with Jeff. In prior meetings, I think that I became equally uncomfortable with the silence, then left the situation. This wasn't helping Jeff. He desperately needs someone to identify with, and although it left him "off the hook," so to speak, I also helped him suppress expression.)

In the discussion that followed the distribution of food, I saw attempts to move into a whole unit as never before. But along with this movement came more frequent intermember criticisms. These criticisms were not really harsh and judging, but more "joking" with underlying attempts to justify individual positions. There was a subtle battle between Randy and Mike over athletic abilities. Mike is smaller but seemingly more knowledgeable on the sport of football. Randy explained his advantage in terms of strength and experience on the midget football team. I want to note that it was not an argument, but more of a "jockeying for position" as suggested in the TACIT approach. Up until this point, each boy seemed to hold an almost equal position in the group with respect to other group members. However, I believe that the need has emerged in each of them to find a somewhat "higher" position.

Ricky also became involved in this jockeying for position, but in a much different way. It is not in his nature to compete in this sense. He is not as conscious of his peers and their recognition. His needs seem to lie more with self-recognition. In this meeting, it seems as though he felt the need to become a stronger member, and acted upon this need. The boys were into a discussion about girls, and Ricky (who seems uninterested in the subject himself) didn't let this hold him back from participating. Instead, his involvement in the conversation was focused on different members, showing that he cared about their "girlfriends." This caring and being interested in other members is very real and the other boys realize this. As a result, Ricky constantly gains position, not by artificial means of a type of "proving" method that others employ, but by being himself.

As all this overt jockeying finally emerged, Darren was overwhelmed. The position that he had found very comfortable was being challenged and he didn't know what to do. Most of the previous clues that Darren had put forth were verbal. But his reaction to others taking over, in a sense, led me to adopt the skill of "interpreting clues of nonverbal language." From Darren's previous behavior, I would have expected him to react to the situation in a much different manner. But as I learn more about the functioning of members within groups, I find that nothing should be based upon mere expectations. So many things happen that initiate deviations from a pattern of behavior. What's more, threatening or uneasy situations can change that behavior altogether.

Darren wasn't quiet, but he certainly wasn't as physically and verbally aggressive as he usually is. It was surprising, but I thought that maybe it was just a bad day or that he was becoming comfortable enough with his position that he could just sit back now. But after a while I realized that the lack of communication was a type of communication in itself. I began to understand that his silence was both because of his leader position being threatened and also a reaching out. After he grasped what was happening (a real withdrawal from the group) he communicated the need to be noticed, reached, and recognized (an artificial form of withdrawal which he probably felt would be manipulative). Through this experience, I realized that all along I had been using the skill of "identifying patterns of behavior," without really identifying this skill. From the time the group began, I developed an understanding of repetitious forms of behavior. Because I understood Darren's verbal system of communication, it was easy for me to interpret his nonverbal signs and signals.

When the party was over, we decided to go outside to perform the breaking-in exercise. Darren showed deliberate defiance of what everyone else was doing—the simple matter of wearing a coat outside. With arms folded, Darren refused to get his coat. Seeking status, he implied that he was tough enough to go without one. I knew that if I let him go through with this, he would have achieved that powerful feeling that he wanted. It would have blocked his recognition of what he was actually feeling, because he would have regained his position in his own mind, not in the group's. I told him that we would not go out until he got his coat. Perceiving his facial expressions, I sensed his feeling that everyone wanted his position of power and leadership, even me. So I portrayed feelings of caring, not authority. I told him that I would feel terrible if he caught a cold and got sick. He looked at me a few moments, then went to get his coat. We all went outside to do the "breaking-in" exercise. It turned out to be a game of strength and cunning. The underlying question of who was strong enough and smart enough to get in the circle was present. Just as everyone completed his turn, the time was up and we didn't have time to talk about it. Joy told them to think about the exercise until next week.

Meeting 6

(The excitement of the boys as we begin the sessions seems to be increasing with each meeting. This seems to reinforce me. I see the excitement and view it as a very positive channel in which I can work. I am seeing my own role much more clearly with each meeting, which is another thing that determines my effects on the group. I really believe that I am growing and learning through this experience, just as they are. I am providing them with help and direction; they are giving me feedback which serves as a basis for my continued help and direction.)

The boys were so excited that we had some trouble getting started. The boys were playfully pushing each other all over the room. They were running around, laughing, and having a good time with each other. All except Chris. He was standing high on a bookshelf, alone, at a corner of the room. He didn't seem very interested in what the other members of the group were doing. (At that moment I realized that I had possibly been ignoring Chris, unintentionally. There is something that has been holding Chris back, and I've known this. But just recognizing it is not enough. It is very difficult to get Chris involved in the group and maybe I've been subconsciously hoping that the group would take the responsibility of doing this. When I saw Chris alone like that, I really felt terrible. Not only would emergence of his feelings and attitudes help him, but he would also be a positive contribution to the whole group. I had noticed this in the very beginning, but failed to act upon it. As a result, Chris is not getting very much from the group. And even though the members like him, they are not getting as much as they could from him. As I realized this today, I found that it was my fault, and I learned something very important about group work. It seems as though it is very easy to pick up on what certain members do and say. Some of them are simply easier to understand; even some members with negative feelings give adequate feedback upon which the worker can proceed. But then you have a member in your group who is much more difficult. You feel for that person and care very much but he is very hard to understand. You want to take that person somewhere for the whole hour and concentrate on what is wrong. But that is not group work.)

(All along, I have been working very hard to prevent dependency on me. Now I realize that I have become dependent on group members to help me. It wasn't the most wonderful thing to realize, but I'm glad that I have. Throughout the rest of the meeting, I worked with Chris as I should have before. It was difficult for both of us, but we both accomplished a lot.)

I walked over to where Chris was as Joy waited for the others to get settled. I asked him why he was up there. He said he was up there waiting for everyone to go outside. I asked him to come down with the group. He jumped off the shelves and joined them. I told the boys that we had a lot of plans today and wanted to get a lot done. Chris looked disgusted when we told them our plans to do the same exercise again. No one else seemed very pleased either, but no other suggestions were made. I explained that there was a purpose behind the exercise and asked them to restate the theme. I wanted them to understand how the exercise related to the purpose of the group and asked them to think about how it felt when they couldn't get into the group. They seemed a little curious and started to decide who would go get the coats. (Some of the boys' coats are on the second floor because that is where their classroom is.) We have established a rule that only one boy gets everyone's coat. Randy and Mike were having a little battle over who was going to go. They were both begging with me to be the one to get the coats. I asked them to decide between themselves. They couldn't decide and the others were getting impatient so I put my keys behind my back and told them to choose a hand. They were both satisfied with their choice; Mike won, and Randy took it well.

It was cold so the exercise was a fast one and we all ran into the school together. Everyone helped to push the desks back so we could make room for our circle. We began with the go-around technique, asking each boy to take his turn, expressing how he felt first being outside of the group, then becoming a part of it. Ricky and Mike said they felt mad when no one would let them in. Ricky said he was mad because he liked to be in the group more than being outside. Darren said he felt bad because he was cold and it was warmer in the group. Then he thought some more and added that he liked to be a part of the group. Chris had trouble as he usually does when asked about his feelings. He didn't have too much to say; he followed through with expression like the others. Jeff is really coming out of his shell a lot more now. It takes a while for him to express himself. Sometimes that expression becomes suppressed because others get impatient and start moving around, uncomfortable with his silence. When this happened today, Joy and I reminded them of the ground rule "speak as I," and immediately went back to Jeff. It was really wonderful how Jeff responded to this. Instead of forgetting or losing grasp of what he was saying before, he looked at us, and continued. (He is developing much more self-confidence in the group and is very happy about this. I believe that he is finally understanding that he is an equal member. I was so glad to see this, because as I mentioned earlier, I have been trying to help him by showing that I won't let go when he has something to say. He understands this now, and is also dealing with those silent moments when he collects his thoughts.)

(Randy has really overcome the need for my attention and because of this, he is relating to the other members in a much more positive way. For a while, I thought that some hostility was developing toward me. But now he accepts my role; he seems to accept everyone else's role, and most important, his own. I treated Randy in such a way that he understood the importance of equality in the group. He saw that while I didn't give *all* my attention to him, I didn't give it *all* to anyone else either.)

After we finished talking about the exercise, I immediately proposed the idea of a fantasy. (I have learned that there needs to be some structure in the meetings, especially when dealing with this age-group. They can, for the most part, deal with silence, but if Joy and I would sit there with no specific purpose in mind, they would detect this, I'm sure. It has happened before and I've learned through those experiences. In fact, this meeting was a very good one because we adopted the subtheme and planned to work on it. We didn't have to fight, so to speak, to direct them away from physical activities. The structure that we had was not an authoritative device. We suggested procedures and they had every opportunity not to accept them.)

I told them that no one could talk during the exercise and asked them to close their eyes and think about the group at this moment. I told them to remember what it was like before we had our group. I gave them many things to think about such as what they would be doing at that time on Tuesday morning, how they felt about other members before we were together as a group, and so on. Then I asked them to remember the first meeting and what they were feeling then, and also how their feelings might have changed with each meeting. In ending, I brought them back to the group as it was, asking them to think awhile about what they have learned about themselves and others in the group.

What followed proved to be a very meaningful experience for all of us. The boys understood the fantasy much more than I had imaged they would. Everyone seemed very content to listen to other's explanation of what they thought about the fantasy. Ricky said that Joy and I were showing how nice it is to care about people. Everyone agreed, as Chris put his head on the floor. I asked Chris if he was learning anything and he just shook his head. I said, "What are you learning, Chris?" and he said that he learned to know everyone better. (When Chris is asked a question about his feelings, he becomes very uncomfortable. He usually bites his lip and looks around a lot. He is also relieved when his turn is over as we go on around the circle. He hasn't been verbally contributing anything in the sense of commenting on subjects that we discuss, unless it is his turn or he is asked.)

Everyone was talking about what they were learning about the group, paying attention to the "speak as I" ground rule, but Chris was just lying on the floor with his head down again. I took advantage of a moment of silence and confronted Chris, saying, "Aren't you interested in what we are discussing, Chris?" He said, "Yea, I am." I asked him why he hardly ever looked at people when they were talking, and he shrugged his shoulders. For a long time I used the skill of "getting with the other's feelings." I was truly empathetic with Chris, I could feel his uneasiness, and this time I was going to work at surfacing those feelings by helping him understand them. I said that I could understand why he wouldn't want to talk or comment if he didn't like what we were discussing or if he didn't like the group experience. He said no, that wasn't true. He didn't know what was wrong. As I tried to get Chris' feelings, I used the skill of "making the problem the group's." I said, "Now I could be wrong: does anyone else think that Chris is quiet a lot?" Everyone responded to this by acknowledging Chris' behavior. I said that maybe we could all help him understand why he didn't feel like getting into the group. I explained that he was part of the group and if one part of the group is troubled, it will affect the whole group. I stated my skill to them: "We are going to make this one problem, the group's problem, so that we can all help Chris." Everyone responded in a very positive way, truly concerned about Chris.

Now Chris was looking up at the clock and moving around uncomfortably. I moved down into the same position that Chris was in. Everyone followed; we were all lying on our stomachs, very close together. The group was ready to tackle the problem. Chris sensed everyone's sincerity and everyone was silent as he felt that concern. I asked him if this was his usual behavior, wanting to know if he acted like this in school. Everyone answered "no" for him, and he smiled. Apparently, his behavior in school was completely opposite. But he slowly implied that the school situation doesn't call for a projection of feelings. Then I realized that his withdrawal from the group had come about mostly in the last meetings when we were engaging in activities other than physical sports. He is comfortable in those situations, has confidence in himself, and knows that others accept him. His fears of intimacy seem to stem mainly from his need for someone to reach out and help him express the closeness and good feelings that he evidently has toward group members. I also believe that another factor affecting his behavior is his age. (He is thirteen; the others are ten.) In many ways the other members look up to him, his physical abilities, and his age. Because of the great consciousness of peers, someone with this image must find it very difficult to admit feeling hurt, disillusioned, or frustrated.

Someone asked him what he does outside of school and he started explaining how he stands in front of Kentucky Fried Chicken and waits for them to close every night. The people who work there give him free chicken that they haven't sold.

At first it was very painful for Chris to know that he was, in a sense, in the "limelight" of the group experience. But as he talked, he became more comfortable and feelings came out about how much he appreciated what those people did for him.

He had desperately needed the reassurance from the group that he belonged, and I could feel his happiness that everyone was listening and caring. He went on to say that a new boy was coming into their class, and we all talked about how it would feel to be a newcomer. (We related this to being outside of a group and then being accepted.)

Something very wonderful had happened to Chris, and he began talking with group members about everything that was brought up. There was little direction needed in the following discussions, because they were all very happy that we had helped someone in the group. No one mentioned going outside at all. It was almost as if I was sitting there watching them gradually move into a cohesive unit. It was a unique experience for me. I had such good feelings at that moment, that I knew if I didn't share them with the group, I would be holding in a very needed expression. I told them that I felt very good about the group and that they made me feel very happy. I explained that I thought they were grasping the purpose of the experience.

Many members started talking, including Chris. Darren also had something to offer at that moment, and he apparently felt that he had been interrupted. He started to yell very angrily, about how it wasn't fair, defending himself with our ground rule. He said that we made a rule to talk one at a time and it wasn't fair because he was interrupted. He kept repeating this; Joy and I permitting him to express his anger. I didn't say anything until he finished, arms folded and pouting. I told Darren that I was sure no one interrupted him intentionally and everyone agreed. Darren has a habit of violating the ground rule himself, but then remembers it and lets the person go on. I reminded him of this, not by way of throwing the situation on him, but in order to bring to his attention that sometimes interruptions were accidents. He agreed with this, stating that he does it unintentionally. But all of a sudden, the entire blame went to Chris. Darren said it was his fault; he was the guilty person who didn't want Darren to talk, and he began to call Chris all sorts of names.

This was a very intense moment and everyone was quiet. We had just done something very meaningful for Chris (Darren was very helpful in that), and now someone was overtly attacking him. I was pleased at how Chris handled the whole situation. The confidence he had obtained just minutes before seemed to be very real. He was most expressive in telling Darren that he hadn't meant to interrupt, asking him to go ahead and proceed with what he wanted to say. Darren refused, telling us to look at Chris and his big white teeth. He certainly was trying everything. The concern that he had shown for Chris was seen as a threat to Darren. He hasn't felt comfortable with the equality that everyone else is feeling. His role as leader could be very helpful to the group if he understood that "leading" doesn't mean running the show. I really want to help him with this, and I tried very hard to explain the equality of each member, how everyone was just as important, and so on.

Just then, all of the kids from the other groups started to come into the room. Every member in the group yelled at them to go away for a few minutes. They were very involved with the problem and very united. Chris walked over and stood beside Darren. The time factor bothered me and I wanted so much to be able to solve the problem. But I knew that I had to leave the problem with Darren and Chris. We decided that we would talk about the problem next week. Darren said that he wanted that.

Summary

The Autonomy stage brings on a crisis of power and control in the group. Members seek positions, statuses, and roles for themselves to influence the allocation of group resources and norms which protect their fears of losing security. The group tends to stylize and some members get their needs met at the expense of others. Frequently, work is avoided or evaded and members are constricted in their inability to confront the taboo of the authority theme.

The counselor needs to function highly as provider and processor and only moderately as catalyst and director to help the group through this stage. The skills for assuming these functions effectively include responding to feelings and content in a personalizing manner, illuminating process, activating the here-and-now, sharing the counselor's own feelings, reaching behind conflicts and decisions, reaching for feelings and perceptions, demanding work, and invoking the contract. These skills can enable members to be aware of their conflicts and needs and the hurts and putdowns of others, and to compare these processes with their contract and goals. Members can risk the security of trust in structure and move toward the trust in each other as people. This discovery recommits members to each other, the theme, and the group's purpose and initiates the Closeness stage of TACIT development.

Critical Incidents

Critical Incident 4

Subtheme.　Being Responsible for Ourselves

Context of Incident.　This event occurred during the early part of the third meeting. The counselor had begun the meeting by stating the subtheme "Being Responsible for Ourselves" and asked members to take a few moments to think about this theme. When discussion was encouraged, a long, uneasy silence ensued. Then one member who appeared especially tense during the silence turned to the counselor.

Choice Point

Cheryl: "I'm getting frustrated. I thought you were supposed to start us off and tell us what to do—otherwise, I don't know what to say. We're getting nowhere this way."

The group turns to observe the counselor's reaction.

What would you do at this point? What is your rationale for this response?

TACIT Response. The counselor using the TACIT model would likely use four skills here. The first is personalizing the content, feelings, and goals of Cheryl. The second is gently demanding work. The third is relating the there and then to the here and now. The fourth is illuminating the current authority crisis in the group process: "I certainly sense your frustration and anger at me, Cheryl. I guess you've had these feelings toward me before in the group and you'll probably have them again. You're mad at me, Cheryl, because apparently I haven't lived up to your expectations. You are used to leaders in groups, especially adults, telling you what to do and you expect that from me. However, I see us working differently in this group. The subtheme for this meeting is Being Responsible for Ourselves, which I think requires you to be your own chairperson in this group. This may be difficult for you as I'm sure it is for others here who probably have feelings and expectations similar to yours. One of the major issues I see present in our group at this time is authority. My refusal to tell you all exactly what to do here seems to have a great effect on what is happening in our group. Maybe some other members would like to comment on this."

Rationale. This response legitimizes the genuine expression of feelings of Cheryl and these feelings in other members of the group. It surfaces the underlying issues of leadership, authority, and expected roles. It also invites further expression of these feelings and explorations of these issues. This processing is essential for members' increased awareness of the evolving structure and the opportunity to work more autonomously and responsibly in this group.

Critical Incident 5

Subtheme. Being Responsible for Ourselves

Context of Incident. This critical incident emerged closely after the previous one in the third meeting. The group was attempting to make a decision on its own as to what to discuss for the remainder of the meeting. During the tentative discussion, several members looked closely at the counselor, apparently attempting to see if he approved of the suggested topics. Some of the more aggressive members began to seek concrete rules to follow.

Choice Point

Steve (turning to counselor): "How should we decide what to talk about—by majority vote or should we have everyone agree?"

Chris: "Yeah, and after we make our decision, I'd like to know if you agree with it or go along with it!"

The group now sits silently waiting for your response, apparently in agreement with these two members.

What would you do at this point? What is your rationale for this response?

TACIT Response. The skill used here is reaching behind decisions: "You are asking me how to make decisions in this group. And yet (with a sense of humor in voice), you have *decided* that I can decide this, that my ideas count more than others' about this. I wonder if you want to count all members' ideas and how you will know you have counted these. You know this is the first decision we have talked about as a decision, but we have been making them all along."

Rationale. On the surface, this incident is a straightforward request for information; yet substantive issues deserve recognition. Members are revealing underlying orientations toward leadership and authority, evidencing some dependent and counterdependent behavior in relation to making decisions. The event also reflects some members assuming more power and control over the group and checking this position against the control of the counselor. The response, therefore, must reinforce that the group belongs to the members, that they need to determine how to make decisions. However, the counselor asks only that they consider who they are counting in their decisions and that they are conscious of how these decisions are made.

Critical Incident 6

Subtheme. Being Responsible with Others

Context of Incident. This happened during the early part of the fourth meeting. Two members have been building up, but suppressing, their anger at each other as they have resented each other's attempts to gain leadership in the group. They now exchange these hostilities as the group experiences a tense silence, seemingly immobilized by the confrontation.

Choice Point
Chris: "When Steve said that, I got mad as hell. You really piss me off Steve!"
Steve: "Well I couldn't care less what you think, Chris! Why don't you just shut up and keep your opinions to yourself!"
The two continued to exchange angry looks while the group fell into an uneasy silence.
What would you do at this point? What is your rationale for this response?

TACIT Response.   Two skills are most useful here—illumination of process and reaching behind conflicts. "I believe we are more aware of the tension that has been building between you, Chris, and you, Steve, than our silence lets on. This conflict has been really brewing between you. There are strong feelings and we are stuck, perhaps afraid, as to whether we wish to respond to them. We have feelings about Chris, Steve, and what went on between them. I believe we can stay with them and share our feelings and ideas if Chris and Steve would talk to each other, to respond aloud and tell each other what they think about what they have said to each other."

Rationale.   This response relates to the surface issue of hostile feelings between two group members, but also challenges the group's immobilization in the face of interpersonal conflict. The conflict is made the group's, yet some direction is given to promoting a fuller, more authentic interchange between Chris and Steve. Finally, the illumination suggests that members can provide insight into the nature of the conflict within the context of the position-seeking in the evolving group structure and process and, in turn, can develop more insight into the current power and control obstacles in the group.

8
Closeness

The Closeness stage evolves from the resolution of the overt and covert power and control conflicts of Autonomy and the revision of early group structure. Members move from tentative involvement in the group and the establishment of structural fences to protect them from the catastrophic expectations of the exposure which they fear. The wishes for closeness—for knowing others and being known authentically, for understanding and being understood—begin to motivate behavior in the group. The "I" attaches its identity to the "We," and members initiate discussion of the "It" in terms of these here-and-now "I-We" processes.

Cohesiveness becomes the glue for spontaneous interaction and support and the spur for the challenge of work in the group's real agenda of interpersonal relationships and socioemotional needs. As Yalom (1975) has noted in his research and theory of group cohesiveness, it is the *sine qua non* for members' learning. Cohesiveness in the group process is analogous to relationship in individual counseling. It is the heat that melts the iron. However, while the iron is hot, somebody must shape the horseshoe. The group in Closeness develops a cohesiveness that ultimately moves from the comfort of being part of the whole to support for risking honest and open self-disclosure and feedback. It seeks the differences so vital to Interdependence and mutual aid—to growth.

During Closeness many members may discover for the first time the potential to care about others and to be cared for. The newness of this experience for members—the very experience which makes the counseling group such a powerful medium for change and growth—does produce some awkward and tentative forays of self-disclosure and feedback. In fact, this stage frequently begins with an impasse. The impasse is a period in which the group is stuck and somewhat immobilized. It has given up the old security of hierarchical structure without trusting the new support of authentic concern and interaction. Often for one brief and dramatic moment, or for a total meeting

or two, the group seems to regress totally to the preaffiliation behavior of the early Trust stage. In one sense, they have. They start
over. This beginning is marked, however, by an underlying warmth
and respect so obvious to all members that the group structure is
"buried" with little effort and the group is "reborn" into its transformation to cohesive trust. The doubts for closeness are quickly
relieved. The buds of confidence find sunshine in the group's capacity
to stay with each member, understand, and help. This confidence
flowers in full bloom. The group basks in its glow. The basis of
relationships moves from control to contact, from the power of positions, statuses, and roles to the power of care and concern.

Individual Process

Each member's questions about the "I", the "We," and the "It" during
Closeness relate to disclosure, closeness, and cohesiveness. In relation to the "I," each member experiences such questions as:

> "What can I do to allow these others to know me?"
> "How can I communicate what I am experiencing and who I
>   think I am—both the good and bad?"
> "How can I overcome my fears of being known to achieve my
>   wishes for being known?"
> "How can I contribute to the needs of others that I am dis-
>   covering?"

In relation to the "We," each members asks such questions as:

> "How can I get to know others better?"
> "How can I contribute to developing the trust which they need to
>   be more honest with me?"
> "What will others do to keep this warmth alive?"

In relation to "It" (the counselor and/or content of the experience),
each member wonders:

> "When we get honest will the counselor be able to protect me and
>   others from getting hurt?"
> "Will the counselor now push us toward more disclosure than we
>   are ready for?"
> "Will our discussion lead to so much difference among members
>   that we lose this togetherness?"

"How will we handle the deep problems and feelings that are likely to be shared with us?"

"Can we draw a line between what we handle responsibly and what is too much for us to deal with without anyone being too hurt?"

Members manifest these questions in their risks of self-disclosure and feedback and in their attempts to protect and rescue members whom they perceive may be hurt by exposing more than the group can understand. They assert similarities before differences and are wary of conflicts which threaten cohesiveness. Yet they open up the structure and communication for needs to be shared and, from their underlying caring, discover that conflicts are inherent in the inevitable differences and that these differences are basic to authentic interdependence and mutual aid. They begin to accept both their own autonomy (difference) and interdependency (union with others) not as opposites but as very connected poles in the process of growth and development.

Group Process

In the Closeness stage of the formative group, the theme of intimacy comes to the forefront. The members' attraction for the group, significance attached to it, and strong feeling of bond in its "We-ness" constitutes cohesiveness. As the Autonomy covert (and often overt) conflicts are resolved in the interest of relating as people rather than as roles, the group gradually evolves into a cohesive unit. All members come into, or are directly offered the opportunity to come into, the group. They all share some degree of equal importance to each other and to the group as a whole. Morale increases. So does the commitment to the group's purpose, goals, and themes. This commitment includes a deeper investment in the agenda of dealing with the group's human relations in the service of needs and goals.

A different level of trust is established. While initial trust was based upon shared goals and a predictable structure, trust now entails a feeling that other members can care for each other. Mutual trust grows in people and resources rather than in structural power and control. This trust is an impetus for spontaneous self-disclosures. Members especially disclose their feelings of closeness and their here-and-now responses to the interaction (their feedback). The group really becomes a group in the deepest sense of the concept when absent or silently withdrawn members are really missed for the first time. The group begins to say to itself and to members who have not been previously central to the process, "We're O.K. We have something special to offer to those in need."

While a mutual aid system is developing for meeting closeness needs, the group does tend to suppress feelings which may produce conflict. Compared to the previous stage, there is a calm after the storm. Group interaction can be sugar-coated. Interaction seems to be all sweetness and light at first, as the group basks in the glow of its newly discovered unity. Eventually, however, the group's embrace will seem superficial and ritualistic unless authentic differences are permitted to emerge.

The content tends to dovetail with the process. The themes reflect here-and-now feelings and concerns. The "I-We-It" seems more balanced, as what is discussed relates more to what is being experienced at the moment in the group.

Some initial conflicts may arise in these discussions. Often, however, these conflicts reflect problems with intimacy, not with power. The jealousies which underlie the surface conflicts are those related to closeness, not to status. The group responds to these conflicts and supports initial risks, but tends to smooth them over quickly in the interest of cohesiveness. In fact, the group begins to allocate statuses in this stage on the basis of who embodies the norms of honesty and openness in self-disclosure and feedback or responses to other members. The "good member" is perceived as one who helps the group by taking risks in expressing here-and-now feelings. All members are respected as belonging, however, and the difficulties in risking are appreciated as well. The recommitment to stated group purpose and theme and the discovery of how members may help each other toward more mutual aid lead members to renegotiate the contract. The group now knows what it can accomplish and wishes to incorporate its own model for effective participation and group functioning into its contract. This contract, as renegotiated, can serve as the springboard for the group's entry into Interdependence.

Counseling Process

The group's task is to use cohesiveness to develop authentic closeness and mutual aid. The counselor's parallel task is to enable the self-disclosure and feedback that contributes to closeness and intermember help. This task requires that the counselor function as a catalyst and provider with moderate use of directing and processing. The catalyzing skills include modeling self-disclosure and feedback, encouraging intermember contact, and reaching for empathic feedback. The providing skills are the personalizing ones mentioned in the last chapter, as well as those of genuineness and confrontation. Directing entails following the leads of members and using the skills of clarifying purpose and renegotiating the contract. For processing, the counselor needs to detect and challenge the obstacles to work, especially during the early impasses of Closeness, and to illuminate the process by relating there-and-then concerns to here-and-now process when members themselves do not make these connections.

Skills

Modeling Self-disclosure and Feedback. The members during Closeness seek ways of being known and getting to know others and for building the trust for free-flowing interaction. The procedures for meeting these needs in group process are self-disclosure and feedback. When the counselor models these skills, he or she is providing useful tools for members. A helpful model for understanding the procedures of self-disclosure and feedback and their contribution to group process is the Johari Window (Luft, 1970). In fact, the Johari Window model can be presented to the group to catalyze members' finding ways to interact in behalf of their needs and goals. This "window" is depicted in Figure 8.1.

The "window" is divided into four "panes" using the dimensions of "known or unknown to self" and "known or unknown to others." Any single person in the group, or any single group event, can be characterized by these four quadrants. What is known both to the self and to others (Open Area of Quadrant 1) increases trust. However, members often have had impact on others without knowing how others have experienced them. In other words, this impact as experienced by others is "known to others" but "unknown to self" (Blind Area of Quadrant 2). Then, too, members have aspects of themselves or experiences in the group which have not been shared. This content is "known to self" but "unknown to others" (the Hidden Area of Quadrant 3). Finally, there are forces at work in the here and now that may be largely unconscious; that is, they are "unknown to both self and others" and likely will remain as such (the Unknown Area of Quadrant 4).

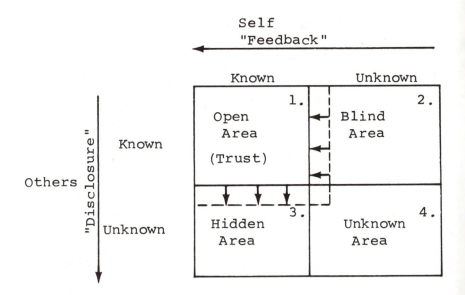

FIGURE 8.1.   Johari Window.

In any interpersonal relationship in which there is growth, trust must be increased. This process is particularly true of the counseling group. The increase of trust demands the enlargement of the Open Area of Quadrant 1 and the shrinking of the Blind and Hidden Areas of Quadrants 2 and 3. This alteration of the panes of the Johari Window, the central trust process in the group, requires disclosure and feedback. Self-disclosure extends the Open Area by shrinking the Hidden Area (depicted by the arrows from Quadrant 1 to Quadrant 3). Feedback enlarges the Open Area by diminishing the Blind Area (depicted by the arrows from Quadrant 1 to Quadrant 2). The greatest way of opening up trust and empathy in the group is for members to exchange self-disclosure (reducing the Hidden Area) and feedback (reducing the Blind Area). As members give ("disclose") and receive feedback, they increase the opportunity for trust and for open, free-flowing communication.

The counselor models these procedures for establishing trust by disclosing his or her own feelings and by providing feedback to members and the group through sharing observations, perceptions, and interpretations. The counselor's feedback, to serve as a model, needs to reflect the principles for effective feedback in groups and other interpersonal systems. The principles are as follows:

1. *Feedback must stem from a concern for the other and a desire to improve your relationship with him, her, or the group.* We are most open with those we care about (Carkhuff, 1969). From this concern, feedback aims to create a shared understanding of the particular relationship. If we give feedback, we should be ready to receive it in return. Feedback is best when we wish the other to know what we perceive about him, her, or the group and we wish to know how the other perceives and feels about us: "I have not felt very close to you in this group [or to you, the group] and I would like to change that. Perhaps I can try to describe what I have been experiencing in relation to you and hear from you how it's been on the other side of our relationship."

2. *Feedback should be descriptive rather than evaluative, whenever possible.* Feedback should be more the message of: "This is how your (specific) behavior affects me"; rather than, "You are a manipulator." In this sense, effective feedback focuses on the nature of observed and perceived behavior rather than on the inferred nature of the person. We share observations rather than inferences. As much as possible we need to suspend our judgments to permit unclouded observations. In addition, we can best give feedback in terms of "more or less" rather than in terms of "either-or." Then we can describe behavior in terms of quantity and patterns rather than in terms of quality or judgments. Judgments come out in terms of good or bad, right or wrong, nice or not nice. Descriptions and observations reflect a continuum of measurement of the meaning of behavior: high participation—low participation; often directs comments to counselor rather than group—seldom directs comments directly to counselor, and so on. An example of effective descriptive feedback is: "This is the third time in this meeting that I noticed your changing the subject when someone was talking about something potentially powerful for them. You seem to be trying to avoid this pain or to protect others and the group from experiencing it. I'm not sure this is helpful to the group at this time. I wonder what is going on for you inside about our dealing with painful topics and about what I am saying to you now."

3. *Feedback should be specific rather than general.* The focus on description rather than evaluation and on behavior rather than the person, as in the above example, helps to keep feedback specific. So

does the focus on the "here and now" rather than the "there and then." The message above was put into such terms as: "This is the third time in this meeting . . ."; not in terms of "Do you always avoid painful topics with others?" The potential for feedback to improve the relationship and to be meaningful to the receiver increases when it is tied to place and time, especially the here and now.

4. *Feedback should be well timed.* The focus on actual time and place helps feedback to be timed more appropriately. This timing is especially appropriate when feedback is given as close as possible to the actual occurrence of the situation which is described. Particularly destructive timing is the accumulation of observations and feelings (especially resentful ones) over a period of time and then the dumping of these all at one time: Not, "I have been concerned from the beginning of this group about your ____" but, "Just now while Jill and I were talking, you ____."

5. *Feedback should be directed toward behavior which the receiver can do something about.* This principle reflects the aim of feedback to be helpful to the receiver and the relationship, not destructive. Included in this principle is the choice of the amount of information given. How much information we give needs to be based on what the person (or group) receiving it can use rather than on the amount we might like to give. For instance, the counselor does not give feedback on the group's size being a deterrent to its interaction, when the group has already been formed and the current size is largely unmodifiable. Nor does the counselor share an informed dissertation about the theory of group size in relation to interactional problems. Instead, the counselor can note that several members have commented in this meeting about the group being experienced as too large for them and therefore serving as an obstacle to their participation. The counselor can then ask the group how it might deal with this perceived obstacle to break down some of this barrier for members.

6. *Feedback should be checked out.* In the group there are two useful ways of checking out feedback to ensure accuracy and communication. The first is asking receivers to paraphrase what they heard in the feedback. The second is asking other members whether this feedback makes sense to them (fits their impressions and opinions of the perceived and described behavior). The feedback that is most useful in the group is that which is more consensual, or shared by others.

There are basically two ways in which effective feedback is shared: by describing one's own feelings ("I feel hurt by what you just

said"; "I like what I saw you doing just now"), and by describing one's
own perception of the other's behavior ("You cut in before I finished
my sentence"). When feelings are shared, it is important that they be
recognized and expressed as temporary and capable of change and not
as permanent attitudes. Compare: "At this point I'm irritated with
you" with "I dislike you and I always will." When the counselor takes
the risk to share feelings in a way that others may get angry or hurt
and puts these in the temporary terms that more accurately reflect
the meaning, members can discover the value of feedback designed to
increase mutual trust. They may be more ready to move beyond their
fears of their own feelings as destructive to themselves and others
and to risk acceptance of their central place in the close, authentic,
and interdependent relationships which we all so desperately need.
The group, like the Velvetine Rabbit, is on its way to becoming really
"real." It is ready to invite this realness from all its members.

Encouraging Intermember Contact. The counselor can catalyze intermember contact by encouraging the use of ground rules, directing
messages to the intended recipient, and amplifying the expression of
the feeling component in intermember communication. The ground
rules which especially aid members to make contact with each other
are "speak as I"; "speak to individuals"; and "own our interaction."
The skills and techniques for establishing and reinforcing these
ground rules (presented in Chapter 5) are most useful. The group in
Closeness has rediscovered purpose and increases motivation for
tapping mutual aid resources. It is frequently very ready to intensify
the use of norms which can be explicated through these ground rules.

Directing messages to the intended recipient refers to the counselor's listening to the "I-Thou" aspect of "We," "They," or "the
Group" communication. The counselor encourages members to consider to whom specifically their messages are really directed and to
try to use more direct communication to meet their needs. The person
who notes that, "We have been getting very close to each other in the
group," is encouraged to express this experience more directly: "With
whom do you feel very close to in the group? Can you tell them this
and what it means to you?" and "With whom do you feel less close to
in the group right now but would like to be closer to? Can you tell
them directly, face to face, what you are feeling and what you want?"

Amplifying the feeling component of interaction between and
among members includes reaching for more concreteness in the
general feelings expressed, helping members get in touch with the
feeling component of their reactions to others, and suggesting activi-

ties which increase the nonverbal expression of feelings toward other members. To amplify general feelings, the counselor can ask directly what these may be: "You told John you thought he didn't like you. How does this perception of your relationship with him make you feel about yourself and him? Can you tell him this?" The counselor can help members get in touch with these feelings more, if they do not tend to be expressed because they are out of awareness, by asking members to take time to tune in to what they are experiencing in feelings: "John and Mary, are you willing to try something right now to help you get more in touch with your feelings about each other? Close your eyes and imagine the two of you at each end of a football field walking toward each other in the middle. As you walk toward each other in your imagination focus on the other and then become aware of what you are feeling. . . . As you get closer and can see each other better, do these feelings change? . . . What feelings do you have when you get toe to toe and nose to nose with each other in the middle of the field? . . . Now open your eyes, look at each other, and share what you wish about what you experienced in this fantasy." Finally, a very frequent dynamic of this stage of development, when members are feeling closeness toward each other, is the spontaneous impulses to make physical contact with each other—to touch—but the repression of these impulses out of the socialized taboo that relates touch to sexual intimacy. Members can find some freedom from the restriction of this taboo for communicating nonsexual intimacy and feelings with the counselor's encouragement. The norms for touch and physical contact can be reformed: "John, you felt like giving Mary a hug. Why don't you?"; "Jill, I want to hug you right now. Can I?" In the previous use of the fantasy activity with John and Mary, the counselor might intensify the emotional contact by actually having them line up at opposite sides of the room, walk toward each other in silence, and when they meet in the middle to let what happens to happen—nonverbally. All of these skills can enable the members of the group to make the emotional contact with each other which grows out of and increases initial closeness and which they very much need and seek at this stage.

Reaching for Empathic Feedback. When members in the group do express intense here-and-now feelings, these churn in the guts of other members (Anderson, 1980a). The chords that are struck are the basis for spontaneous empathic responses. However, members frequently are thrown by the intensity of what these feelings stir up in themselves. Especially during the early part of Closeness, they may be afraid of the intensity and honesty of their own reactions and embarrassed about expressing their responses. The counselor can catalyze this most empathic emotional connection by reaching for these responses.

This skill at this time is really rather easy. The members are more ready than not to share their own feelings as stimulated by those expressed and are drawn toward those who have expressed such intense feelings. They wait largely for permission. The counselor grants this permission and extends an invitation by noting: "We have reacted greatly to Jack's pain/joy/grief/fear [or whatever]. I can sense we have been drawn to him. I think it would be helpful for him and for us if we share some of our reactions with him." Most often this comment, or a similar one which invites response, stimulates a great deal of empathic feedback and self-disclosure in relation to the theme of the particular feelings expressed. In these moments, members often experience their humanity and its connection with all humans most fully, especially in relation to those in the group. They trust the salve of this humanity to heal all wounds. They learn the power of bearing pain for growth when one does not have to suffer alone.

Genuineness. Chief among the providing skills during closeness are the personalizing ones which were covered in Chapter 7. These include personalizing meanings, problems, feelings, and goals. Another skill which enables the group by providing support during closeness is genuineness. Genuineness is the counselor's authenticity—the ability to be honest with others. The counselor's words, in short, are closely related to his or her feelings. Carkhuff (1969) writes about the relationship of the skill of genuineness to such relationship elements as warmth and respect in these words: "In addition to constituting a necessary dimension of the experiential base and indeed the goal of helping, one of the potentially critical dimensions of genuineness is the respect it communicates—we are most genuine with whom we care most" (p. 181). He also conveys the relationship of genuineness to self-disclosure: "Although a helper may be genuine and not self-disclosing or self-disclosing and not genuine, frequently, and particularly at the extremes, the two are related (p. 187)." The counselor's genuineness permits closeness in the group. If other members recognize the counselor's sincerity, they will risk greater genuineness themselves. The bond of genuine closeness increases the odds for the group's dealing with the real needs and concerns of members, not just those deemed safe or socially acceptable. The counselor is genuine when his or her verbal and nonverbal communication is congruent, when it reflects the counselor's here-and-now experience, when it includes both positive and negative feelings, and when it risks challenging his or her relationship with the group or with particular members.

The TACIT approach conceives genuineness as "selective authenticity." What is "selective" about this authenticity is the counselor's focus on the theme and how "It" relates to the counselor as an "I" in the "I-We-It" interaction. In other words, the counselor shares those parts of his or her own life and here-and-now experiences that *relate to the theme.* This function keeps his or her genuineness related to the parallel task and does not pull the counselor into entering the group as a member totally for the purpose of meeting his or her own needs. To be genuine and yet to accomplish the parallel task of enabling group members to meet each other's needs, the counselor may use the ground rule of "disturbances come first." When the counselor finds him- or herself disturbed by a there-and-then situation, especially during the Closeness stage when it does not spark the authority conflicts of Autonomy, he or she can share this disturbance with the group. This confrontation of the disturbance in the here and now usually serves the counselor, as it does members, to move beyond it toward more effective functioning in the group. This selective authenticity does tend to promote more equality and closeness in the group. Again as members experience the counselor as a person with a function rather than a symbol of power authority, they are more ready to experience themselves and others in the same way. In brief, genuineness begets genuineness.

Confrontation. The skill of confrontation is a special case of feedback. Confrontation is feedback specifically addressed to discrepancies in words and deeds. Through confrontation, the counselor provides the group and/or members with a difference to consider in the process of self-awareness and self-evaluation. In effective confrontation, the counselor must feel his or her own sense of caring and the basic understanding of the other, whether member or group. Confrontation springs from this empathy. Then the counselor feeds back discrepancies and the specific directions in which these lead (Carkhuff, 1969). These elements of confrontation are reflected in the following example of the counselor's response to the group member. The group member has said, "I really can't make friends here. I think most of the members are out for themselves. They don't care about me." The counselors confronts, "You say you want to make friends, to get closer to others in this group, yet you seem to be excusing yourself when you find it difficult to reach out to the others here. As long as you make excuses and write them off as not caring, you will feel this emptiness." This confrontation is best, of course, when the member has felt some empathic understanding from the counselor. While confrontation in itself can be most empathic, the understanding part of the message could increase the use of confrontation in providing an opportunity for self-awareness and self-evaluation. For instance, the counselor could follow the above confrontation with: "You're probably hurt by what I've said, but I believe you really want something different for yourself and facing this difference between what you are saying and doing here might be helpful. What do you think? Is there any truth that hits home to you in what I've said?" If confrontation of discrepancies increases the other's awareness of specific contradictions, the other can choose to bring behavior more in line with words. He or she, or the group, can act in ways that contribute more effectively to meeting needs.

Clarifying Purpose. The counselor clarifies purpose by asking the group to weigh its current interactions against its desires. In short, the counselor notes and asks, "This is what we have been doing. Is this what we want to be doing here?" Much of this clarification relates to the leads of the group during Closeness. These leads hint at members' wishes to use the group differently. As the members express their readiness to redefine and recommit themselves to the group's purpose, the counselor makes this message explicit and directs the group to work on stating what they want. For instance, the group which expresses low energy in the beginning of the meeting through difficulty in getting started and through several members' expressing their difficulty in feeling with the group today can be asked to shuttle in fantasy between a place outside of the group— "there and then"— which seems to meet their needs and then to the group—"here and now." This shuttling is encouraged until members discover what is "there and then" that is lacking for them "here and now." Then, they are asked what they want from the here and now and how they can make this a more viable place and time to meet their needs.

In clarifying the purpose, the counselor needs to be alerted to what the group is working on. The major group themes can be surfaced through self-disclosure and feedback or through reaching for feedback in the group. Members are asked, "What are we working on?" and "What do you want to work on?" These questions help to produce a relevant agenda and to energize the group toward activity that is consistent with its achieving its clarified purpose or overriding theme.

Renegotiating the Contract.   During Closeness, when members are involved in knowing what the group resources for their needs really are, members not only are more willing and able to clarify purpose but are also ready to renegotiate a more meaningful contract. The contracting skills covered in Chapter 5 are vital now for this renegotiating. These include clarification of purpose, of roles and responsibility, and of useful ground rules in a simple statement of the theme and relevant subthemes. These also entail the reaching for feedback and making decisions of the contract that are truly consensual reflections of the group's cohesiveness and collective will. The contract at this stage no longer serves to provide structure for the group to discover its own needs. Conversely, the contract now serves as a way for the group to account for its own needs and to develop a structure which promotes the matching of these needs to group resources. The contract, as renegotiated during closeness, operationalizes the group's sense of mutual aid.

Illuminating Process.   The skill of illuminating process, which was introduced and presented in Chapter 7, is used in a special sense during Closeness. The members themselves tend to carry the processing function during this stage. They often demand staying in the here and now and, with little encouragement, self-reflect on their process. Frequently, the counselor can help the group examine whether it has overrestricted the norms for content with this here-and-now implicit rule. The theme demands relating the here and now to the there and then, and members need open content boundaries for addressing this relationship.

   In relating here and now to there and then and vice versa, the counselor illuminates the connection of these processes. The member who shares fears of closeness with friends outside the group is asked who he or she fears getting close to most (and least) in the group. The member who has spontaneously hugged another inside the group is encouraged to reflect upon how he or she might use this behavior in relationships outside the group. The group, while it basks in the warmth of its cohesiveness, can consider what made a difference in this system so that members have a conceptual framework to initiate and influence more closeness in their natural groups in social living. The greatest value of the group experience for members lies in this very ability to relate learnings inside the group to outside situations.

The group itself will not last forever, but the process it sets off in members may.

Detecting and Challenging Obstacles to Work. A special skill in Closeness is the counselor's detecting and challenging the obstacles to work. This skill was also covered in Chapter 7 in relation to the authority theme of Autonomy. In Closeness, it is particularly needed during the early impasse which marks the transition to this stage and later in relation to the intimacy theme.

The major obstacles to work during the impasse are the members' catastrophic expectations and fears as they give up the old belief system of trust in structure and have yet to develop the new one of trust in people (Bloomberg & Miller, 1968). When the environmental supports of group structure and power and control begin to give way to the self-supports of authentic interaction, the members fear a loss of self and are stuck. They seem unsure of where to go or how to get there. The counselor helps the group by naming this obstacle ("We seem stuck. I believe we have reached an impasse") and calling for the experience of both the fears and the wishes ("I wonder what we're afraid of?" and "What is it that you would like to see happening here now, would like to do next, if you weren't afraid?"). Sometimes the group can literally "bury" itself, or have a funeral in which they symbolically reflect an old group culture leaving and a new one being born. In fact, I have found that just suggesting such an activity in the group is enough for the group to move through its impasse by experiencing it and moving on to a new level of work—even though the group did not pick up on the suggestion and go through with the exercise!

The intimacy theme can create an obstacle to work when members hold on so desperately to the warmth and closeness they are experiencing that they fear the disclosure of authentic differences. So, too, can this theme lead to the expectation that the counselor will become a friend and not provide the difference of his or her parallel task and specific function which at times require the demand for work. In these events, the counselor must detect and challenge the obstacles. Again, these are named or feedback about the counselor's observations are given, and members are asked, "Is this what we want? Is this going to help us achieve your goals?" The counselor can self-disclose: "You have been acting like I wasn't here when I asked you if you are working on what you want to work on. I felt a little silly, like I had been a nondrinker at a beer bust. Yet I believe it is important for me to help you by raising the question or I wouldn't have asked. Your reaction leaves me feeling even more that it is important for you to consider if we are going to use these good feelings we have about each other to float along where we are now or to grow together. I really need to ask: Is this what you want? Is this what you're here for?" The counselor who trusts the process knows that members will want to work toward Interdependence and need little more than periodic nudges to confront the obstacles to this process.

Principles for the Closeness Stage

The following principles incorporate these skills as guidelines for the counselor using the TACIT approach during Closeness:

1. The counselor needs to provide the difference to hold members to experiencing the impasse which most often portends the transition from Autonomy to Closeness.
2. The counselor needs to initiate and help members develop the processes of self-disclosure and feedback.
3. The counselor needs to help members learn to give and receive effective empathic feedback through use of the principles for effective feedback.
4. The counselor needs to help members to reclarify the group's purpose and theme and to renegotiate a contract in which members are more genuinely commited to group goals, the selected subthemes, each other, and the ground rules for achieving their goals. The current "I-We-It" is weighed and evaluated against the wanted "I-We-It," and the group chooses procedures to close the gap between the real and the ideal.
5. The counselor needs to help the group get its underlying human relations agenda on the table by encouraging intermember contact, reaching for feelings and empathic feedback, and comparing its contract and needs against the needs and hurts of members.
6. The counselor needs to help the group to transfer here-and-now themes to members' there-and-then situations and to activate there-and-then themes in here-and-now process.
7. The counselor needs to use more freely his or her own "selective authenticity" to risk genuineness, self-disclosure, and feedback (as much as is expected of any other member) with-

in the boundary of the counselor's function and parallel tasks.

8. The counselor needs to reach for the common ground, or similarities in experienced differences, and reach for differences in experienced similarities. Also, he or she reaches for the positives in the negatives and the negatives in the positives.

Example

In the continuing scenario of the group of fifth-graders in school, we find the Closeness stage flowering in Meetings 7 and 8. The facilitation of more authentic autonomy and interdependence in this Closeness stage of development requires more explicit dealing with questions of direction and purpose. In the TACIT approach, the contract can be directly renegotiated through the more authentic commitment to an "I-We-It" balance in relation to member-chosen group goals. The goals must be feasible to sustain effort and to reinforce emerging hopes for success. More commitment can be encouraged for dealing with the agenda of interpersonal relations as well as to the theme. Within this stage members can be involved in interdependent mutual aid; can interact with each other as person to person rather than as role to role, revealing their wishes and fears and asking for and accepting help; and can take responsibility for themselves and others.

Meeting 7

The conflict involving Darren and Chris last week was not yet resolved. As the members sat down in the circle, I could sense that they had not forgotten. This evident concern verified my feelings that "We" concerns were beginning to emerge. I opened the meeting by saying, "We have a discussion to finish, if you all remember." Darren, looking unusually embarrassed, said, "I remember." But before focusing completely on Darren, I asked the group to verbally remember what had happened with the closing of Meeting 6. (I wanted to include the group when taking up the issue again. After all, I had used the skill of "making the problem the group's" and I felt that it was very important to follow through with this. I thought that my suggestions of the importance of unity would reinforce the individual feelings of "We-ness" that were gradually coming to the surface. Another objective in including the group was to permit Darren to understand group concerns, since he had felt threatened in the last meeting.)

(Darren has the potential to be a very healthy component of the group. He has leadership qualities and is a very caring person. I wouldn't want to ignore his anxieties, because the understanding of them is very important to him and the other group members. However, the initial understanding or attempt to understand Darren's anxiety in the last two meetings has to come from me. It is through my understanding that Darren can understand.)

(I have no indication whatsoever that the expressed anger and anxiety have anything to do with any other individual members or even the group situation itself. Instead, it seems to be stemming from conflicts within himself—unfulfillment of personal needs. As I think about the group in between meetings, I have different views of his behavior. I was completely disillusioned and confused with him at the onset of the group experience. Then he moved into the experience displaying behavior which actually defined the direction that the group would move in for a while. I have a very strong feeling that he sensed this almost as much as I did.)

(In last week's recording, I expressed the attitude that Darren must learn to differentiate between a strong but equal member of the group and one who runs the show. I had to admit to myself since then my perceptions and anger with him at that point. Later on, I realized that Darren's behavior had disrupted and imposed a closing conflict on the meaningful meeting that we had all achieved. But conflicts are meaningful too. Perhaps that is one of the most difficult things that the counselor has to understand. I know now that Darren's anger in no way stopped or stunted our togetherness. It gave us yet another device by which to become united. But that was only secondary. The primary consideration was Darren's feelings. He doesn't want to run the show. Instead, he wants to be reassured, just like every other member, that he is an important part of the group. Especially now, as togetherness is being experienced more and more, each member has the need to contribute to that growing unity feeling.)

(His anger with himself because of feeling threatened was imposed on Chris during the last meeting. From what I observed today, he had begun to understand this. He was embarrassed by last week's behavior and told the group that he still thought that it wasn't fair that he had been interrupted. However, this time the blame was shifted toward the situation. No mention was made of Chris being the cause of his anxiety.)

I helped Darren deal with his feelings through using the skill of "redirecting signal to intended recipient." In this case the recipient was Chris. But as I perceived the situation, Chris was the wrong recipient. Actually, the attack he was making was on the situation and himself. I helped him realize this by "reaching for feelings" of how he felt during the situation, then pointing out that what he had just expressed was not anger toward Chris but toward the fact that he had been interrupted. I didn't feel that it would be wise to come right out and say that I thought he felt threatened. Instead, I again stressed the equality of group members, and that he was right when saying that the situation was unfair for him (an equal part of the group). This was very successful. He said that he now understood that it was an accident, and he assumed the very natural role that he had before through the rest of the meeting.

Darren's stable understanding was so real that I felt no reservations when pursuing the issue further. Joy also sensed Darren's ability to deal rationally with the conflict, and together we "reached for feelings" from other group members. We asked them what their reactions were at the time when Darren was expressing his anger. This worked out very well. While Darren spoke, they listened intently. Prior to Darren's disclosure, we included them in restating what had happened. Now we followed through with this, by indicating that their feelings about the situation were also important.

The members are now sharing their feelings with increasingly authentic and real expressions. Ricky immediately offered his feelings, saying, "I was mad at Darren because we helped Chris and then he made him feel bad." He said that the situation also made him feel bad, along with being mad. There were other expressions of feeling bad about what had happened. Randy said that he was upset because Darren kept saying things over and over again, not getting anything accomplished. Darren listened to these comments and reacted beautifully. He didn't see them as an attack, and showed no need to defend himself. We concluded that the whole situation was not exactly pleasant for anyone. Through this experience the entire group had a hand in the problem. Darren was helped to understand his own actions, and the group moved yet another step closer together.

Chris seemed more involved than before because of last week's conflict. He was more comfortable when we talked about "group feelings." He still becomes uneasy at certain moments, but his behavior exhibits more real feelings of belonging.

Jeff was quiet for a while in this meeting and the group jumped at the chance to deal with that also. They pointed out the fact that he was quiet a lot in school. Ricky said that when he went to visit Jeff at home, he wasn't quiet. He also told us that if Jeff went to visit him, he was afraid to go into Ricky's house. Jeff agreed with this and laughed. Then he told us that sometimes he just didn't have anything to say. Even Jeff is feeling that he belongs to the group. Even though expression is not frequent, it is put forth with less confusion. His explanations of his behavior are moving away from the "I don't know," toward real attempts to bring his feelings into words.

We discussed ideas of things that we could do as a group. Someone suggested singing songs. Everyone agreed, and Chris got the music books. Everyone had a good time singing together, clapping, and laughing at our mistakes. We planned a football game with Don and Audrey's group, but before we went out we pushed the chairs and desks back together. Everyone waited together in the hallway and we had a pep talk. The game was competitive, but they handled it well. We lost, and they handled that even better. Chris said, "We'll get them next time," and everyone ran into the school.

Meeting 8

We formed our circle; everyone very enthusiastic. (I'd like to note the procedure that we have developed in forming the circle. It was Darren's idea, a few meetings ago. Upon his words, "Let's go!" we all hold hands, forming a circle. We remain holding hands, until we all are seated on the floor in our circle. It is beautiful. The feelings of "We-ness" that shine through as we do this is amazing. If someone outside of the group were to enter the room as we join hands to form our circle, it may seem insignificant. But working with the group all these weeks, nothing is small. Everything is so important. As we formed our circle today, I took a few moments to reflect upon our meetings; starting from the first. We have come a long way).

Everyone had a turn at sitting in the middle of the group. Then we used the go-around technique, each member saying one thing that he liked about the person who was sitting in the middle. This exercise worked out so well that it practically lasted throughout the whole meeting. It seems as though the members could go on and on about each other's good qualities. In fact, some of the boys got impatient if the person before them was taking too long. They couldn't wait to have their turn.

I was so happy with Jeff's participation. Ricky was first to go into the circle and Jeff listened intently, watching Ricky being in the center. I was surprised because as we finished with Ricky, Jeff took a deep breath and said he would like to be next. As he first entered the circle, he was a bit uneasy, but very proud that he had volunteered. I was proud of him too. It took a lot of courage. In fact, as I remember every other exercise, Jeff was always at the end of the line. Even then, he hesitated to participate. Jeff just glowed with happiness as his fellow members verbally expressed to him that he was "O.K.," that he "belonged." It was wonderful to see the other members reinforce Jeff's conception of himself. It is definitely not just Joy and me who help the less confident members. It is a group effort now, and as a result, the confidence level of those members has increased significantly. Jeff has obviously been the most withdrawn member. It had been evident to every boy in the beginning; they almost ignored his silence because they were uncomfortable with it. But the comments that they gave to him today brought out such a positive reaction. They turned his periodical silence into something meaningful for the whole group. Darren said, "I like Jeff because he never interrupts anyone." Mike said that he liked Jeff because in the last couple of meetings he "joined" the group.

The boys did such a very responsible job with the exercise. Not only did they understand what we were doing, being very serious about it, but they also gave examples, as they explained why they liked a person. I had to hold myself back from running to Jeff and giving him a big hug as he left the group. Smiling, he said "thank you." He really meant it.

(I am learning a lot about holding myself back when need be. I care so much about the members, but many times, directly displaying those feelings could be very wrong. Jeff has gained independence while he was in the circle. If I would have acted upon my feelings [giving Jeff a hug as I explained] I would have taken away from that newly found freedom the autonomy that is now emerging. I realized that indirectly we had all embraced him.)

No one mentioned an outdoor activity. Everyone was having a great time being together. The comments about members were taken very seriously. But we also laughed and had a good time discussing past experiences that we have had. "We" statements were frequent throughout the entire meeting.

(We are now a cohesive unit. My role in this meeting mainly involved sitting back and understanding how we got here. To be truthful, I could never have imagined this success during our first meeting. We have grown together. I have learned so much through each one of the boys and I feel that they have learned from me. My main goal for the group has gradually been met. And I certainly didn't do it by myself. Our theme of learning to get along with others is in full focus now. Today, I sat back and watched the shared responsibility and shared leadership. I observed and participated in the intimacy that we all enjoyed.)

(I also tried to prepare myself for the termination of this experience. I believe that much of my reflection on past meetings today had a lot to do with the realization of the few meetings that we have left. My direction was vital in the beginning. They have responded positively to this and have reached a point where they can direct themselves. However, they will need as much help leaving the group as they did coming in. My goal now is to direct them toward applying what they have learned here to experiences outside of the group. What they have learned today should provide a basis for deeper evaluation. I would like this to be the focus for next week.)

Summary

During Closeness members build and use a culture of mutual trust and cohesiveness. They confront the impasse in the transition of the security of structure in Autonomy and the yet-discovered security of real trust in others. They move on to develop processes of self-disclosure and feedback and procedures for these. The purpose of the group becomes clearer for members. They recommit themselves to the goals explicit in this purpose and theme and they renegotiate and live the contract more fully.

The counselor enables the evolution of this culture through high use of the catalyzing and providing functions and more moderate use of the directing and processing functions. Catalyzing requires the skills of modeling self-disclosure and feedback, encouraging intermember contact, and reaching for empathic feedback. Providing involves personalizing, genuineness, and confrontation. Directing entails clarifying purpose and renegotiating the contract. Processing comes from relating here-and-now themes to there-and-then themes. These skills enable the group to risk more authentic interaction. This interaction inevitably confronts the differences in members that surface when they trust the process enough to be themselves. The experience of these differences and their use in the members' process within and outside the group mark the beginning of true mutual aid—of Interdependence.

Critical Incidents

Critical Incident 7

Subtheme.   Responding to Others

Context of Incident.   This incident occurred in the sixth meeting. The group had been discussing such values as trust, intimacy, sharing, and group norms for the disclosure of personal problems. During this discussion, one member of the group remained quiet and seemed fearful of joining in group discussions. Finally, two other members noticed this situation and commented.

Choice Point
Tom: "Mark, I notice you haven't said anything or contributed in any way to our discussion."
Judy: "Yeah, I noticed that, too. Why haven't you said anything?"
Mark (with emotion in his voice): "I'll tell you why! I don't feel I can trust you guys not to laugh at me or make fun of me if I make a mistake or say something personal and foolish."

     This statement appears to have immobilized the other group members and they all focus their attention on Mark.
What would you do at this point? What is your rationale for this response?

TACIT Response.   The counselor uses self-disclosure and some confrontative feedback and encourages intermember contact: "I'm really excited to hear you say what you did, Mark, because I experience a very honest statement and one that I respect. I believe your sharing these feelings is a big risk for you. I feel that while you say you've been afraid of the risk to talk up, your statement to the group represents a greater risk than in remaining silent and not disclosing yourself. I wonder what impact Mark's statements make on the rest of us, and I bet Mark does, too."

Rationale.   The surface issue is the reluctance of Mark to share in the group discussion and risk personal disclosure. At a deeper level, the issue involves trust, the level of disclosures, and mutual concern for other members. The counselor needs to enable the establishment of norms that permit freedom to deal with personal issues at many levels and that therefore can support this group process as it strengthens a climate of trust and closeness. The counselor responds to Mark's concerns as well as attempts to establish the responsibilities of group members for each other. In doing this, the counselor also models some self-disclosure and feedback.

Critical Incident 8

Subtheme. Responding to Others

Context of Incident. In this meeting after members responded supportively to Mark, especially to affirm the risk he took and their appreciation of it, a brief silence ensued. During the silence, another member who had remained silent through most of the discussion suddenly began to cry.

Choice Point
Sandra (crying): "I wouldn't want anyone to open up inside, not anyone! It's horrible and it can make you miserable. I've tried it and I know! It's too big a risk to take!" Sandra continues crying.

The other members appear shocked and taken aback by this incident, some silently looking at Sandra and a few at you.
What would you do at this point? What is your rationale for this response?

TACIT Response. The most preferred response initially is silence, or the active containment of a response. This containing by the counselor can encourage the group to make contact with Sandra's pain and fears. If the group seems immobilized, the counselor can model self-disclosure and feedback: "Sandra, I know you're hurting right now, and I respect your saying you aren't willing to risk disclosing your insides. Yet I appreciate what you've shared. I feel much closer to you now than while you were silent. I don't know how the others feel, and I hope they might tell you, but you've had an impact on me. When you risk disclosing your insides as you just did, I am drawn to you, wanting to get even closer to you."

Rationale. The surface issue is deciding whether to respond personally to Sandra's distress. The underlying issues center around the group's concerns about trust, closeness, and fears of closeness and risk. The trust issues for the group are: "How can I trust myself—and others?" "How far can I go in revealing myself?" "How far do I want other members to go?" "What are the responsibilities of members to those who choose to reveal personal data?" "Will I be hurt or will I hurt others when we open up?" The counselor needs to respond to Sandra with genuine care and concern, share the impact she had made on him, and reach for the empathic response and contact of other members (if the group is not ready to initiate these responses).

Critical Incident 9

Subtheme. Helping Others in the Group

Context of Incident. This was toward the end of the seventh meeting. The group had made a few tentative thrusts at dealing with emotional issues. Several members revealed some personal concerns to the group, accompanied by some appropriate emotional expression. Following these disclosures, the group responded supportively, then tended toward quietness and a tranquility with members reaffirming the importance of personal disclosures. Some inertia has evolved in relation to the emotional intensity leading to a group collusion to avoid future painful issues. It appears that the group considers their responses to be a final, token gesture to the emotional aspects of the group's work. They want to close the group on this more calm and supportive atmosphere and fear opening up more painful conflict. Several members actively take this stance.

Choice Point
Jane: "I really feel close to Sandra after our talk; I think I know, now, how she *really* feels.
Gomez: "I think we're all closer than we've ever been. It seems we really trust each other."
Chris: "I feel the same way. This group really seems together."
Steve: "You know what we ought to do? We should all get together and go somewhere and have a party."

Other members continue the discussion along the same lines, none of them actually picking up on the idea of the party.
What would you do at this point? What is your rationale for this response?

TACIT Response. The counselor here clarifies purpose, begins to renegotiate the contract, illuminates process, and detects and challenges the obstacles to work: "I think it would be helpful if we stopped and looked at what might be happening here. We are feeling closer to each other, but I sense a closure in what you are saying. It's like we have gotten here through some pain and it feels better now so we don't want to open any more wounds. I think we now know what potential we have to help each other—to achieve our purpose in this group. I wonder if you really want group process to end like this— that you don't want to go any deeper in honest disclosure and confrontation? And I wonder what we may be afraid of now?"

Rationale. The counselor attempts to illuminate both surface and underlying issues in terms of both positive and negative aspects of the process—to support the disclosure and cohesiveness, while at the same time gently demanding work by subtly discouraging a premature closure of authentic emotional expression and contact. This requires enabling the group to clarify purpose and goals and to decide how to work in the direction of achieving them. The counselor both supports prior work and challenges toward future growth. Otherwise, the group can avoid movement by reacting to emerging conflict and tensions by holding onto early closeness, circling round and round the work it has done to reach this sense of well-being by restating its history rather than looking to its future.

9
Interdependence

In Interdependence the group moves from the mutual trust of Closeness to mutual aid. The trust and cohesiveness permit the emergence of difference. When these differences become resources for individual member learning and group growth, the interdependent mutual aid system in the group is established.

"Mutual aid" is a phrase first coined by Kropotkin (1925) in his seminal study of animal and human evolution. His study suggests that the species that have survived and progressively developed have not been the dominant, destructive, or competitive ones. The "fittest" have been those most able to cooperate with one another through interdependent mutual aid. This mutual aid marks both the healthy person and the healthy group.

Ruth Benedict (Maslow & Honigmann, 1970), the anthropologist, discovered a similar interdependence in her study of healthy cultures. She termed this mutual aid "synergy." In cultures with synergy, members' own selfish and vital need-meeting is interdependently connected with others'. Most acts toward self-actualization contribute simultaneously both to the good of the self and the good of the group. In synergy, or mutual aid, there is no inherent conflict between individual and group needs and goals. Members build a healthy system on which they depend for their own growth and development. This interdependent mutual aid relationship is readily assumed by members during the Interdependence stage of TACIT group development.

Individual Process

The three sets of questions which members have regarding the "I," "We," and "It" of this group process during Interdependence are not experienced so separately as in the earlier stages. These elements of group process fuse for members. In fact, the work of the group is marked by this fusion. The questions by this stage also tend more to be statements. Individual members now experience their own needs as these dovetail with the group resources. Their autonomy and differences as well as their interdependence and sense of group needs come out in such statements about "I" as:

"I want to grow."
"I'm O.K."
"I am different from yet similar to you."

In relation to the "We," the statements involve:

"We can grow together."
"We're O.K."
"We are different yet similar."
"We do know and have known what we've been doing together."
"We know what we can do to maximize the growth of all members of this group."

Toward the "It," or the counselor and the counseling process, each member directs.

"It—this group—can and will help us as we help each other."
"It—this group—knows its resources, including the counselor, and will tap these as needed to achieve our purpose, theme, and goals."
"It—this group—will stay on target and will meet individual member's needs in proportion to what these needs are."
"It—this group—will help each and every member to discover their special and unique self and to use this self as the basis for authentic and close relationships with others."

The overriding question, which members seldom ask but consistently work on, is: "What can we do before we end and while we have these resources to meet the needs of all members, starting with those whose needs seem strongest and most pressing for their individual growth?" In brief, each member assesses and acts to contribute as fully as possible to achieving the purpose of the group.

Group Process

The Interdependence stage is marked by several dynamic balances of members' and the group's needs. Members fuse autonomous and interdependent concerns. Cohesion strengthens and balances work for the "I," the "We," and the "It." This balance anchors the connection of here-and-now process to content—both in the here and now and as related and transferred in learning to the there and then. The interaction, while consistent with purpose and attending to these dynamic balances, is fluid, spontaneous, and creative.

Members of this mature work group face reality. Through "valid communication" (Bennis & Shephard, 1956), members reflect a consensual reality in which individuals and the group as a whole are expressively aware of what they are doing together. Members responsibly and spontaneously sense what self and others need to achieve their common tasks and purpose; and members are given what they need in proportion to their needs. This consciousness of mutual aid taps the group resources for work at the "I," the "We," and the "It" levels as these needs emerge. The group's awareness of needs springs from open feedback channels. The Open Area of the Johari Window presented in Chapter 8 has enlarged to the point that members know what self-disclosure and feedback are most immediately pertinent to the needs of individual members and of the group. Members' differences are accepted, reached for, and used to achieve the group's goals. This process very much includes a respect for the counselor's difference in expertise and experience and the contribution of this difference, valued no more than any other member's, to the group's growth and learning.

Counseling Process

The group's task in Interdependence is to tap its resources for mutual aid. The counselor's parallel task is to enable the group to use its mutual aid resources. Toward this end, it is best for the counselor to stay out of the way of the group's process and to serve as a consultant to the group when the group perceives this need and calls upon him or her. The counselor, as a member, functions in providing and processing (much as any other member). As consultant, the counselor may be called upon to function in directing and catalyzing. The skills for providing and processing are those presented in previous chapters—

personalizing, self-disclosure, feedback, genuineness, and illuminating processes. The new skills for directing and catalyzing require offering experimental activities, exercises, or techniques which may serve as tools for members to resolve the specific themes which emerge.

Skills

Offering Experimental Activities. This skill for serving as a consultant to the group is really quite complex. It requires the counselor to have the creativity borne of study and experience to set up experiments as based on the group's needs for learning and a compendium of activities and techniques which can be used differentially in response to specific needs.

The "experiment" is a cornerstone of experiential learning (Zinker, 1977). It entails structuring a situation in the group in which the member can try (and "try out") new behavior and study the consequences for self and others within the safety of the lab. The results, if successful, can then be risked in behavior outside of the group. Experiments especially help members enact wishes in ways never tried before.

Zinker (1977, 1980) particularly describes the use of experiments in this stage of group development. As he notes about this stage (Zinker, 1980): "The group takes on more clarity, thematic pointedness and elegance in resolution. The leader tracks the themes of the ongoing action effectively and suggests original ways of resolving group dilemmas [through experiments]. The leader reveals himself or herself as a group member with a special task rather than as an insulated role-bound genius" (pp. 69–70). As Zinker reflects, these experiments cannot be preplanned. They must evolve and be in response to the emergent themes in the here-and-now group process. They may be a part of the counselor's repertoire because they have been developed before in similar situations, or were used as a structured exercise. Often, they are created on the spot by the counselor and/or members.

If the counselor is listening for expressed wishes, he or she can play these through in terms of how they may be enacted in the group. For instance, the member who discloses that he or she wants to be freer in expressing nonverbal affection can be asked to try an experiment wherein he or she goes to each member of the group and expresses experienced affection nonverbally and differently to each. Metaphors in the individual member's or group's themes can be enacted in experiment. A member who expresses a desire for a fresh start can be "reborn" through the group's acting out the metaphor together of giving birth.

In enacting group wishes and metaphors, the members are especially creative, spontaneous, and involved during Interdependence. In fact, this creativity is often the best source of the counselor's experiments. The counselor, when asked by the group what he or she can do to help a member resolve a particular theme, can ask the group what might be done to create an experiment where the member can try to resolve the theme in action in the here-and-now in a way that he or she wishes. Also, the member himself or herself might be able to design this experiment. When the particular member or the group seems stuck, then perhaps the counselor can draw on his or her own knowledge and experience to construct a relevant experiment. The key principle is to translate wishes into how they may be enacted and to structure a laboratory experiment in the group in which the member or members can try this enactment—to try the new behavior on for size for them to see if it fits, if it meets wishes or needs. Most often, the group is ready to help the member process the experience itself. They share the impact on them through feedback and seek the meaning through self-disclosure. They generate the data needed to assess the results, positive and negative, of the experiment. If this processing were not initiated by the group itself, it is imperative that the counselor seek it.

Using Structured Exercises. Structured exercises are also experiments and should always be presented as such. However, these are experiments that have been used by others and are available in catalogues or compendiums by experienced group leaders. The definition, research, and general principles which I have evolved in another source (Anderson, 1980b) for the use of structured exercises were introduced in Chapter 3. I will expand on some of these ideas here.

A structured exercise is the counselor's intervention in group process that involves a set of specific orders, instructions, or prescriptions for the behavior of group members (Lieberman et al., 1973, p. 409). These prescriptions specify certain members' behavior alternatives at a particular moment in the group. For example, if the counselor says, "Pick out the member of this group you feel most different from and we'll go around for each of you to tell that person how you feel, why you think you feel that way, and what you appreciate about his or her difference," he or she is using a structured exercise. Each group member can choose whether or not to carry out the directive. However, if the member chooses to participate, the behavior alternatives are limited by the interactions. The exercise calls for trying out specific new behavior as focused on a particular identified theme.

On the other hand, if the counselor says, "How different do you feel from other members of this group?" he or she is not using a structured exercise. In this example, the worker specifies the content of the interaction but members can choose how to approach this content—the process of this interaction. A particular member may discuss his or her perspective of one other member. Or he or she may address feelings about the counselor or the group as a whole. Or the member may describe feelings about several particular members. This question, therefore, does not constitute a structured exercise. It does not instruct the group in both the content and process of its interaction and consequently limit its choices for participation for the duration of the exercise.

A structured exercise may take only a few minutes—"Tell Jack why you feel closest to him in the group"—or it may consume most of the group meeting (Pfeiffer & Jones, 1979). It may be primarily verbal or nonverbal ("Stand up, Jack and Jill, face and walk toward each other, and without talking, let happen whatever happens"). Finally, the exercise may involve a number of different participant combinations:

1. The group as a whole: "Sculpturing"—arranging members into a group statue which represents their image of the group.
2. One member vis-à-vis the group: "Breaking in"—one member attempts to break into the group physically while the others form a tight circle with arms interlocked and attempt to keep him or her out so that the member has to use his or her own power to get in.
3. The entire group as individual members: "Go-around"— each member in a "go-around" is to give, in order, his or her opinion of what the group could do in the next ten minutes to begin to meet its most pressing need.
4. Pairs: "Mirroring"—the group is broken into twos and each pair is to "mirror" (or imitate) nonverbally the behavior of each other in order.
5. One particular pair: "Arm wrestling"—two members who are afraid of their own power are asked to arm wrestle each other.

6. Each of the members independent of the group: "Fantasy trip"—the members are asked to imagine individually taking a trip through the woods and visiting a wise person in a mountain retreat to whom they ask a very important question for which they need a particular wise answer.

7. One particular member: The "empty chair"—a member is requested to have a dialogue that gives voice to two conflicting forces of his or her current internal life and to move to the empty chair when it represents the other side of the conflict, such as the fear of confrontation which opposes one's desire to assert oneself more.

The counselor can develop a mental file of these structured exercises from the various catalogues of them which have been published (for instance, Garr & Sayer, 1979; Johnson, 1972; Johnson & Johnson, 1973; Lewis & Streitfield, 1970; Malmud & Machover, 1965; Otto, 1970; Saretsky, 1977; Schutz, 1967, 1971; Stevens, 1971). There is a danger that the counselor familiar with this compendium of structured exercises will draw upon those too often, especially early in the group when members are struggling for structure and the interaction wanes. The research (summarized in Chapter 3) suggests that these exercises can become a serious obstacle to TACIT development and rob members of their opportunity to develop authentic autonomy and interdependence. In brief, it is only when the members do not need these exercises for structure but seek a particular structured intervention for meeting a particular need of the group or its members that they are useful. Then they are truly perceived and used as "experiments" (such as during Closeness and particularly during Interdependence).

In Chapter 3 I have offered (Anderson, 1980b) five principles for the use of these structured exercises at any point in the group's TACIT development. These principles are derived from the theory and research on these exercises and on my own experience as a recipient and purveyor of their use. These are:

1. *Don't use structured exercises to enliven the group or its members emotionally.* Too often structured exercises seem to be used as emotional space fillers, or as something interesting to do when the group seems at loose ends. This is a mistake. Members of the group are alive, and if they seem to need to be energized by the counselor, if meetings seem listless, if the counselor believes he or she must constantly spark more lively activity, the problem most likely lies

within the group process and will only be compounded by accelerating devices. This developmental obstacle can best be explored rather than circumvented. The counselor and the group need to consider together the obstructions to members' involvement through attention to such areas as the current norms operating in the group, the relationship of these norms to the group's goals and to each member's primary tasks, and the members' perceptions and feelings toward the counselor, each other, and the experience. This principle is not to suggest that the counselor refrain from asking members to stand up and stretch, for instance, when they seem physically fatigued and therefore stuck in devoting energy to the task at hand. However, it instructs the counselor to control any impulse to use a structured exercise to enliven interaction solely for the sake of energizing or "sparking" emotional expressivity.

2. *Don't use structured exercises to accelerate "breakthrough."* Similar to the first principle, this one is concerned about the proclivity in practice for accelerating interaction in the group. Indeed, structured exercises are effective for accelerating groups to bypass the early, "slower" stages of development and plunging members quickly into "instant intimacy" through the expression of positive and negative feelings. But they do not accelerate the individual and group growth process through these "breakovers." It is the "breakthrough" which can significantly aid this growth. Counselors can best help the group and its members *through* anxiety, *through* the impasses or difficulty stages, rather than *over* them. It is the struggle with timidity, with mistrust, with resistance, with authority, with developing mutual aid relationships and the development of competencies to move beyond them in real relationships with others that is the very stuff of growth in group process, not an impediment to it. It is these skills that are transferred to the world outside of the immediate group experience in behalf of one's further development.

3. *Use structured exercises to increase awareness of group process.* This principle evolves from the second, in that structured exercises used to control rather than to illuminate group process create more obstructions than they prevent. Exercises to increase closeness by bypassing the "trust" and "autonomy" stages of group development rob members of the opportunity to develop the skills to confront structural barriers to interpersonal closeness and mutual aid and to experience the power of their own choice to work through these obstacles within and outside of the group. On the other hand, there are structured exercises that can be introduced to, or created by, the group for the purpose of increasing the group's awareness of what is occurring in its structure and process so that it can *choose* to alter its focus and participation in line with individual and group goals. Contrary to bypassing these obstacles to group development, they are designed to confront them directly. Some of these are activities such as suggesting that members compile a list of what they think the current norms are in the group—the do's and don'ts about how to become a "good group member" if someone new to the group wanted this information; asking members to place themselves physically in the room in a place they believe represents their position in the group at that point in time in the group process; having a "go-around" in which members share their reactions as to what the most (or least) meaningful part of the group experience (or meeting) was for them thus far. Always, these exercises are best introduced as "experiments" and as optional for the group or any members to try, and what members do with the "data" they collect from this "experiment" is their own choice.

4. *Use structured exercises to increase autonomy and interdependence.* The activities suggested in the third principle and the way they are introduced and used are designed to increase, not decrease, a member's autonomy and interdependence. The counselor is suggesting a means to discover more about important aspects of the group's structure and process, not a preconceived end of how this information is used by it. It is the group's responsibility, and each member's, to choose what will be done with what they know. In the further interest of helping the group and its members increase their awareness of what they do, the counselor can provide or solicit more information on what they did do with their awareness, including perhaps denying that it is so. But here, too, the choice must be theirs to act on their awareness. The autonomy and their interdependence in achieving their goals for the group experience is theirs, as it must be, and the degree to which they experience this through the counselor's behavior is the degree to which they can be able to use it on their own behalf, both within and outside the group.

5. *Help the group and its members to evaluate realistically the structured exercises that are used.* Because the research consistently demonstrates that structured exercises feed the omnipotent mystique of the counselor, and result in the erroneous evaluation of a powerfully effective group for members in their own eyes, it is most important that members get help to put the experiences that are used into a proper, more realistic, perspective. Group members can be aided in their awareness that the structured exercises that are perceived as especially meaningful to an individual member's growth or to the group as a whole were tools to their awareness on which they *chose* to act. There is nothing magical about them or those who suggested them. They served, for the most part, as a way of concentrating awareness on what is. There are many other ways to increase our awareness if we stop, look, and listen. This awareness is an important step, but only a step, in the process of growth. It is the responsibility that members of the group took to act upon this awareness that likely made the difference in the actual growth experienced. And in the final analysis, only they could do this for themselves.

Principles for the Interdependence Stage

There are few principles for guiding the counselor's work with the TACIT theme-centered group during Interdependence. These are:

1. The counselor needs to trust the group.
2. The counselor needs to maintain a consultant role to the group, keeping interventions few and far between.
3. When called upon, the counselor needs to make experiments, exercises, and techniques available to the group at the appropriate level of the group process—the "I," the "We," and the "It."

Example

Meetings 8 and 9 of the ten meetings demonstrate Interdependence and the counselors' function in the preadolescent groups in school. Meeting 8 was included in the last chapter (Chapter 8) and should be reviewed with the ninth meeting, which follows.

The Interdependence stage is marked by several dynamic balances of member's concerns which the counselor has attempted to influence from the beginning. The mature group involves processes of "valid communication" in which it seems to know what it is doing. The theme is approached realistically with a balanced fusion of autonomous and interdependent concerns. Cohesion remains strong and is the anchor for focusing on the here-and-now confluence of the "It" (content) and the "We and I" (process). Members spontaneously sense what self and others need to achieve their common task, and members are given what they need in proportion to what their needs are. With a consciousness of the mutual aid in the group and how it can be used for accomplishing individual, interpersonal, and group theme-related work, the "I-We-It" is both differentiated and integrated through open feedback channels among members and between members and the counselor.

Meeting 9

(Along with the Interdependence stage has come decreased defensiveness among members. Because of this, they seem to have discovered a freedom to experiment with each other. I noticed the rediscovery of fellow members. Questions directed toward members contain curiosity of why others feel and react as they do. This was all very evident in today's exercise.)

They were very responsive when we told them about the "secret" exercise. As I handed them pieces of paper, they stressed the importance of being alone to write their secrets, as much as Joy and I did. In comparing their participation in exercises from beginning meetings until now, there is a remarkable difference. In the beginning, there was much ambiguity over such exercises because of fears and unclear understanding of our purpose. Although the exercises that we do now are of the same type, the boys' responses are much different. The declining reluctance to participate in these awareness activities showed me increasingly clear conceptions of the theme in relation to our existence as a group. This has resulted in enthusiasm and enjoyment of the exercises. Before, the boys almost demanded knowing the purpose before involving themselves. Now they know that the purpose of the exercise can only be realized to the fullest extent through participation and post-discussion. They trust our direction and their own.

Everyone took this exercise as a very serious matter. Even Randy, who has a tendency to joke around about everything, sat in his corner, very involved in his secret.

There were questions about the exercise from those who did not clearly understand. In emphasizing our progress, I will again reflect back on earlier meetings. If we would be doing an exercise early in the experience, questions weren't asked, even though they were present. They would rather write anything than reveal that they were confused. Now, trust has developed, permitting them to expose the true confusion or misunderstanding that they experience from time to time.

Each person read the secret that he had chosen, freely commenting on how he felt about it. There was such a variety of secrets. But everyone, no matter how varied from the one before, showed much concentration on inner feelings.

There were two secrets in particular that dealt with feelings about the group. Chris read the first one, which said that the group had provided that person with very good feelings about himself and others. We talked about this for a while, relating it to the them. It was the first secret, and the true owner of it had come forth. Mike quietly said, "I'd like to tell you all that it is my secret." Darren felt that this type of thing shouldn't be a secret. He said that it is something important to the group and should be voiced instead of kept quiet. Darren's contribution wasn't hostile or joking at Mike's secret. Instead, he was displaying the real type of disclosure that he had learned in the group. He knows that our experience permits freedom of opinion. What's equally important is that Mike understood what Darren was saying. As I "reached for Mike's feelings," I discovered why he chose this as a secret. His thoughts during this meeting were concentrated on the unity that had emerged. It was all a secret to him simply because he felt that he had never voluntarily come out to say how meaningful the group was to him. His positive feelings had always been voiced because we used the go-around technique. Now, he did want everyone to know how he felt. I noted his good feeling about getting it out. This also showed me that Mike clearly understood the purpose of our group. To me, there is a visible difference between expressions that come out because of norms that have developed and expressions of feelings that are truly experienced and real.

Ricky's secret, which was directed toward the group experience, was read by me. Darren jumped in again, saying that for some reason he didn't feel this should be a secret. This gave me a very good opportunity to discuss means by which our group situation could be beneficial in the area of self-actualization. I initiated a discussion of looking at reasons why individual feelings can be helpful to the group. I asked the boys why they thought our group had become so close. There were different responses all pertaining to the fact that we had all engaged in some form of self-disclosure. (i.e., "It happened because we say what we think"). We discussed the fact that this type of interaction enabled us to learn more about each other. It was very meaningful because the discussion focused on the connectedness that interdependence is based on. I tried to emphasize the individual autonomy; we all had the choice of accepting or rejecting those relationships.

(Darren's theme-centered feelings had been expressed, and they were worked through and understood by group members. What is most important is the fact that the Closeness stage did not become so illuminated that the members could not understand that "I" is separate from "We." They have realized that being a group is rewarding and wonderful. But at the same time, there has been spontaneous actualization that "I" am at the core of my experiences. For the most part, members have shown me realization of their individuality, even at the peak moments of our togetherness.)

Summary

When Interdependence evolves, the group begins its own synergistic mutual aid system. It quickly resolves any remants of the prior stages, in order, and monitors itself for the most pressing needs of members. These needs are met in proportion to what they are. The creative, spontaneous, and purposeful interaction assures a balance of the "I-We-It" in behalf of the group's and each member's growth.

The counselor stays out of this process. He or she serves as a consultant only when group members request this expertise. Then the counselor can help the group and/or members enact wishes through experiments, exercises, or techniques. These are offered and used as trials or experiments and are designed to increase awareness of wishes and behavioral alternatives within and outside of the group. Basically, however, the counselor, no less than the group members, needs to trust the group process and its growing capacity for mutual aid. This aid guides the group and the counselor to need-meeting interaction and activities until Termination.

Critical Incidents

Critical Incident 10

Subtheme. Developing Mutual Aid

Context of Incident. During the eighth meeting the group followed the needs which seemed most pressing for individual members. These needs became most immediate for the group as a whole. Interactions were sharpened. When the group finished one such interaction, they sensed a few loose threads but some completion. They just finished talking about why a particular group member—Jane—did not risk a response to a member who reached for her feedback and what they could have done to help her and to help the group.

Choice Point
Judy: "I guess we can move on."
Gomez: Yeah, but I feel like she's still on a hot seat, kind of. . . ."
Steve: "I feel that too. But I don't know what else to do. I feel like we're on a dime."
Cheryl: "I feel like she's on a dime."
Jerry: "I feel like we all are, and we can't move from here!"
What would you do at this point? What is your rationale for this response?

TACIT Response. The counselor uses a structured exercise designed to extend members' individual awareness as well as offer them a "break" in the interaction: "I'd like to suggest something. At this point I suggest we just take a couple of minutes, stand up, and turn around with our backs toward the group, and think what you could personally do when we come back to get us off the dime. Otherwise we might just sit here and be stuck. Would you be willing to try that?"

Rationale. The surface issue and real issue are the same: When has an issue been worked? How can we moved on without avoiding issues or imposing group needs on individuals? The members, with the help of a break in the action through a structured exercise, can resolve this issue themselves.

Critical Incident 11

Subtheme. Using Mutual Aid

Context of Incident. This critical incident occurred during the tenth meeting. The group had talked primarily about personal feelings, rather than task issues, over the last several meetings. During the middle of a personal disclosure by one group member, another group member asserted a nonconnected question about planning a party.

Choice Point
Tom: "I've been really preoccupied lately with death. I've been afraid of dying all my life and I feel really alone since my dad died last year. In here, I've been afraid that I'm going to lose some of you and this feeling makes me think a lot about my own death."

Steve: "I wonder if we could discuss the party we're supposed to have so we can start planning for refreshments and entertainment."
Jane: "How can you talk of something like that after what he just said!"
Mark: "Hey, man, didn't you hear what he just said? How can you completely ignore his feelings? Don't you give a damn about him?"
Jerry: "Did what Tom say about death scare you, Steve?"
What would you do at this point? What is your rationale for this response?

TACIT Response.   Trust the group. Do nothing.

Rationale.   The group members have demonstrated that they wish to confront this issue themselves. They have indicated that they can respond to this with responsibility for others and accountability for what they and others do to each other. They can tap this mutual aid and develop it further through use of the group's own potency of mutual aid.

Critical Incident 12

Subtheme.   Using Mutual Aid

Context of Incident.   This event occurred in the twelfth meeting, close to the termination of the life of the group. Up to this point all members had been working toward helping each other within and outside of the group, especially sharing very deep, meaningful feelings and information about themselves. Now, a dramatic shift is evident. The members begin the meeting talking about lighthearted irrelevant or amusing things, as if deliberately to avoid further involvement on a personal level. This has continued for almost five minutes into the meeting. Finally, one member who has expressed considerable sensitivity and empathy over the last several meetings begins to speak.

Choice Point
Gomez: "You know something? I wonder why we're talking about all these things. It's almost like we're all withdrawing from the group even though we have three meetings left after this."

     The group remains silent, considering its past behavior.*What would you do at this point? What is your rationale for this response?*

TACIT Response   Trust the group. Do nothing. (If the group cannot increase awareness of its own process on its own, and wants to, the counselor could use the "shuttling fantasy" structure exercise, as described in Chapter 5.)

Rationale.   Both surface and underlying issues have been recognized and dealt with by a group member. In doing this, Gomez is fulfilling the processing function of a group leader—instilling in others the responsibility for distributive leadership. This is a sign of Interdependence growth in the group.

10
Termination

Termination does not necessarily follow Interdependence. The group can end at any point in TACIT development. When groups end during Trust or Autonomy, or the early stage of Closeness, the termination is marked by decreased confidence and hopes and high fears in interpersonal relationships. The members regret and project the blame for expectations unfulfilled. They mistrust.

The group which terminates following Interdependence, or at least the latter phases of Closeness, may experience increased ambivalence about separation, but members basically sense the power of their own autonomy and responsibility to meet their needs more effectively in interpersonal relationships. They increase their basic trust. Whenever Termination occurs, it is a stage in which members need the counselor's difference for them to use it to its fullest advantage. This counseling task can be very difficult because the counselor, too, is experiencing the end. He or she may share the members' regrets and/or their desire to hold on to the illusion that the group will not really terminate. Many of the models of stages of group development assume the Termination stage without separate coverage of it. Tuckman (1965), for instance, added adjourning to his stages of forming, storming, norming, and performing only after revisiting research of these stages in a later review (Tuckman & Jensen, 1977).

On the other hand, some models, such as Garland et al. (1973), cover this stage in detail. Several students of small-group process have focused exclusively on Termination (Banet, 1976; Husband & Scheunemann, 1972; Kauff, 1977; Lawler, 1980; Lewis, 1978). In general, the particular processes of Termination, as discovered by others, reflect the group stages of death as first conceptualized by Kübler-Ross (1969). It begins in denial, avoidance, and some shock, moves through anger, regression, and flight, to a period of bargaining (when members communicate that they still need the group). From the bargaining evolves the first step in facing the reality of the impending ending, as in dying, through depression and grief or sadness, and then the acceptance that leads to review, evaluation, and transfer to the new state of being, or what Kübler-Ross (1969) calls "decathexis." The members, if helped through this process, are ready to face the new beginnings of life without the group that all endings bring on.

Individual Process

Each member experiences the process of stages of ending mentioned above. The group's ending is experienced symbolically as a death for each individual member. If the group terminates after Interdependence, each member also experiences a set of questions toward the "I," the "We," and the "It." About "I," each member asks:

> "Can I transfer what I have learned here to life outside of the group?"
> "Can I be captain of my own ship as I was in this group?"
> "Did I do everything I could to get the most from this experience?"
> "Will I be able to do more in the future if I were to be in such a group?"
> "Do I still need the group?"

In relation to "We," each member asks:

> "What will become of the others when the group ends?"
> "Will I find others elsewhere who are as strong and understanding?"
> "Will we continue to meet after the group ends?"
> "Do they still need the group?"

Toward "It," members wonder:

> "Will the counselor ever work with another group like ours?"
> "Does this really have to end?"
> "What was it that we did that we can take into our other groups?"
> "Will we always remember this experience together?"

As members manifest the behavior which seeks to answer these silent questions, the Termination stage evolves. It may last for one or several meetings and is often stimulated by the counselor's reminding members of their already sensed inevitable ending. The group process takes on a special character for the remainder of this stage in the group.

Group Process

Again, Termination can come at any time in the life cycle of the group, even though its date, as in the TACIT approach, is often set when the group begins. If the group separates after the latter stages of Closeness and Interdependence, members emerge with a strong sense of competence in relation to their lives outside of the group— even with renewed ambivalences. The wishes for autonomous and interdependent human relations that satisfy needs far outweigh the fears. Feelings of alienation decrease and trust and hopes for synergistic mutual aid relationships increase. Members feel willing and able to captain their own ships to the shores of interpersonal growth.

These outcomes are colored by regression to behavior more characteristic of early TACIT stages. Members may seem detached and losing their affiliation with the group. This behavior, based on some insecurity, is less a rejection of the group than an insinuation that members still need each other, the counselor, and the group. The group moves from denial, then anger, to this bargaining for extension or continuance of time together. When this bargaining fails, the group faces its underlying grief and sadness, its depression through inactivity, and then its painful acceptance and final closure through involvement in its ending work and movement away from the group and toward life situations outside.

If Termination occurs during the earlier TACIT stages, the reverse is likely. Members experience feelings of inadequacy, fears stronger than wishes, increased mistrust and alienation, and less faith in their own potential for self-actualization. The feelings about separation are denied awareness and expression even more strongly, preventing an effective ending process. Absences and dropouts are likely to increase. Unstated regrets and resentments predominate.

Because the group often avoids the unpleasant work of termination, the counselor must help it keep this task in focus. The end of the group can be a real loss for the counselor as well as for members. All gradually come to the realization that it can never really be reconvened. Even if they continue relationships with certain members, the group as an entity is gone forever. It will be missed. For all, it could have been a place of pain, conflict, and fear but also a place of love, joy, and great meaning. Some of life's most poignant and fulfilling moments can occur in the microcosm of a developed group. The counselor, therefore, like all other members of the group, must go through the ending process. His or her acceptance in the face of ambivalence is vital for enabling members to terminate effectively.

Counseling Process

The task of members is to terminate effectively. The parallel task of the counselor is to enable separation and the transfer of learning from the group. This enabling usually requires that the counselor carry all four functions of group leadership at a high level: catalyzing, providing, processing, and directing. The catalyzing and processing skills require initiating termination, focusing, and reaching for feelings and evaluation. The providing skills demand sharing one's own feelings. Directing involves holding out the ending and facilitating closing. In addition, there are counselor skills for the post-group phase. These skills include evaluation and follow-up.

Skills

Initiating Termination. The counselor initiates termination by pointing out the ending. Because of the difficulty members have in facing feelings about ending through denial, the counselor must provide time for these feelings to be sorted out. This time comes from the counselor's pointing out endings, or reminding the group of its impending ending (Shulman, 1979). It is through this reminder that the counselor initiates termination. This catalyzing is followed by helping members focus on their ending feelings.

Focusing. Focusing comes from acknowledging the behavior and feelings which reflect the ending. The counselor reflects the denial and sadness which comes from members starting to come late for meetings, having difficulty getting started, creating lulls in the interaction, and so on. As the counselor focuses the group and specific member's attention on these behaviors and reflects their feelings, he or she is able to reach for these ending feelings more directly and specifically to catalyze their expression.

Reaching for Feelings and Evaluation. The counselor reaches for members' feelings about ending by encouraging members to share these and to stay with them. Indirect cues of anger and grief are responded to directly. As always, it is most important that the counselor reach for the ambivalences in these feelings. When the positives are expressed—the sense of accomplishment, for instance—the counselor reaches for the negative—the sense of loss. When negatives are expressed (the anger), the counselor reaches for the positives (the love).

Similarly, the counselor reaches for evaluation. Members are asked for their feedback about the group, themselves, and the counselor. Again, he or she reaches behind the positives for the negatives—what the counselor did that they did not appreciate as well as what they appreciated, for instance—and behind the negatives for the positives—what the group did accomplish as well as what was left unfinished. The counselor must particularly help the group avoid the "fairwell party syndrome" (Shulman, 1979) wherein no negatives are faced. Especially important in this evaluation is helping members to credit themselves. Almost as with a graduation ceremony, the members' fears of "going it alone" may detract from their experienced confidence that they are taking something new in themselves with them. The counselor needs to help members credit themselves for what they have accomplished as individuals and as a group—to graduate with "honors" due them.

Sharing the Counselor's Own Feelings. A particular skill which provides the group with the support for working through the ending is the counselor's sharing of his or her own feelings. Often counselors must risk their own feelings of endings first for members to feel free to risk themselves. Both may feel vulnerable, but it is part of the counselor's function and a measure of professional skill to take the first, hard step. The counselor, in this expression, best models the importance of tuning into and sharing *both* the positives and the negatives. The reality of ambivalences, even though one side of the feeling may outweigh the other in intensity, is as ubiquitous for the counselor as for the members during Termination.

Holding Out the Ending. The counselor assumes the directing function by unyieldingly holding out the ending and demanding work through it. He or she must especially avoid being seduced into the denial phase by joining the group's taboo of mentioning it, or permitting members to decide to extend the group meetings or to party their way through it. This requires that the counselor stay tuned to his or her own feelings so that they do not blind him or her to the meaning of the group's process at this time.

The counselor holds out the ending not only in the process but also in the substantive content of the group—the "It" as well as the "I" and "We." Here the counselor directs the group to identify major learnings and directs members to identify areas for future work. The counselor also helps members to connect this difficulty in ending to endings in their relationships outside of the group and to discuss how they can transfer their learnings in the group to their life situations outside.

Closing.   Closing is providing a way for members to say their final good-byes to each other in the group. It is the structure for leaving. An exercise or ritual is suggested (if the group has not developed one of its own) for this purpose. I prefer to use a "symbolic closing exercise" that requires the group to go outside together nonverbally and to follow me to an open space where we can form a circle. As we look at each other in the circle for almost the last time, I am the only one who talks. I then ask members to turn their backs to the group and walk out far enough so that they can't see any other members out of the corner of their eyes. When they reach this spot, they are to become aware of their separateness from the group and to take several minutes to tune in to the meaning of this. After these few minutes, during which most members feel their sadness *and* their strength, I instruct them to walk back to the center slowly and to literally bump up against each other into a solid circle of bodies. After a minute of experiencing the strength of this solidness, I ask them to form a circle again with our arms around each other. When face to face and arm in arm, I suggest that this is our very last opportunity in the group itself to say what we want to say so that we won't regret not having said it in the group. When everyone who wants to has had his or her say, I instruct the group once more to spread out as they were and to take a brief moment when they are out of peripheral vision to become aware in silence of what they as individuals are taking from the group. With this accomplished, the exericse, the meeting, and the group, as such, end.

Evaluation.   The special skill of counselor evaluation refers to the assessment of specific outcomes of the group. This skill requires a knowledge of evaluation research methodology and its use in counseling. This methodology will not be covered here and often is not used in its strictest sense of measuring outcomes. I do suggest, however, that whenever possible, counselors try to operationalize group outcomes in ways that instruments may be used for precise measurements of the results. There are a variety of instruments with demonstrated validity and reliability that are available for measuring process and outcome variables in groups. When these are used in pre- and post-tests, the counselor has some additional data for evaluating the group's success and/or lack of success in accomplishing particular goals. While this procedure lacks controls and therefore places great limits on the validity of the findings, nevertheless, the counselor has data which tend to be more reliable than the testimonies of group members. These instruments and measurements can also reflect particular needs in follow-up.

Follow-up. Follow-up skills are those which enable the counselor to check on graduated group members to provide further support for changes, to encourage more transfer of the learning, or to get additional counseling or other service if needed. This follow-up can range from a self-addressed and stamped postcard asking members to check how they are doing in particular areas, to a questionnaire, telephone call, or personal interview. It is usually best to wait until about three to six months after the group ends for this follow-up. The research indicates that change is maintained or not after this period as much as after any longer period (Lieberman et al., 1973). Most counselors have some informal follow-up of group members, whether or not they initiate this procedure. Usually, this follow-up involves those members who were high changers and doing well in their own life situations, or, conversely, those who were negative changers or casualties who are in further, or perhaps even deeper, trouble. This skill is designed to formalize the procedures for this follow-up. The concerned counselor does not forget about his or her responsibility to (not *for!*) members after the group terminates.

Principles for the Termination Stage

During Termination, the functions and skills of the counselor suggest some overall guidelines for the TACIT theme-centered counseling process. These principles are:

1. The counselor needs to initiate the ending process by reminding the group of its impending ending in time for it to work through members' feelings.
2. The counselor needs to be aware particularly of his or her

own feelings during Termination and to share these with the group.

3. The counselor needs to reach for both the positives and negatives of the members' feelings and evaluations during separation.
4. The counselor must hold the group (and him- or herself) to the ending time and its work on ending.
5. The counselor needs to credit members and the group for what was accomplished.
6. The counselor needs to help the group relate the here-and-now ending process to members' there-and-then-content—the "I-We" to the "It" as a there-and-then theme. This enables members to transfer their learning.
7. The counselor needs to seek or provide a procedure for closing the group.
8. The counselor needs to consider methods for formal evaluation and follow-up.

Example

The following example reflects the last, or Termination, stage meeting in the group we have been considering throughout Part II. The preadolescent group meeting (No. 10) reflects the dynamics of ending. This section also includes the data and their analysis used to evaluate the "efforts" and "effects" of the counseling groups in the project in which this group was involved.

Now let us turn to the final meeting of the preadolescent group and the data used to evaluate outcomes of the TACIT theme-centered approach for these participants.

Meeting 10

I got to the meeting ten minutes late. The boys were all very happy to see me, and one of them was worried that I had been in a car accident. Darren ran to greet me, telling me how he was afraid that I wasn't going to be there to say good-bye. He has been very conscious of this ending for the past few meetings. He has truly understood this experience and has benefited from it. Darren and I have become very close, which is ironic when viewing our first meeting. I would have expected him to be a definite barrier to the group's progress. Instead he became one of the most important contributors to the group's growth. I have learned so much about being the counselor within a group through him. Many times I could have very easily denied him the opportunity to be aggressive, bold, and very physically active. For a while his actions did bother me and the other group members, and there were ways that I could have stopped it, but I didn't. The important point is that my allowing him to "act out" was an experiment. Of course, I wanted him to understand his actions, but I have never worked with a group before. I didn't know what would result from my behavior. But I did learn from this that I had reacted to Darren in the way which provided him with the best means to understand his own behavior. It helped me tremendously with other members. I gradually learned more about my own goals in helping others. Darren's behavior is right for Darren. It is natural and need not be changed, but more fully understood by him. I really believe that I have helped this understanding take place through our experience. Throughout the entire meeting, Darren stayed close to me, repeatedly saying that he would really miss me. At one point, he whispered to me that I had helped him to want to be nice to other people. He had also been doing a lot of reflecting back to earlier stages of our experience. He even asked me if I remembered how he "used" to act. He felt that I liked him more now than I did in the beginning. I explained that it may seem that way because of the process of getting to know each other. He agreed that people can show each other their feelings much more after a bond of trust has been developed. He truly understood, giving me the example of how he used to act with Jeff. He used to "pick on" Jeff, more because of not knowing how to react to their differences than because of actually disliking him. He explained to me that because he and Jeff were in the same group, he got to "know him a lot better, and like him more."

I sat down to join the party. It took only a few moments for me to see the chaotic state that was present. For the most part, fears of all members have been resolved through our experience. These resolutions freed us all of barriers that could have prohibited us from real interaction. But today there was another type of fear present. It was evident that there were fears of ending our group. This took many different forms. Some of the members simply chose to ignore that our experience was over. Others repeatedly expressed feelings about the separation. But there was one thing common to all group members: regression to behavior that was characteristic of earlier meetings.

For the first time in many, many meetings, Chris again retrieved the ball that had been his outlet for uncomfortable feelings. He continuously bounced it all around, as he had done before. Randy joked around about the ending of our group, just as he had with the beginning. Ricky was as serious as ever about our group, expressing his sadness over the ending.

Every member, no matter what behavior they retreated to, was very aware of our task of termination. They all knew that our group would soon be an experience of the past. I tried to help them deal with this, while using the go-around technique, asking them to say a few words which expressed their feelings at this point. It seemed as though everyone wanted to be first to explain his feelings. But once a few members had their turns, it became even more evident that we were going to leave each other in this situation. The go-around technique didn't really work. As in an earlier meeting, I would have had to push too hard for its completion. Darren put his head down on the desk and wouldn't look at the rest of the group. I explained that throughout our lives we become involved with many groups, none of them exactly the same. I said that it's not easy to say good-bye to people whom we have grown to know and love in certain degrees. But I asked them to think back to how we gradually got to know each other. I "shared my feelings," telling them that I felt sadness in saying good-bye, but that everyone of them had brought me learning and happiness that I'll never forget. I told them that the experience has been something that we can take with us—what we have learned here can be applied to other groups. (I must admit that I was happy to have the role of giving direction in this meeting. If I had not been so aware of the need for this, I could have easily behaved in similar ways. The group has given me more than I could ever explain, and I felt very confused about the termination myself. This was evident as I think about my personal preplanning for this meeting. This time it wasn't as extensive. I feel this is partly because of me as a member [I probably wanted to ignore the termination more than I really was aware of] and partly because of my role as a leader [I really had no idea of what to plan or expect today from the members]. But as I saw the strong need for my direction, I thought of nothing else. I assumed the leader role, wanting to provide as much for them now as I ever did.)

As in Trudy and Joy's group, the workers were able to use the TACIT approach to help group members achieve both group and individual developmental tasks. The student counselors were able to use themselves and theme-relevant program activities to influence the group process toward mutual aid. This movement occurred to a degree in all treatment groups and in all cases culminated in the group project of a party in which members took pride in the accomplishment of group goals. The contract formulation and renegotiation as related to theme work also stood as a gauge in all treatment groups for successful efforts at both using the TACIT methodology and achieving the developmental objectives.

Data Analysis: Evaluation of Effects

The data were analyzed via the *t*-test for all pre- and post-test scores. The total scores on the Behavior Checklist rated by teachers are reflected on Table 10.1. The student counselor ratings of behavior in the group with this checklist could not be used in analysis as inter-rater reliability was only .59. However, teacher ratings showed an increase in desirable behavior in the classroom in all but six of the forty members. The highest increase was in the members of the group used in the above case study (Group 4). The total increase and its statistical significance were as true for the behavior of boys as of girls.

Table 10.2 includes the subscales of the Behavior Checklist. Two of these subscale changes are statistically significant. Greatest change occurred in the decrease in physical agression ($p < .03$). However, increases were consistent in the other four subscales: decreased attention-seeking deviant behavior ($p < .07$) and increased sensitivity to other ($p < .06$), expression of feelings ($p < .05$), and collaborative behavior ($p < .07$). All subscale changes approach significance. One of the major behavioral outcomes appears to be the movement from physically aggressive behavior to express feelings toward more frequent verbalization of feelings. This change is reflected in the statistically significant findings of these two subscales of the Behavior Checklist.

The Group Survey is a sociometric rating scale which enabled two additional evaluation scores: an empathy score and a self-concept score. In this instrument members were asked to rank each group member, including him- or herself, on three criteria: ability to cooperate, confidence in self, and caring about the group. On the basis of deviancy or accuracy with the pooled group ranking, an individual member empathy score was derived. Empathy is therefore operationalized as an ability to perceive (rank) the self and others as consensually perceived (ranked). The self-concept score was derived from the total of each member's own rank on the three subscales. Used in pre- and post-tests, this scale allowed measurement of

TABLE 10.1
Behavior Checklist Scores

Boys

Group	Member	Pre	Post	Difference
1	1	22	23	+ 1
(Total increase = +21)	2	13	22	+ 9
	3	18	23	+ 5
	4	27	23	− 4
	5	14	24	+10
2	6	13	17	+ 4
(Total increase = +23)	7	28	30	+ 2
	8	17	22	+ 5
	9	16	30	+14
	10	15	16	+ 1
	11	15	12	− 3
3	12	9	12	+ 3
(Total increase = +20)	13	21	25	+ 4
	14	26	28	+ 2
	15	13	19	+ 6
	16	24	29	+ 5
4	17	9	22	+13
(Total increase = +55)	18	12	26	+14
	19	8	23	+14
	20	20	27	+ 7
	21	26	30	+ 4
	22	26	29	+ 3

Girls

Group	Member	Pre	Post	Difference
5	23	23	28	+ 5
(Total increase = +29)	24	21	25	+ 4
	25	17	26	+ 9
	26	21	31	+10
	27	9	14	+ 5
	28	28	24	− 4
6	29	23	32	+ 9
(Total increase = +13)	30	14	16	+ 2
	31	28	30	+ 2
	32	12	12	0
	33	30	30	0
7	34	16	16	0
(Total increase = +24)	35	19	22	+ 3
	36	26	28	+ 2
	37	26	28	+ 2
	38	10	22	+12
	39	30	32	+ 2
	40	14	17	+ 3
Totals	40	367	433	+66
$\overline{X}$		18.95	23.63	
s.d.		18.08	22.55	
s^2		326.92	505.58	

$t = 1.440$

$p < .07$

TABLE 10.2
Behavior Checklist Subscale Scores

Subscale	Pre	Post	Difference	*t*	*p*
Sensitivity to other's needs	Sum = 156 Mean = 3.9 s.d. = 1.234	Sum = 183 Mean = 4.6 s.d. = 2.438	+27	1.620	< .06
Action against group norms	Sum = 168 Mean = 4.2 s.d. = 2.150	Sum = 196 Mean = 4.9 s.d. = 2.210	+28	1.434	< .07
Use of physical aggression	Sum = 185 Mean = 4.6 s.d. = 2.441	Sum = 222 Mean = 5.6 s.d. = 2.338	+37	2.041	< .03
Collaborative behavior	Sum = 145 Mean = 3.6 s.d. = 1.319	Sum = 167 Mean = 4.2 s.d. = 2.158	+22	1.422	< .07
Free expression of feelings	Sum = 150 Mean = 3.7 s.d. = 1.234	Sum = 175 Mean = 4.4. s.d. = 2.338	+25	1.670	< .05

empathy development and self-concept change during the experience—two of the major objectives of the program.

Table 10.3 summarizes the data on empathy development for members. All members increased in their ability to perceive themselves as others perceived them and to perceive others as others perceived themselves within their group. This development of empathy was statistically significant ($t = 2.632$; $p < .01$). As predicted in theory, this empathy development does appear to be influenced by the TACIT group experience. In addition, the empathy scores highly correlated with related behavioral changes ($r = .40$; $p < .01$).

Self-reported self-concept scores increased similarly to the empathy scores. All but seven members increased their self-concept (esteem) via their self-ratings. Table 10.4 reports these data. This change in self-esteem, operationalized as perception of self as increased cooperativeness, confidence, and caring about the group, was the most statistically significant finding ($t = 4.710$; $p < .001$). As predicted, members seem to have developed more sense of self-worth as a result of TACIT group accomplishments. Unlike empathy, however, this change did not correlate significantly with rated behavioral changes ($t = .21$; NS).

TABLE 10.3
Empathy Scores

Boys

Group	Member	Pre	Post	Difference
1	1	11	22	+11
(Total	2	7	22	+15
increase	3	9	22	+13
= +59)	4	14	20	+6
	5	8	24	+16
	6	7	19	+12
2	7	14	30	+16
(Total	8	9	22	+13
increase	9	8	27	+19
= +81)	10	8	20	+12
	11	8	17	+9
	12	5	22	+17
3	13	12	25	+13
(Total	14	14	28	+14
increase	15	8	20	+12
= +72)	16	13	29	+16
	17	5	25	+20
	18	7	28	+21
4	19	5	24	+20
(Total	20	11	27	+16
increase	21	13	30	+17
= +110)	22	13	29	+16

Girls

Group	Member	Pre	Post	Difference
5	23	11	26	+15
(Total	24	10	25	+15
increase	25	9	20	+11
= +74)	26	11	25	+14
	27	5	20	+15
	28	14	18	+4
6	29	12	30	+18
(Total	30	8	20	+12
increase	31	15	27	+12
= +58)	32	6	13	+7
	33	19	20	+1
	34	8	16	+8
7	35	10	22	+12
(Total	36	13	24	+11
increase	37	13	26	+13
= +75)	38	5	22	+17
	39	20	30	+10
	40	7	19	+12
Totals		392	935	
$\overline{X}$		9.8	23.37	
s.d.		4.51	4.41	
s^2		20.34	19.45	

$t = 2.632$

TABLE 10.4
Self-esteem Scores

	Boys					Girls			
Group	Member	Pre	Post	Difference	Group	Member	Pre	Post	Difference
1	1	8	12	+ 4	5	23	13	15	+ 2
(Total	2	11	14	+ 3	(Total	24	11	16	+ 5
increase	3	6	11	+ 5	increase	25	8	14	+ 6
= +22)	4	5	11	+ 6	= +19)	26	9	12	+ 3
	5	9	13	+ 4		27	13	15	+ 2
2	6	10	12	+ 2		28	16	17	+ 1
(Total	7	18	18	0	6	29	3	11	+ 7
increase	8	17	17	0	(Total	30	16	16	0
= +2)	9	14	16	+ 2	increase	31	9	11	+ 2
	10	17	17	0	= +29)	32	3	12	+ 9
	11	15	13	− 2		33	9	15	+ 6
3	12	18	17	− 1	7	34	16	16	0
(Total	13	13	17	+ 4	(Total	35	12	13	+ 1
increase	14	17	18	+ 1	increase	36	18	17	− 1
= +10)	15	15	16	+ 1	= +15)	37	15	17	+ 2
	16	8	12	+ 4		38	14	16	+ 2
4	17	12	18	+ 6		39	9	15	+ 6
(Total	18	10	17	+ 7		40	12	16	+ 4
increase	19	7	16	+ 9	Totals	471	601		
= +39)	20	8	16	+ 8	X̄	11.77	15.03		
	21	12	18	+ 6	s.d.	4.135	1.430		
	22	15	18	+ 3	s^2	17.10	2.05		

$t = 4.710$
$p < .001$

231

In sum, the findings indicate an increase in classroom acceptable behavior and a decrease in unacceptable behavior. This change is most significant in the ability to express feelings in more acceptable ways while decreasing such unacceptable expressions as physical aggression. Members also increased their ability to empathize (accurately perceive) with other members and their self-esteem in relation to self-report ratings.

Interpretation of Findings

These findings must be viewed cautiously as there were no controls to increase confidence in the TACIT group experience as the cause of these outcomes. That changes did occur there is no doubt. The majority of these changes do relate to the theoretical hypotheses both of the developmental tasks of preadolescents and the TACIT group counseling approach. Certainly a plausible explanation is the direct influence of the TACIT experience, capably facilitated by the student counselors, on these outcomes. The permanence of these changes, as much as the other possibly strong influences on them, depend upon the classroom experiences of the youngsters involved. There seemed to be a great deal of reciprocal reinforcement between the counseling group attitudes and behavior and those of the classroom.

Conclusion

Both the "efforts" and the "effects" evaluations support the efficacy of TACIT group counseling with preadolescents in school. Group members were able to increase their empathic perception of each other and their sense of self-esteem during the experience. Their classroom behavior increased in interpersonal sensitivity, ability to collaborate, and ability to express feelings appropriately. Their classroom behavior decreased in physical expression of aggression and in attention-seeking deviance from classroom norms. These behavioral changes are the *sine qua non* of appropriate classroom learning norms vital to the achievement of the school's objective for the child.

The TACIT group counseling approach, as used in this project, seems especially applicable to operationalizing the counselor's function of mediating between the need of the child to use the school and the need of the school to serve the child. The results of this project attest to the fruitful possibilities of this approach, the developmental needs and strengths of the preadolescents involved, the actual skills of the student counselors, and the desire of the school to serve the child.

Summary

Termination, whenever it occurs, is marked by ambivalence for the counselor, members, and the group as a whole. Termination early in TACIT development has the negative balance more intense than the positive. After Closeness and/or Interdependence, the positive outweighs the negative and the members can experience the ending process effectively. They can move beyond the group by working through the separation.

The counselor enables this process by catalyzing, processing, providing, and directing. He or she comes to terms with his or her own feelings and uses this difference to help members to understand what they have accomplished and to package their experience in such a manner that they can unwrap it and discover the gift of their own abilities to make what happened for them in the group more real for them in their separate social worlds. This end, then, is a real beginning for them.

Critical Incidents

Critical Incident 13

Subtheme.   Focusing Learning

Context of Incident.   This incident came in the thirteenth meeting. During the meeting, members discussed how their learning in the group had helped them outside. Most comments were positive, yet not very intense. One member has been looking very hurt and pained.

Choice Point
Jerry (in a strained voice): "I've had trouble using what I've learned here in school. They don't seem to care about me. When I get honest with people there, as I am in here, they come down harder on me. I really wonder what to do about this!"

A few members attempt to offer some help, mostly reassurance, but with little success. Finally, the group falls silent.

What would you do at this point? What is your rationale for this response?

TACIT Response.   The counselor focuses on the ending and reaches for feelings and evaluation: "I believe we have difficulty owning the negative feelings and evaluations we have now that we are close to ending. Jerry has started to express this negative in his experience. It is as if we will feel less good about our experience together if we accept that some aspects of this group experience haven't worked. This stance prevents our really helping Jerry. Perhaps we can talk about some of our less positive feelings and evaluations about our group and its ending and then come back to Jerry and his specific situation. Is that O.K. with you, Jerry?"

Rationale.   Group members can help Jerry but they are blocked because of how his comments stir up their avoided feelings about ending. The surface issue of transfer of learning from the group is a real one for all members, clouded here by the underlying issue of the group experience and its ending.

Critical Incident 14

Subtheme.   Preparing for Termination While Still Working

Context of Incident.   This was the fourteenth meeting and the incident involved one member's expressed anger during a discussion when several members disclosed what they assessed as unfinished business for themselves as the group was drawing to a close. The member's anger was intense and displaced.

Choice Point
Chris (in a very angry tone): "You guys are kidding yourselves. If that much is unfinished for you, its your own fault! You could have gotten more from this group if you would've tried harder!"
        The group seems taken aback by Chris' outburst and lapses into silence.
What would you do at this point? What is your rationale for this response?

TACIT Response.   The counselor shares his own feelings and reaches for the positives behind negatives and the negatives behind positives: "Chris, you're really angry because you don't want members to have any bad feelings about this group. I wonder if maybe that is because you're fighting your own feelings which aren't so positive about the group and having to leave it. I ask because I was aware of something like that in me as Cheryl, Sandra, and Tom were talking about unfinished business for themselves. I felt good about their honesty and the awareness they took from the group. Yet I was aware of some anger and realized this was from my own frustration about not finding ways to help them with some more of this in the group. Then I realized that there is always unfinished business, that this is life. A part of me wants to hold onto this group. It has been such a good experience for me and I will always remember it so much more positively than negatively. Yet these negative comments have me thinking about working with future groups and I appreciate this feedback for my learning. Perhaps we can all try to share both the positive and negative feelings we now have about ourselves and the group experience. I would especially appreciate both the positive and negative feedback each of you could give me about my function and role in this group."

Rationale. Members will manifest individual styles centered on the same underlying issues regarding ending. Most will be more immediately aware of one side of their positive/negative ambivalences. Chris reacts to the negatives in others, displacing anger perhaps related to her own frustrations, and the surface issue becomes the tension of her hostility censoring honesty in the group. Chris and the other members need encouragement to confront the ending authentically, both with positives and with negatives. The counselor shares these, and the difficulty in being in touch with them in ending, in a manner which tends to defuse the hostility and tension and legitimizes ambivalence in disclosure and feedback.

Critical Incident 15

Subtheme. Saying Good-byes

Context of Incident. This event occurred during the fifteenth and final group session. Group members had generally finished saying their good-byes and the atmosphere was one of resignation and sadness. In general, all unfinished business had been completed and there was a reluctance to stay and yet a greater reluctance to break up the group and leave. The majority of the group members were quiet and contemplative, feeling a sense of intimacy and yet not really knowing how to express the sensation of "oneness" with the group.

Choice Point
The members sit in silence, feeling somewhat peaceful, yet sad and depressed. A few sighs are expressed and the silence appears long. *What would you do at this point? What is your rationale for this response?*

TACIT Response.   The counselor uses the skill of holding out the ending by directing the closure: "It's always hard to say good-bye, especially to people we've grown quite close to. I don't know of any way of really saying it that can escape the sadness yet the appreciation we feel. I'd like to suggest something at this point that may help us express our good-byes in a meaningful way. I want each of us to close our eyes for about one minute and get in touch with our feelings about ourselves and each other. At the end of a minute, I want us to get up slowly with our eyes still closed, move about the room, and simply do whatever we feel like doing—all without talking. Let's just see how we all end up, without planning or thinking, or talking, and then we'll all leave. O.K., let's close our eyes. . . ."

Rationale.   The issue, both surface and underlying, is needing direction for a significant and meaningful way to say good-bye and leave. The counselor provides a closing exercise which deals directly with the group's expression of feelings and permits members to balance their autonomy and interdependence in the termination as throughout the group process.

Afterword

This book has been about group process. This process is a holistic reality, so much more than the sum of its parts. At this level it cannot really be analyzed. To describe such a process, as I have done in this book, is somewhat a contradiction. TACIT group process is more than the sum of principles and elements which I have included for understanding it. What I have done is to attempt to sketch a map of this process, a model for understanding and negotiating its territory. As Schumaker (1977) notes:

> One way of looking at the world as a whole is by means of a map, that is to say, some sort of plan or outline that shows where various things are to be found—not all things of course, for that would make the map as big as the world, but the things that are most important for orientation: outstanding landmarks, as it were, which you cannot miss or which, if you did miss them, leave you in total perplexity [p. 87].

What I have done in this book is to draw a map of the territory which may help you to negotiate group process in your counseling. You know from traveling that the map is not the territory. If you have traversed the group process terrain, you know that this map is a TACIT model of group process, not the process itself. It is a two-dimensional representation of a three-dimensional reality. To the degree that it helps you negotiate the territory of group process without too much perplexity or without getting lost, it is useful.

If your goals are to help members balance their inevitable polarities of autonomy and interdependence, this map includes some valuable landmarks. I can think of no nobler or more pertinent goals for counseling through group process. In life, we are alone and we are not alone. We are separate and we are united. We are autonomous and we are interdependent. The road to this discovery is the TACIT one.

Through TACIT development in group process we continuously confront the paradox of this growth in the questions attributed first to Rabbi Hillel over a thousand years ago:

> If I am not for myself, who will be for me?
> If only for myself, what am I?
> If not now, when?

If not now, when?

Appendix
Instrument to Measure TACIT Skills

Scale

0	1	2	3	4
Not used	**Poor**	**Ineffective**	**Minimally effective**	**Good**

Stage, Function, and Skill	Operational Definitions		Scale
Trust Stage			
Providing			
1. Attending	a.	Leans forward, faces other squarely, maintains eye contact	0 1 2 3 4
	b.	Arranges setting to promote interaction	0 1 2 3 4
2. Observing		Actively notices and accurately reads nonverbal communication	0 1 2 3 4
3. Active listening and empathy	a.	Responds to content	0 1 2 3 4
	b.	Responds to feelings	0 1 2 3 4
	c.	Connects feelings and content	0 1 2 3 4
Directing			
4. Contracting	a.	Clarifies purpose	0 1 2 3 4
	b.	Clarifies roles and responsibilities	0 1 2 3 4
	c.	Reaches for feedback	0 1 2 3 4
	d.	Establishes theme	0 1 2 3 4
	e.	Introduces ground rules	0 1 2 3 4
Catalyzing/Processing			
5. Clarifying	a.	Surfaces individual goals	0 1 2 3 4
	b.	Questions toward specificity	0 1 2 3 4
	c.	Reaches inside silences	0 1 2 3 4

Scale

0	1	2	3	4
Not used	Poor	Ineffective	Minimally effective	Good

Stage, Function, and Skill		Operational Definitions	Scale
6. Elaborating	a.	Moves from general to specific	0 1 2 3 4
	b.	Contains responses	0 1 2 3 4
	c.	Requests more information	0 1 2 3 4
Autonomy Stage			
Processing			
7. Illuminating	a.	Actively recognizes process	0 1 2 3 4
	b.	Surfaces group tensions	0 1 2 3 4
	c.	Shares own feelings as linked with process	0 1 2 3 4
	d.	Increases members' awareness of process	0 1 2 3 4
8. Relating here-now to then-there		Interprets the relation of content to group process in the here and now	0 1 2 3 4
9. Reaching behind conflicts and decisions	a.	Checks for underlying ambivalences	0 1 2 3 4
	b.	Shares own reactions	0 1 2 3 4
	c.	Surfaces all sides of conflict	0 1 2 3 4
	d.	Reaches for empathy in members	0 1 2 3 4
	e.	Reflects norms used in decision making	0 1 2 3 4
Providing			
10. Personalizing	a.	Personalizes meaning	0 1 2 3 4
	b.	Personalizes problems	0 1 2 3 4
	c.	Personalizes feelings	0 1 2 3 4
	d.	Personalizes goals	0 1 2 3 4
Catalyzing			
11. Reaching for feelings and perceptions	a.	Checks for underlying ambivalences	0 1 2 3 4
	b.	Supports communication in taboo areas	0 1 2 3 4
	c.	Reaches for individual response	0 1 2 3 4
	d.	Reaches for group response	0 1 2 3 4
Directing			
12. Demanding work	a.	Challenges illusion of work	0 1 2 3 4

Scale

0	1	2	3	4
Not used	Poor	Ineffective	Minimally effective	Good

Stage, Function, and Skill	Operational Definitions	Scale
	b. Reaches for work when obstacles threaten	0 1 2 3 4
	c. Focuses group on problem solving and mutual aid	0 1 2 3 4
13. Invoking the contract	Questions about what is happening in relation to contract	0 1 2 3 4

Closeness Stage

Catalyzing

14. Encouraging inter-member feedback	a. Encourages use of ground rules	0 1 2 3 4
	b. Directs messages to intended recipient	0 1 2 3 4
	c. Amplifies feeling messages	0 1 2 3 4
15. Reaching for empathic content	Invites intermember responses	0 1 2 3 4
16. Confrontation	Feeds back discrepancies between words and deeds	0 1 2 3 4

Providing

17. Modeling self-disclosure and feedback	a. Discloses appropriately	0 1 2 3 4
	b. Uses feedback consistent with principles	0 1 2 3 4
18. Sharing own feelings	Shares own feelings and ideas in relation to theme and members	0 1 2 3 4

Processing

19. Clarifying purpose	a. Aids group in discovering what it wants	0 1 2 3 4
	b. Encourages group to weigh interactions against desires	0 1 2 3 4
20. Illuminating process	Brings there-then to here-now	0 1 2 3 4
21. Detecting and challenging obstacles to work	a. Names obstacles	0 1 2 3 4
	b. Reaches for ambivalences	0 1 2 3 4
	c. Elicits feedback about obstacles	0 1 2 3 4

Directing

22. Renegotiating the contract	a. Reclarifies purpose	0 1 2 3 4
	b. Reclarifies roles and responsibilities	0 1 2 3 4
	c. Reclarifies theme, sub-themes, and ground rules	0 1 2 3 4

Scale

0	1	2	3	4
Not used	**Poor**	**Ineffective**	**Minimally effective**	**Good**

Stage, Function, and Skill	Operational Definitions	Scale
Interdependence Stage		
Providing/Processing/		
Catalyzing/Directing		
23. Offering experimental activities	a. Helps group design experiments related to individual member's needs	0 1 2 3 4
	b. Uses structured exercises appropriately	0 1 2 3 4
Termination Stage		
Directing		
24. Initiating termination	Points out ending	0 1 2 3 4
25. Holding out ending	a. Continually presents the reality of ending	0 1 2 3 4
	b. Gently demands work on ending	0 1 2 3 4
26. Closing	Provides structure for final good-byes	0 1 2 3 4
Processing		
27. Focusing on ending	Acknowledges the behavior and feelings which reflect ending	0 1 2 3 4
28. Evaluating and following up	Assesses specific outcomes	0 1 2 3 4
Providing		
29. Sharing own feelings	a. Expresses positive and negative feelings in ending	0 1 2 3 4
	b. Credits individual members and the group for efforts and effects in their own behalf	0 1 2 3 4
Catalyzing		
30. Reaching for feelings and evaluation	a. Encourages expressing and staying with feelings related to termination	0 1 2 3 4
	b. Reaches for *both* positive and negative feelings	0 1 2 3 4
	c. Reaches for *both* positive and negative feedback	0 1 2 3 4

References and Bibliography

Abramowitz, S. I. & Abramowitz, C. V. (1974). Psychological-mindedness and benefit from insight-oriented group therapy. *Archives of General Psychiatry, 30,* 610–615.

Adler, A. (1956). *Individual psychology.* New York: Basic Books.

Ahumada, J. L., Abiuso, D., Baiguera, N., & Gallo, A. (1974). On limited-time group psychotherapy: I. setting, admission, and therapeutic ideology. *Psychiatry, 37,* 254–260.

Anchor, K. N. (1979). High and low-risk self-disclosure in group psychotherapy. *Small Group Behavior, 10,* 279–283.

Anderson, A. R. (1969). Group counseling. *Review of Educational Research: Guidance and Counseling, 39,* 209–230.

Anderson, A. R., & Johnson, D. L., (1968). Using group procedures to improve human relations in the school social system. *School Counselor, 15,* 334–342.

Anderson, J. D. (1975). Human relations training and social group work. *Social Work, 20,* 195–199.

Anderson, J. D. (1978). Growth groups and alienation: A comparative study of Rogerian Encounter, Self-Directed Encounter, and Gestalt." *Group and Organizational Studies, 3,* 85–107.

Anderson, J. D. (1979). Social work with groups in the generic base of social work practice. *Social Work with Groups, 2,* 281–293.

Anderson, J. D. (1980). The communication of feelings in today's groups: An evolutionary perspective. *Social Work with Groups, 3,* 51–59. (a)

Anderson, J. D. (1980). Structured experiences in growth groups in social work. *Social Casework, 61,* 277–287. (b)

Angell, D. L., & Desau, G. T. (1974). Rare discordent verbal roles and the development of group problem-solving conditions. *Small Group Behavior, 5,* 45–55.

Anspacher, H. L., & Anspacher, R. (Eds.) (1956). *The individual psychology of Alfred Alder.* New York: Basic Books.

Anthony, E. J. (1967). The generic elements in dyadic and in group psychotherapy. *International Journal of Group Psychotherapy, 17,* 57–70.

Appleby, D. G., & Winder, A. E. (1973). *Groups and therapy groups in a changing society.* Washington, D. C.: Jossey-Bass.

Arlow, J. A. (1963). Conflict, regression, and symptom formation. *International Journal of Psychoanalysis, 44,* 12–22.

Ashkenas, R., & Tandon, R. (1979). An eclectic approach to small group facilitation. *Small Group Behavior, 10,* 224–241.

Assagioli, R. (1965). *Psychosynthesis.* New York: The Viking Press.

Assagioli, R. (1973). *The act of will.* New York: The Viking Press.

Austin, D. (1957). Goals for gang workers. *Social Work, 2,* 43–50.

Babad, E. Y., & Amir, L. (1978). Bennis and Shephard's theory of group development: An empirical examination. *Small Group Behavior, 9.*

Bach, G. R. (1954). *Intensive group psychotherapy.* New York: Ronald Press.

Bach, G. R. (1965). Marathon group dynamics: III. disjunctive contacts. *Psychological Reports 1,* 255–269.

Baekeland, F., & Lundwall, L. (1972). Dropping out of treatment: A critical review. *Psychological Bulletin, 82,* 738–783.

Bales, R. F., & Strodtbeck, F. L. (1951). Phases in group problem-solving. *Journal of Abnormal and Social Psychology, 46,* 485–495.

Banet, A. G. (1976). Yin/yang: A perspective on theories of group development. In J. W. Pfeiffer & J. E. Jones (Eds.), *The 1976 handbook for group facilitators.* La Jolla, Calif.: University Associates, pp. 169–189.

Bassin, A. (1962). Verbal participation and improvement in group therapy. *International Journal of Group Psychotherapy, 12,* 369–373.

Baute, B. (1975). Termination and the autonomy chair: A new ritual for group intimacy. *Transactional Analysis Journal, 5,* 180–182.

Bean, B. W., & Houston, B. K. (1978). Self-concept and self-disclosure in encounter groups. *Small Group Behavior, 9,* 549–554.

Beaulieu, E. M., & Karpinski, J. (1981). Group treatment of elderly with ill spouses. *Social Casework, 62,* 551–557.

Beck, A. P. (1981). A study of group phase development and emergent leadership. *Group, 5,* 48–54.

Bednar, R. L., & Battersby, C. P. (1976). The effect of specific cognitive structure on early group development. *Journal of Applied Behavioral Science, 12,* 513–522.

Bednar, R. L., & Lawlis, G. (1971). Empirical research in group psychotherapy. In *Handbook of psychotherapy and behavior change: An empirical analysis.* A. Bergin & S. Garfield (Eds.), New York: Wiley, pp. 420–439.

Bednar, R. L., Melnick, J., & Kaul, T. J. (1974). Risk, responsibility, and structure: A conceptual framework for initiating group counseling and psychotherapy. *Journal of Counseling Psychology, 21,* 31–37.

Bennis, W. G. (1964). Patterns and vicissitudes in T-group development. In L. P. Bradford, W. G. Bennis, & R. A. Shepard (Eds.), *T-group theory and laboratory method: Innovation in re-education.* New York: Wiley, pp. 248–278.

Bennis, W. G. (1968). Toward a genetic theory of group development. *Journal of Group Psychoanalysis and Process, 1,* 23–36.

Bennis, W. G. & Shepard, H. A. (1956). A theory of group development. *Human Relations, 9,* 415–457.

Bennis, W., et al. (1957). A note on some problems of measurement and prediction in a training group. *Group Psychotherapy, 10,* 328–341.

Benson, R., & Blocker, D. (1967). Evaluation of developmental counseling with groups of low achievers in a high school setting. *The School Counselor, 14,* 215–220.

Bergental, J. F., & Haigh, G. W. (1965). *Residential basic encounter groups.* Los Angeles: Psychological Service.

Berger, D. M. (1976). The multidiscipline patient care conference: Learning in groups. *Canadian Psychiatric Association Journal, 21,* 135–139.

Berne, E. (1961). *Transactional analysis in psychotherapy.* New York: Grove Press.

Berne, E. (1963). *The structure and dynamics of organizations and groups.* New York: Grove Press.

Berne, E. (1966). *Principles of group treatment.* New York: Oxford University Press.

Bernstein, J. (1949). *Charting group progress.* New York: Association Press.

Berstein, S. (1950). There are groups and groups. *The Group, 13,* 3–10.

Bertcher, H. J., & Maple, F. F. (1977). *Creating groups.* Beverly Hills, SAGE Publications.

Berzon, B., Pious, C., & Farson, R. (1963). The therapeutic event in group psychotherapy: A study of subjective reports by group members. *Journal of Individual Psychology, 19,* 203–212.

Binder, J. A. (1976). A method for small group training of psychiatric ward staff. *Psychiatry, 39,* 364–375.

Bion, W. R. (1959). *Experiences in groups and other papers.* New York: Ballantine Books. (1966).

Blocher, D. (1966). *Developmental counseling.* New York: Ronald Press.

Bloomberg, L., & Miller, C. (1968). Breaking through the process impasse. *Voices,* 33–36.

Blumberg, A. (1971). Sensitivity training: Process problems and applications. Syracuse: Syracuse University Press, pp. 19–32.

Bonney, W. D. (1969). Group counseling and developmental process. In G. M. Gazada (Ed.), *Methods of group counseling in the schools.* Springfield, Ill.: Charles C. Thomas, pp. 157–180.

Bonney, W. D. (1974). The maturation of groups. *Small Group Behavior, 5,* 445–461.

Bonney, W. D., & Foley, W. J. (1963). The transition stage in group counseling in terms of congruity theory. *Journal of Counseling Psychology, 10,* 136–158.

Bordin, E. S. (1965). The ambivalent quest for independence. *Journal of Counseling Psychology, 12,* 339–345.

Borkman, T. (1976). Experiential knowledge: A new concept for the analysis of self help groups. *Social Service Review, 50,* 445–456.

Braden, W. W., & Bradenburg, E. (1955). *Oral decision-making.* New York: Harper and Brothers, 1955.

Bradford, L. P. (1978). Group formation and development (2nd ed.). In L. P. Bradford (Ed.), *Group Development,* La Jolla, Calif.: University Assoc.

Braeten, L. J. (1974/75). Developmental phases of encounter groups and related intensive groups: A critical review of models and a new proposal. *Interpersonal Development, 5,* 112–129.

Bramer, L. M., & Shostram, E. L. (1976). *Therapeutic psychology: Fundamentals of counseling* and *psychotherapy* (3rd ed.). Englewood Cliffs, N.J.: Prentice-Hall.

Breton, M. (1982). A strategy for the use of stress in social work groups. *Social Work with Groups, 5,* 71–80.

Buchanon, P. C. (1965). Evaluating the effectiveness of laboratory training in industry. In *Explorations in human relations training and research,* No. 1. Washington, D.C.: National Training Laboratories, pp. 14–32.

Bugen, L. A. (1978). Expectation profiles. *Small Group Behavior, 9,* 115–123.

Butler, T., & Fuhrman, A. (1980). Patient perspective on the curative process: A comparison of day treatment and outpatient psychotherapy groups. *Small Group Behavior, 11,* 371–388.

Campbell, J. T., & Dunnette, M. D. (1968). Effectiveness of T-group experiences. In *Managerial Training and Development, Psychological Bulletin, 70,* 73–104.

Caple, R. B. (1978). The sequential stages of small groups. *Small Group Behavior, 9,* 470–476.

Carkhuff, R. R. (1969). *Helping and human relations: A primer of lay and professional helpers (Vol. II). Practice and research.* New York: Holt, Rinehart and Winston.

Carkhuff, R. R. (1980). *The art of helping* (Vol. IV). Amherst, Mass.: Human Resource Development Press.

Carkhuff, R. R., & Berenson, B. (1967). *Beyond counseling and therapy.* New York: Holt, Rinehart and Winston.

Carmer, J. C., & Rouzer, D. L. (1974). Healthy functioning from the Gestalt perspective. *The Counseling Psychologist, 4,* 20–23.

Carr, J. E. (1965). The role of conceptual organization in interpersonal perception. *Journal of Psychology, 59,* 159–176.

Carrasquillo, C. Ing., L. L., Kuhn, S., Metzger, J., Schuburt, R. H., & Silveira, G. L. (1981). Group counseling with persons with developmental disabilities. *Social Casework, 62,* 486–490.

Cartell, R. B. (1948). Concepts and methods in the measurement of group syntality. *Psychological Review, 55,* 48–63.

Cartwright, D. (1951). Achieving change in people: Some application of group dynamic theory. *Human Relations, 4,* 381–392.

Cartwright, M. H. (1976). A preparatory method for group counseling. *Journal of Counseling Psychology, 23,* 75–77.

Charrier, G. O. (1974). Cog's Ladder: A model of group development. In J. W. Pfeiffer & J. E. Jones (Eds.), *The 1974 handbook for group facilitators.* La Jolla, Calif.: University Associates, pp. 142–147.

Chessick, R. D. (1965). Empathy and love in psychotherapy. *American Journal of Psychotherapy, 19,* 205–219.

Chin, R. (1969). The utility of systems models and developmental models for practitioners. In W. G. Bennis, K. D. Benne, & R. Chin (Eds.), *The planning of change* (2nd ed.). N.Y. Holt, Rinehart and Winston, pp. 297–312.

Churchill, S. (1959). Prestructuring group content. *Social Work, 4,* 52–59.

Churchill, S. (1974). A comparison of two models of social group work: The treatment model and the reciprocal model. In P. Glasser, R. Sarri, & R. Vinter (Eds.), *Individual change through small groups.* New York: The Free Press, pp. 266–280.

Clark, J. V., & Culbert, S. S. (1965). Mutually therapeutic perception and self-awareness in a T-group. *Journal of Applied Behavioral Science, 1,* 180–194.

Coffey, H. (1952). Socio and psycho group process: Intergrative concepts. *Journal of Social Issues, 8,* 65–74.

Cohen, A. I. (1971). Process in T-groups: Some observation. *Journal of Contemporary Psychology, 3,* 127–130.

Cohen, A. M., & Smith, D. R. (1976). *The critical incident in growth groups: Theory and techniques.* La Jolla, Calif.: University Associates, pp. 155–217.

Cohn, R. C. (1969–70). The theme-centered interactional method: Group therapists, as group educators. *Journal of Group Psychoanalysis and Group Process, 2,* 19–36.

Cohn, R. C. (1970). Therapy in groups: Psychoanalytic, experimental and Gestalt. In J. Fagen & I. L. Shepherd (Eds.), *Gestalt therapy now.* New York: Harper & Row, pp. 130–139.

Cohn, R. C. (1972). Style and spirit of the theme-centered interactional method. In C. J. Sager & H. S. Kaplan, (Eds.), *Progress in group and family therapy.* New York: Brunner/Mazel, pp. 852–878.

Colman, A. D. (1975). Group consciousness as a developmental phase. In A. D. Coleman & W. H. Bexton (Eds.), *Group relation reader.* Sausalito, Calif.: GREX.

Conyne, R. K. (1980). Developmental patterns: A context and guideline for special issues. *Journal for Specialists in Group Work, 5,* 2–4.

Cooley, C. H. (1956). *Human nature and the social order.* New York: The Free Press.

Cooper, C. L., & Mangham, I. C. (Eds.) (1975). *Theories of group process.* New York: Wiley.

Copeland, H. (1980). The beginning group. *International Journal of Group Psychotherapy, 30,* 201–212.

Corazzini, J. G., & Anderson, S. M. (1980). An apprentice model for training group leaders: Revitalizing group treatment. *Journal for Specialists in Group Work, 5,* 29–35.

Corey, G. (1981). *Theory and practice of group counseling.* Monterey, Calif.: Brooks-Cole.

Corey, G., & Corey, M. S. (1977). *Groups: Process and practice.* Monterey, Calif.: Brooks-Cole.

Corsini, R. (1957). *Methods of group psychotherapy.* Chicago: William James Press.

Corsini, R., & Rosenberg, B. (1955). Mechanisms of group psychotherapy:

Processes and dynamics. *Journal of Abnormal and Social Psychology, 51*, 406–411.

Cowger, C. D. (1979). Conflict and conflict management in working with groups. *Social Work with Groups, 2*, 309–320.

Cozby, P. C. (1973). Self-disclosure: A literature review. *Psychological Bulletin, 79*, 73–91.

Crandall, R. (1978). The assimilation of newcomers into groups. *Small Group Behavior, 9*, 331–336.

Crews, C. Y., & Melnick, J. (1976). Use of initial and delayed structure in facilitating group development. *Journal of Counseling Psychology, 23*, 92–98.

Criss, F. C., & Goodwin, R. C. (1970). Short-term group counseling for parents of children in residential treatment. *Child Welfare, 49*, 45–48.

Crocker, J. W., & Wroblewski, R. G. (1975). Using recreational games in counseling. *Personnel Guidance Journal, 53*, 453–458.

Crowell, L., & Scheidel, T. M. (1961). Categories for analysis of idea development in discussion groups. *Journal of Social Psychology, 54*, 155–168.

Culbert, S. A. (1968). Trainer self-disclosure and member growth in two T-groups. *Journal of Applied Behavioral Science, 4*, 47–73.

Culbert, S. A. (1970). Accelerating laboratory learning through a phase progression model for trainer intervention. *Journal of Applied Behavioral Science, 6*, 21–38.

Culbert, S. A. (1972). Accelerating participant learning. In W. G. Dyer (Ed.), *Modern theory and method in group training*. New York: Van Nostrand Reinhold.

Curran, T. F. (1978). Increasing motivation to change in group treatment. *Small Group Behavior, 9*, 337–348.

D'Angelli, A. R. (1973). Group composition using interpersonal skills. *Journal of Counseling Psychology, 20*, 531–534.

Day, M. (1967). The natural history of training groups. *International Journal of Group Psychotherapy, 17*, 436–446.

De Julio, S., Bentley, J., & Cockayne, T. (1979). Pregroup norm setting: Effects on encounter group interaction. *Small Group Behavior, 10*, 368–388.

Dell, P. F., Shelly, M. D., Pulliam, G. P., et al. (1979). Family therapy seminar. *Journal of Marriage and Family Counseling, 4*, 43–48.

Derman, B. (1976). The Gestalt thematic approach. In E. W. L. Smith (Ed.), *The growing edge of Gestalt therapy*. New York: Brunner/Mazel, pp. 151–159.

Diamond, M. J., & Shapiro, J. L. (1973). Changes in locus of control as a function of encounter group experiences: A study and replication. *Journal of Abnormal Psychology, 82*, 514–518.

Dickenson, W. A., & Truax, C. B. (1966). Group counseling with underachievers. *Personnel and Guidance Journal, 95*, 243–247.

Dickhoff, H., & Lakin, M. (1963). Patients views of group psychotherapy: Retrospections and interpretations. *Journal of group Psychotherapy, 14*, 61–73.

Dies, R. R. (1979). Group psychotherapy: Reflections on three decades of research. *Journal of Applied Behavioral Science, 15,* 361–373.

Dies, R. R., & Hess, A. K. (1971). An experimental investigation of cohesiveness in marathon and conventional group psychotherapy. *Journal of Abnormal Psychology, 77,* 258–262.

Dinkmeyer, D. (1970). Developmental group counseling. *Elementary School Guidance and Counseling, 4,* 267–272.

Dinkmeyer, D. C., & Muro, J. J. (1971). *Group counseling: Theory and practice.* Itasca, Ill.: F. E. Peacock Publisher, pp. 189–196.

Doverspike, J. E. (1973). Group and individual goals: Their development and utilization. *Educational Technology, 13,* 24–26.

Dreikurs, R. (1951). The unique social climate experienced in group psychotherapy. *Group Psychotherapy, 3,* 292–299.

Drum, D. J., & Knott, J. E. (1977). *Structured groups for facilitating development: Acquiring life skills, resolving life themes, and making life transitions.* New York: Human Services Press.

Duncan, J. A., & Gazda, G. M. (1967). Significant content of group counseling sessions with culturally deprived ninth-grade students. *Personnel and Guidance Journal, 46,* 11–16.

Dunnette, M. D. (1969). People feeling: Joy, more joy, and the slough of despond. *Journal of Applied Behavioral Science, 5,* 91–112.

Dunphy, D. C. (1966). Social change in self-analytic groups. In *The general inquirer: A computer approach to content analysis.* Cambridge, Mass.: MIT Press.

Dunphy, D. C. (1968). Phases, roles and myths in self-analytical groups. *Journal of Applied Behavioral Science, 4,* 195–224.

Durkin, H. E. (1964). *The group in depth.* New York: International Universities Press, pp. 36–61.

Dyer, W. W., & Vriend, J. (1977). *Counseling techniques that work.* New York: Funk and Wagnalls.

Egan, G. (1970). *Encounter: Group processes for interpersonal growth.* Belmont, Calif.: Brooks/Cole, pp. 69–71.

Egan, G. (1975). *The skilled helper: A model for systematic helping and interpersonal relating.* Monterey, Calif.: Brooks/Cole.

Elliot, J. (1976). *The theory and practice of encounter group leadership.* Berkeley, Calif.: Explorations Institute.

Erikson, E. H. (1950). *Childhood and society.* New York: W. W. Norton.

Estes, R. H., & Henry, S. (1979). The therapeutic contract in work with groups. *Social Service Review, 50,* 611–632.

Evans, N. J., & Jarvis, P. A. (1980). Group cohesion: A review and reevaluation. *Small Group Behavior, 11,* 359–370.

Farrell, M. P. (1976). Patterns in the development of self-analytic groups. *Journal of Applied Behavioral Science, 12,* 523–542.

Feinberg, N. (1980). A study of group stages in a self-help setting. *Social Work with Groups, 3,* 41–49.

Felton, G. S., & Biggs, B. E. (1972). Teaching internalization behavior to collegiate low achievers in group psychotherapy. *Psychotherapy: Theory, Research and Practice, 9,* 281–283.

Felton, G. S., & Biggs, B. E. (1973). Psychotherapy and responsibility: Teaching internalization behavior to black low achievers through group therapy. *Small Group Behavior, 4,* 147–155.

Felton, G. S., & Davidson, H. R. (1973). Group counseling in the classroom. *Academic Therapy, 8,* 461–468.

Fiebert, M. S. (1968). Sensitivity training: An analysis of trainer intervention and group process. *Psychological Reports, 22,* 829–838.

Fike, D. F. (1980). Evaluating group intervention. *Social Work with Groups, 3,* 41–52.

Fisher, A. B. (1974). *Small group decision-making: Communication and the group process.* New York: McGraw-Hill, chap. 7.

Flack, F. F. (1971). Group approaches in medical education. In H. I. Kaplan & B. J. Sadock (Eds.), *Comprehensive group psychotherapy.* Baltimore: Williams and Wilkins.

Flesher, J. (1957). The economy of aggression and anxiety in group formations. *International Journal of Group Psychotherapy, 7,* 31–39.

Foley, V. (1974). *An introduction to family therapy,* New York: Grune & Stratton.

Foley, W. J., & Bonney, W. C. (1966). A developmental model for counseling groups. *Personnel Guidance Journal, 42,* 576–580.

Follet, M. P. (1943). *Creative experience.* New York: Longmans, Green, chap. 3.

Forisha, B. L., Hoffman, M., & Holtzman, R. (1979). The Gestalt growth group experience. *Small Group Behavior, 10,* 332–342.

Foulds, M. L. (1971). Changes in locus of internal-external control: A growth group experience. *Comparative Group Studies, 2,* 293–300.

Foulds, M. L. (1972). The experiential-gestalt growth group experience. *Journal of College Personnel, 13,* 48–52.

Foulds, M. L., Guinan, J. F., & Worehing, R. G. (1974). Marathon group: Changes in perceived locus of control. *Journal of College Student Personnel, 15,* 8–11.

Foulkes, S. H., & Anthony, E. J. (1957). *Group psychotherapy: The psychoanalytic approach,* London: Penguin Books.

Frank, J. (1955). Some values of conflict in therapeutic groups. *Group Psychotherapy, 8,* 142–151.

Frank, J. D. (1957). Some determinants, manifestations, and effects of cohesiveness in therapy groups. *International Journal of Group Psychotherapy, 7,* 53–63.

Frank, J. (1959). The dynamics of the psychotherapeutic relationship. *Psychiatry, 22,* 17–39.

Frank, J., & Ascher, E. (1941). The corrective emotional experience in group therapy. *American Journal of Psychiatry, 108,* 126–131.

Frank, M. (1972). Phases of development of a multinational training group. *Comparative Group Studies, 3,* 3–50.

Frankl, V. E. (1965). *The doctor and the soul: From psychotherapy to logotherapy* (2nd ed.). New York: Alfred A. Knopf.

Freedman, S. M., & Hurley, J. R. (1979). Maslow's needs: Individual perceptions of helpful factors in growth groups. *Small Group Behavior, 10,* 355–367.

Freedman, S. M., & Hurley, J. R. (1980). Perceptions of helpfulness and behavior in groups. *Groups, 4,* 51–58.

Friedman, W. H. (1979). *How to do groups.* New York: Jason Aronson.

Fromm, E. (1956). *The art of loving.* New York: Bantam Books.

Frost, R. (1962). *In the clearing.* New York: Holt, Rinehart and Winston.

Fullmer, D. (1971). *Counseling: Group theory and system.* New York: Intext Educational Publishers.

Garland, J. A. (1981). Loneliness in the group: An element of treatment. *Social Work with Groups, 4,* 95–110.

Garland, J. A., & Frey, L. A. (1970). Applications of stages of group development to groups in psychiatric settings. In S. Bernstein (Ed.), *Further explorations in group work.* Boston: Boston University School of Social Work.

Garland, J. A., Jones, H. E., & Kolodny, R. L. (1973). A model of development for social work groups. In S. Bernstein (Ed.), *Explorations in group work.* Boston: Milford House, pp. 17–71.

Garland, J. A., & Kolodny, R. L. (1981). *Treatment of children through social groupwork: A developmental approach.* Boston: Charles River Books.

Garr, B. A., & Sayer, J. E. (1979). *May I join you?* Sherman Oaks, Calif.: Alfred Press.

Garvin, C. D. (1981). *Contemporary group work.* Englewood Cliffs, N.J.: Prentice-Hall.

Gauron, E. F., & Rawlings, E. I. (1975). A procedure for orienting new members to group psychotherapy. *Small Group Behavior, 6,* 293–307.

Gawrys, J. Jr., & Brown, B. O. (1963). Group counseling: More than a catalyst. *The School Counselor, 12,* 206–213.

Gazda, G. M. (1971). *Group counseling: A developmental approach.* Boston: Allyn & Bacon.

Gazda, G. M. (1975). Group counseling: A developmental approach. In G. M. Gazda (Ed.), *Basic approaches to group psychotherapy and group counseling* (2nd ed.). Springfield, Ill.: Charles C. Thomas, pp. 375–452.

Gazda, G. M., Duncan, J. A., & Meadows, M. E. (1967). Group counseling and group procedures: Report of a survey. *Counselor Education and Supervision, 6,* 306–310.

Gazda, G. M., & Larsen, M. J. (1968). A comprehensive appraisal of group and multiple counseling research. *Journal of Research and Development in Education, 1,* 57–132.

Gazda, G. M., & Peters, R. W. (1975). An analysis of research in group psychotherapy, group counseling, and human relations training. In G. M. Gazda, (Ed.), *Basic approaches to group counseling* (2nd ed.). Springfield, Ill.: Charles C. Thomas, pp. 38–54.

Geller, J. J. (1962). Paratoxic distortion in the initial stages of group relationships. *International Journal of Group Psychotherapy, 12*, 27–34.

Gendlin, E. T., & Beebe, J. (1968). Experiential groups: Instructions for
groups. In G. M. Gazda, (Ed.), *Innovations in Group Psychotherapy.*
Springfield, Ill.: Charles C. Thomas, pp. 190–206.

Gibb, J. R. (1964). Climate for trust formation. In L. P. Bradford, J. R. Gibb, &
K. D. Benne (Eds.), *T-group theory and laboratory method.* New York:
Wiley, pp. 279–309.

Gibb, J. R. (1970). Sensitivity training as a medium for personal growth and
improved interpersonal relationships. *Interpersonal Development, 1*, 6–
31.

Gibb, J. R., & Gibb, L. M. (1965). Humanistic elements in group growth. In J.
A. Brugenthal (Ed.), *Challenges of humanistic psychology.* New York:
McGraw-Hill, pp. 161–170.

Gibbard, G. S., & Hartman, J. J. (1973). The oedipal paradigm in group
development. *Small Group Behavior, 4*, 305–354.

Gill, S. J., & Barry, R. A. (1982). Group-focused counseling: Classifying the
essential skills. *Personnel and Guidance Journal, 60*, 302–305.

Glasser, W. (1965). *Reality therapy: A new approach to psychiatry.* New York:
Harper & Row.

Goldberg, C. (1970). *Encounter: Group sensitivity training experience.* New
York: Science House.

Goldberg, C., & Goldberg, M. C. (1973). *The human circle: An existential
approach to the new group therapies.* Chicago: Nelson-Hall Company.

Goldstein, M. J., Bednar, R. L., & Yandell, B. (1979). Personal risk associated
with self-disclosure, interpersonal feedback, and group confrontation in
group psychotherapy. *Small Group Behavior, 9*, 579–887.

Golembiewski, R. T. (1962). *The small group.* Chicago: University of Chicago
Press.

Gordon, T. (1955). *Group-centered leadership.* Boston: Houghton Mifflin.

Greenwald, J. (1972). The ground rules of Gestalt therapy. *Journal of Contemporary Psychotherapy, 5*, 3–120.

Grotjahn, M. (1972). Learning from dropout patients: A clinical view of
patients who discontinued group psychotherapy. *International Journal
of Group Psychotherapy, 22*, 306–319.

Guetztow, H., & Dill, W. R. (1957). Factors in the organizational development of task-oriented groups. *Sociometry, 20*, 175–204.

Gundlach, R. H. (1967). Outcome studies in group psychotherapy. *Journal of
Group Psychotherapy, 17*, 196–210.

Gurman, A. S., & Gustafson, J. P. (1976). Patients' perceptions of the therapeutic relationship and group therapy outcomes. *American Journal of
Psychiatry, 133*, 1290–1294.

Hall, J., & Watson, W. H. (1970). The effects of a normative intervention on
group decision-making performance. *Human Relations, 23*, 299–317.

Hall, R. (1976). A schema of the Gestalt concept of the organismic flow and its
disturbance. In E. W. L. Smith (Ed.), *The growing edge of Gestalt therapy.*
New York: Brunner/Mazel, pp. 53–57.

Hampden-Turner, C. M. (1966). An existential 'learning theory' and the integration of T-group research. *Journal of Applied Behavioral Science, 2*, 367–386.

Hamsher, J. H., Geller, J. D., & Rotter, J. B. (1968). Interpersonal trust, internal-external control, and the Warren Commission Report. *Journal of Personality and Social Psychology, 9*, 210–215.

Hansen, J. C., Warner, R. W., & Smith, E. J. (1980). *Group counseling: Theory and process* (2nd ed.). Chicago: Rand McNally.

Hare, A. P. (1967). Small group development in the relay assembly room. *Social Inquiry, 37*, 169–182.

Hare, A. P. (1973). Theories of group development and categories for interaction analysis. *Small Group Behavior, 4*, 259–303.

Harrison, R. (1965). Group composition models for laboratory design. *Journal of Applied Behavioral Science, 1*, 409–432.

Harrison, R. (1967). Problems in the design of human relations training. In *Explorations in human relations training and research*. Washington, D.C., NTL Institute for Applied Behavioral Science, pp. 1–9.

Harrison, R., & Lubin, B. (1965). Personal style, group compositions, and learning—Part 2. *Journal of Applied Behavioral Science, 1*, 286–294.

Hartford, M. E. (1972). *Groups in social work*. New York: Columbia University Press.

Hartman, J. J., & Gibbard, G. S. (1974). Anxiety, boundary evolution, and social change. In G. S. Gibbard, J. J. Hartman, & R. D. Mann (Eds.), *Analysis in groups*. Washington, D.C.: Jossey-Bass.

Harvey, O. J., & Schroder, H. M. (1963). Conceptual organization and group structure. In O. J. Harvey (Ed.), *Motivation and social interaction: Cognitive determinants*. New York: Ronald Press.

Hearn, G. (1957). The process of group development. *Autonomous Group Bulletin, 13*, 1–7.

Heckel, R., Holmes, G., & Rosecrans, C. J. (1971). A factor analytic study of process variables in group therapy. *Journal of Clinical Psychology, 27*, 146–150.

Heckel, R. V., Holmes, G. R., & Salzberg, H. C. (1962). Emergence of distinct verbal phases in group therapy. *Psychological Reports, 10*, 14.

Heckel, R. V., & Salzberg, H. C. (1967). Predicting verbal behavior change in group therapy using a screening scale. *Psychological Reports, 20*, 403–406.

Heiniche, C., & Bales, R. F. (1953). Developmental trends in the structure of small groups. *Sociometry, 16*, 7–38.

Henry, S. (1981). *Group skills in social work*. Itasca, Ill.: F. E. Peacock.

Hill, B., Lippitt, L., & Serkownek, K. (1979). The emotional dimensions of the problem-solving process. *Group and Organizational Studies, 4*, 93–102.

Hill, W. F. (1975). Further considerations of therapeutic mechanisms in group therapy. *Small Group Behavior, 6*, 421–429.

Hill, W. F. (1976). Systematic group development (SGD) therapy. In A. Jacobs & W. W. Spradlin (Eds.), *The group: An agent of change*. New York: Behavioral Publications, pp. 252–276.

Hill, W. F., & Gruner, L. A. (1973). A study of development in open and closed groups. *Small Group Behavior, 4,* 355–381.

Hobart, C. W. (1965). Types of alienation: Etiology and interrelationships. *Canadian Review of Sociology and Anthropology, 2,* 92–107.

Hock, E., & Kaufer, G. A. (1955). A process analysis of 'transient' therapy groups. *International Journal of Group Psychotherapy, 5,* 415–421.

Hogan, D. B. (1977). Competence as a facilitator of personal growth groups. *Journal of Humanistic Psychology, 17,* 35–54.

Holt, R. R. (1959). Personality growth in psychiatric residents. *AMA Archives of Neurology and Psychiatry, 81,* 203–215.

Howitz, L. (1967). Training groups for psychiatric residents. *International Journal of Group Psychotherapy, 17,* 421–435.

Hulse, W. C. (1950). The therapeutic management of group tension. *American Journal of Orthopsychiatry, 20,* 834–838.

Hurley, J. R., & Pinchea, S. K. (1978). Interpersonal behavior and effectiveness of T-group leaders. *Small Group Behavior, 9,* 529–539.

Husband, D., & Scheunemann, H. R. (1972). The use of group process in teaching termination. *Child Welfare, 41,* 505–513.

Imbar, S. D., Lewis, P. M., & Loiselle, L. S. (1979). Users and abusers of the brief intervention group. *International Journal of Group Psychotherapy, 19,* 39–49.

Israel, J. (1971). *Alienation: From Marx to modern sociology.* Boston: Allyn & Bacon.

Ivancevich, J. M. (1974). A study of a cognitive training program: Trainer styles and group development. *Academy Management Journal, 17,* 428–439.

Ivancevich, J. M., & McMahon, J. T. (1976). Group development, trainer style, and carry-over job satisfaction. *Academy Management Science, 19,* 395–412.

Ivey, A. E. (1973). Demystifying the group process: Adapting microcounseling procedures to counseling in groups. *Educational Technology, 13,* 27–31.

Jacobs, A. (1974). The use of feedback in groups. In A. Jacobs & W. W. Spradline (Eds.), *The group as an agent of change.* New York: Behavioral Publications, pp. 31–49.

Jeske, J. O. (1973). Identification and therapeutic effectiveness in group therapy. *Journal of Counseling Psychology, 20,* 528–530.

Joe, G. E. (1971). Review of the internal-external control construct as a personality variable. *Psychological Reports, 28,* 619–640.

Johnson, D. W. (1972). *Reaching out.* Englewood Cliffs, N.J.: Prentice-Hall.

Johnson, D. W., & Johnson, F. P. (1973). *Joining together: Group theory and group skills.* Boston: Houghton Mifflin.

Johnson, J. A. (1963). *Group therapy: A practical approach.* New York: McGraw-Hill.

Jones, J. E. (1973). A model of group development. In J. W. Pfeiffer & J. E. Jones (Eds.), *The 1973 handbook for group facilitators.* La Jolla, Calif.: University Associates, pp. 127–129.

Jourard, S. (1971). *Self-disclosure: An experimental analysis of the transparent self.* New York: Wiley.

Jung, C. G. (1926). *Psychological types.* New York: Harcourt Brace.

Jurma, W. E. (1978). Leadership structuring style, task ambiguity, and group-member satisfaction. *Small Group Behavior, 19,* 124–234.

Kaneshige, E. (1973). Cultural factors in group counseling and interactions. *Personnel and Guidance Journal, 51,* 407–412.

Kaplan, S. (1967). Therapy groups and training groups: Similarities and differences. *International Journal of Group Psychotherapy, 17,* 473–504.

Kaplan, S. R. (1974). Characteristic phases of development in organizations. In D. S. Milman & J. D. Goldsmith (Eds.), *Group process today: Evaluation and perspective.* Springfield, Ill.: Charles C. Thomas.

Kaplan, S. R., & Roman, M. (1963). Phases of development in an adult therapy group. *International Journal of Group Psychotherapy, 13,* 10–26.

Kauff, P. F. (1977). The termination process: Its relationship to the separation-individuation phase of development. *International Journal of Group Psychotherapy, 27,* 3–18.

Kaul, T. J., & Bednar, R. L. (1978). Conceptualizing group research: A preliminary analysis. *Small Group Behavior, 9,* 173–192.

Kellerman, H. (1979). *Group psychotherapy and personality: Intersecting structures.* New York: Grune & Stratton.

Kemp, C. G. (1970). *Group counseling: A foundation for counseling with groups.* Boston: Houghton Mifflin.

Keniston, K. (1965). *The uncommitted: Alienated youth in American society.* New York: Harcourt, Brace and World.

Kepner, E. (1980). Gestalt group formation. In B. Feder & R. Ronall (Eds.), *Beyond the hot seat: Gestalt approaches to group.* New York: Bruner/Mazel, pp. 5–24.

Kindelsperger, W. L. (1957). Stages in group development. In *The use of groups on welfare settings.* New Orleans: Turlane University, pp. 8–12.

King, P. D. (1975). Life cycle in the Tavistock study group. *Perspectives in Psychiatric Care, 13,* 180–184.

Klein, A. F. (1972). *Effective groupwork: An introduction to principle and method.* New York: Association Press, 57–175.

Knight, D. J. (1974). *Developmental stages in T-groups.* Doctoral Dissertation. Cincinnati: University of Cincinnati.

Knowles, M., & Knowles, H. (1972). *Introduction to group dynamics* (rev. ed.). New York: Association Press, pp. 10–74.

Koran, L. M., & Costell, R. M. (1973). Early termination from group psychotherapy. *International Journal of Group Psychotherapy, 23,* 346–359.

Koziey, P. W., Loken, J. O., & Field, J. A. (1971). T-group influences on feelings of alienation. *Journal of Applied Behavioral Science, 7,* 724–731.

Kravetz, D. F., & Rose, S. D. (1973). *Contracts in groups: a workbook.* Dubuque, Iowa: Kendall/Hunt.

Kropotkin, P. (1925). *Mutual aid: A factor of evolution*. New York: Alfred A. Knopf.

Kübler-Ross, E. (1969). *On death and dying*. New York: Macmillan.

Kurtz, R. R. (1975). Structured experiences in groups: a theoretical and research discussion. In J. E. Jones and J. W. Peiffer (Eds.), *The 1975 Annual handbook for group facilitators*. LaJolla, CA: University Associates, pp. 167–171.

Lacoursiere, R. (1974). A group method to facilitate learning during the stages of a psychiatric affiliation. *International Journal of Group Psychotherapy, 24*, 342–351.

Lacoursiere, R. (1980). *The life-cycle of groups: Group development stage theory*. New York: Human Services Press.

Lakin, M. (1972). *Interpersonal encounter: Theory and practice in sensitivity training*. New York: McGraw-Hill.

Lakin, M., & Carson, R. C. (1964). Participant perception of group process in group sensitivity training. *International Journal of Group Psychotherapy, 14*, 116–122.

Landreth, G. L. (1973). Group counseling: To structure or not to structure? *The School Counselor, 20*, 371–374.

Langer, J. (1969). *Theories of development*. New York: Holt, Rinehart and Winston.

Larsen, J. A. (1980). Accelerating group development and productivity: An effective leader approach. *Social Work with Groups, 3*, 25–39.

Lawler, M. (1980). Termination in a work group: Four models of analysis and intervention. *Groups, 4*, 3–27.

Leak, G. K. (1980). Effects of highly structured versus nondirective group counseling approaches on personality and behavioral measures of adjustment in incarcerated felons. *Journal of Counseling Psychology, 27*, 520–523.

Leavitt, H. J. (1951). Some effects of certain communication patterns on group performance. *Journal of Abnormal and Social Psychology, 46*, 38–50.

Lee, F., & Bednar, R. L. (1971). Effects of group structure and risk-taking disposition on group behavior, attitudes, and atmosphere. *Journal of Counseling Psychology, 24*, 191–199.

Lefcourt, H. (1976). *Locus of control*. Princeton, N.J.: Lawrence Erlbaum.

Leik, R. K., & Matthews, M. (1968). A scale for developmental processes. *American Sociological Review, 33*, 62–75.

Levin, E. M., & Kurtz, R. R. (1974). Participant perceptions following structured and nonstructured human relations training. *Journal of Counseling Psychology, 21*, 514–532.

Levine, B. (1979). *Group psychotherapy, practice and development*. Englewood Cliffs, N.J.: Prentice-Hall.

Levine, N. (1971). Emotional factors in group development. *Human Relations, 24*, 65–89.

Levitsky, A., & Perls, F. S. (1970). The rules and games at Gestalt therapy. In

J. Fegan & I. L. Shepard (Eds.), *Gestalt therapy now*. New York: Harper & Row, pp. 140–149.

Lewis, B. F. (1978). An examination of the final phase of group development. Small Group Behavior, *9*, 507–517.

Lewis, H. R., & Streitfield, H. S. (1970). *Growth games*. New York: Harcourt, Brace, Jovanavich.

Lieberman, M. A., Yalom, I. D., & Miles, M. B. (1973). *Encounter groups: First facts*. New York: Basic Books.

Lindt, H. (1958). The nature of therapeutic interaction of patients in groups. *International Journal of Group Psychotherapy, 8,* 55–69.

Long, L. D., & Cope, C. S. (1980). Curative factors in a male felony offender group. *Small Group Behavior, 11,* 389–398.

Lowen, A. (1958). *The psychical dynamics of character structure*. New York: Grune & Stratton.

Lubin, B., & Zuckerman, M. (1967). Affective and perceptual-cognitive patterns in sensitivity training groups. *Psychological Reports, 21,* 365–376.

Luft, J. (1970) *Group processes; An introduction to group dynamics*. Palo Alto, Calif.: National Press Books, chap. 4.

Lungren, D. C. (1971). Trainer style and patterns of group development. *Journal of Applied Behavioral Science, 7,* 689–709.

Lungren, D. C. (1977). Developmental trends in the emergence of interpersonal issues in T-groups. *Small Group Behavior, 8,* 179–200.

Lungren, D. C., & Knight, D. J. (1978). Sequential stages of development in sensitivity training groups. *Journal of applied Behavioral Sciences, 14,* 204–222.

Mackey, R. A. (1980). Developmental processes in growth-oriented groups. *Social Work, 25,* 26–29.

Maier, N. R. F., & Hoffman, L. R. (1960). Using trained 'developmental' discussion leaders to improve the quality of group decisions. *Journal of Applied Psychology, 44,* 247–251.

Malmud, D., & Machover, S. (1965). *Toward self-understanding: Group techniques in self-confrontation*. Springfield, Ill.: Charles C. Thomas.

Mann, J. (1951). Analytically oriented study groups. *Journal of Psychiatric Social Work, 20,* 137–143.

Mann, J. (1955). Some theoretic concepts of the group process. *International Journal of Group Psychotherapy, 5,* 235–250.

Mann, R. D. (1966). The development of member-trainer relationship in self-analytic groups. *Human Relations, 19,* 85–115.

Mann, R. D. (1967). *Interpersonal styles and group development*. New York: Wiley

Mann, R. D. (1975). Winners, losers, and the search for equality in groups. In C. L. Cooper (Ed.), *Theories of group process*. London: Wiley.

Martin, E. A., & Hill, W. F. (1957). Toward a theory of group development: Six phases of therapy group development. *International Journal of Group Psychotherapy, 7,* 20–30.

Martin, L., & Jacobs, M. (1980). Structured feedback delivered in small groups. *Small Group Behavior, 11,* 88–107.

Maslow, A. (1962). *Toward a psychology of being.* Princeton, N.J.: Van Nostrand.

Maslow, A. H. (1970). *Motivation and personality* (2nd ed.). New York: Harper & Row.

Maslow, A. H., & Honigmann, J. H. (1970). Synergy: Some notes of Ruth Benedict. *American Anthropologist, 72,* 320–33.

Masterson, J. F. (1972). *The treatment of the borderline adolescent: A developmental approach.* New York: Wiley.

Maxmen, J. S. (1973). Group therapy as viewed by hospitalized patients. *Archives of General Psychiatry, 48,* 404–408.

May, R. (1970). *Love and will.* New York: Harper and Row.

McLachlan, J. F. (1972). Benefit from group therapy as a function of patient-therapist match on a conceptual level. *Psychotherapy: Theory, Research, and Practice, 9,* 317–323.

Mead, G. H. (1962). *Mind, self, and society.* Chicago: University of Chicago Press.

Melnick, J., & Rose, G. S. (1979). Expectancy and risk taking prospensity: Predictors of group performance. *Small Group Behavior, 10,* 389–401.

Melnick, J., & Woods, M. (1976). Analysis of group composition research and theory for psychotherapeutic and growth-oriented groups. *Journal of Applied Behavioral Science, 12,* 493–512.

Mezzano, J. (1967). A consideration for group counselors: Degree of counselee investment. *The School Counselor, 14,* 167–169.

Miles, M. B. (1953). Human relations training: How a group grows. *Teachers College Record, 55,* 90–96.

Miles, M. B. (1970). Human relations training: Processes and outcomes. *Journal of Counseling Psychology, 7,* 301–306.

Mills, T. M. (1964). *Group transformation: An analysis of a learning group.* Englewood Cliffs, N.J.: Prentice-Hall.

Mills, T. M. (1967). *The sociology of small groups.* Englewood Cliffs, N.J.: Prentice-Hall.

Mintz, E. E. (1967). Time extended marathon groups. *Psychotherapy: Theory, Research, and Practice, 42,* 65–70.

Modlin, H. C., & Faris, M. (1956). Group adaptation and integration in psychiatric team practice. *Psychiatry, 19,* 97–103.

Moreno, J. L. (1974). The creative theory of personality. In A. Greenberg (Ed.), *Psychodrama: Theory and therapy.* New York: Behavioral Publications, pp. 73–84.

Napier, R. W, & Gershenfeld, M. K. (1973). *Groups: Theory and experience.* Boston: Houghton Mifflin.

Near, J. P. (1978). Comparison of developmental pattern in groups. *Small Group Behavior, 9,* 493–506.

Neilsen, E. H. (1978). Applying a group development model to managing a class. In L. P. Bradford (Ed.), *Group Development* (2nd ed.). La Jolla, Calif.: University Associates.

Northen, H. (1958). Social group work: A tool for changing behavior of disturbed acting-out adolescents. In *Social work with groups 1958*. New York: National Association of Social Workers.

Northen, H. (1969). *Social work with groups.* New York: Columbia University Press, pp. 116–238.

O'Banion T., & O'Connell, A. (1970). *The shared journey: Introduction to encounter.* Englewood Cliffs, N.J.: Prentice-Hall.

Occhetti, A. E., & Occhetti, D. R. (1981). Group therapy with married couples. *Social Caseworker, 62,* 74–49.

O'Day, R. (1974). The T-group trainer: A study of conflict in the exercise of authority. In G. S. Gibbard, J. H. Hartman, & R. D. Mann (Eds.), *Analysis of groups.* Washington, D.C.: Jossey-Bass, pp. 327–394.

Ohlsen, M. H. (1970, 1977). *Group counseling.* New York: Holt, Rinehart and Winston.

Ohlsen, M. M., & Pearson, R. D. (1965). A method for the classification of group interaction and its use to explore the influence of role factors in group counseling. *Journal of Clinical Psychology, 21,* 436–441.

Osbert, J., & Berlinger, A. K. (1956). The developmental stages in group psychotherapy with hospitalized narcotic addicts. *International Journal of Group Psychotherapy, 6,* 436–447.

Otto, H. (1970). *Group methods to actualize potential.* Beverly Hills: Holistic Press.

Page, R. C. (1979). Developmental stages of unstructured counseling groups with prisoners. *Small Group Behavior, 10,* 271–278.

Paradise, R. (1968). The factor of timing in the addition of new members to established groups. *Child Welfare, 47,* 524–529.

Parker, S. (1958). Leadership patterns in a psychiatric ward. *Human Relations, 11,* 287–301.

Parloff, M. B., & Dies, R. R. (1978). Group therapy outcome instrument: Guidelines for conducting research. *Small Group Behavior, 9,* 243–286.

Parloff, M. B., Waskow, I. E., and Wolfe, B. E. (1978). Research on therapist variables in relation to process and outcomes. In S. E. Garfield and A. E. Bergin (Eds.), *Handbook of psychotherapy and behavior change: an empirical analysis.* New York: Wiley, pp. 110–148.

Passons, W. R. (1972) Gestalt therapy interventions in group counseling. *Personnel and Guidance Journal, 51,* 183–189.

Passons, W. R. (1975). *Gestalt approaches to counseling.* New York: Holt, Rinehart, and Winston.

Paterson, J. G. (1966). Group supervision: A process and philosophy. *Community Mental Health, 2,* 315–318.

Pattison, E. M. (1965). Evaluation studies of group psychotherapy. *International Journal of Group Psychotherapy, 15,* 282–397.

Perls, F. S. (1967). Group vs. individual therapy. *ETC, 24,* 306–312.

Perls, F. (1969). *Gestalt therapy verbatim.* New York: Bantam Books.

Peters, L. N., & Beck, A. P. (1982). Identifying emergent leaders in psychotherapy groups. *Groups, 6,* 35–40.

Pfeiffer, J. W., & Jones, J. E. (1979). *Reference guide to handbooks and annuals* (3rd ed.). La Jolla, Calif.: University Associates.

Philip, H., & Dunphy, D. (1959). Developmental trends in small groups. *Sociometry, 22,* 162–174.

Phillips, H. U. (1957). *Essentials of social group work skill.* New York: Association Press.

Phillips, N. K., Gorman, K. H., & Bodenheimer, M. (1981). High-risk infants and mothers in groups. *Social Work, 26,* 157–161.

Piper, W. E., Doan, B. D., Edwards, E. M. & Jones, B. D. (1979). Pretraining for group psychotherapy: A cognitive-experiential approach. *Archives of General Psychiatry, 36,* 1250–1256.

Pollack, H. B. (1971). Changes in homogeneous and heterogeneous sensitivity training groups. *Journal of Consulting and Clinical Psychology, 37,* 60–66.

Powdermaker, F. B., & Frank, J. D. (1953). *Group psychotherapy.* Cambridge, Mass.: Harvard University Press.

Powles, W. E. (1959). Psychosexual maturity in a therapy group of disturbed adolescent. *International Journal of Group Psychotherapy, 9,* 429–441.

Psathas, G., & Hardert, R. (1966). Trainer interventions and normative patterns in the T-group. *Journal of Applied Behavioral Science, 2,* 149–169.

Reddy, W. B. (1972). Interpersonal compatability and self-actualization in sensitivity training. *Journal of Applied Behavioral Science, 8,* 233–241.

Ribner, N. G. (1974). Effects of an explicit group contract on self-disclosure and group cohesiveness. *Journal of Counseling Psychology, 21,* 116–120.

Rogers, C. R. (1961). The process equation of psychotherapy. *American Journal of Psychotherapy, 15,* 4–21.

Rogers, C. R. (1962). Their interpersonal relationship: The core of guidance. *Harvard Educational Review, 32,* 416–429.

Rogers, C. (1970). *On encounter groups.* New York: Harper & Row, chap. 2.

Rohrbaugh, M., & Bartels, B. (1975). Participants' perception of curative factors in therapy and growth groups. *Small Group Behavior, 6,* 430–456.

Ronall, R. (1980). Intensive Gestalt workships: Experiences in community. In B. Feder & R. Ronall (Eds.), *Beyond the hot seat: Gestalt approaches to group.* New York: Bruner/Mazel, pp. 179–211.

Rose, S. D. (1973). *Treating Children in Groups.* San Francisco: Jossey-Bass.

Rosenbaum, M. (1969). The resonsibility of the group psychotherapy practitioner for a therapeutic rationale. *Journal of Group Psychoanalysis and Process, 2,* 5–17.

Rosenberg, P., & Fuller, M. (1957). Dynamic analysis of the student nurse. *Group Psychotherapy, 10,* 22–37.

Rosenfeld, L. B. (1973). *Human interaction in the small group setting.* Columbus, Ohio: Charles E. Merrill.

Rosenzweig, S. P., & Folman, R. (1974). Patient and therapist variables affecting premature termination in group psychotherapy. *Psychotherapy: Theory, Research, and Practice, 11,* 76–79.

Rothman, A., & Marx, H. (1974). Expectations versus perceptions of a first year law class. *Journal of Legal Education, 26,* 349–362.

Rotter, J. B. (1966). Generalized expectancies for internal versus external control of reinforcement. *Psychological Monographs, 80* (Whole No. 609).

Runkel, P. J., Holmes, R. S., & Foster, B. F. (1971). Stages of group development: An empirical test of Tuckman's hypothesis. *Journal of Applied Behavioral Science, 7.*

Saravay, S. M., (1978). A psychoanalytic theory of group development. *International Journal of Group Psychotherapy, 28,* 481–507.

Saretsky, T. (1977). *Active techniques and group psychotherapy.* New York: Jason Aronson.

Sarri, R. K., & Galinsky, M. J. (1964). A conceptual framework for teaching group development in social group work. In *A conceptual framework for the teaching of social group work method in the classroom.* New York: Council on Social Work Education, pp. 20–36.

Sarri, R., & Galinsky, M. (1967). A conceptual framework for group development. In R. D. Vinter (Ed.), *Readings in group work practice.* Ann Arbor, Mich.: Campus Publishers, pp. 75–95.

Sarri, R. G., & Galinsky, M. J. (1974). A conceptual framework for group development. In P. Glasser, R. Sarri & R. Vinter (Eds.), *Individual change through small groups.* New York: The Free Press, pp. 71–88.

Scheidel, T. M., & Crowell, L. (1964). Idea development in small groups. *Quarterly Journal of Speech, 50,* 140–145.

Scheidlinger, S. (1964). Identification: The sense of belonging and of identity in small groups. *International Journal of Group Psychotherapy, 14,* 291–306.

Scheidlinger, S. (1966). The concept of empathy in group psychotherapy. *International Journal of Group Psychotherapy, 16,* 413–424.

Scheidlinger, S. (1980). The psychology of leadership revisited: An overview. *Group, 4,* 5–17. (a)

Scheidlinger, S. (Ed.). (1980). *Psychoanalytic group dynamics: Basic readings.* New York: International Universities Press. (b)

Schopler, J. H., & Galinsky, M. J. (1978). Common elements in group development. In A. Fink (Ed.), *The fields of social work* (6th ed.). New York: Holt, Rinehart and Winston, pp. 263–288.

Schopler, J. H., & Galinsky, M. J. (1981). When groups go wrong. *Social Work, 26,* 424–429.

Schumaker, E. (1977) *A guide for the perplexed,* London: Jonathon Cape.

Schutz, W. C. (1958). *FIRO: A three-dimensional theory of interpersonal behavior.* New York: Holt, Rinehart, and Winston. (a)

Schutz, W. C. (1958). The interpersonal underworld. *Harvard Business Review, 36,* 123–135. (b)

Schutz, W. C. (1967). *Joy: Expanding human awareness.* New York: Grove Press.

Schutz, W. C. (1971). *Here comes everybody.* New York: Harper & Row.

Schutz, W. C. (1973). *Elements of encounter.* Big Sur, Calif.: Joy Press.

Schwartz, W. (1971). On the use of groups in social work practice. In W.

Schwartz & S. Zalba (Eds.), *The practice of group work*. New York: Columbia University Press, pp. 3–24.

Schwartz, W. (1976). Between client and system: The mediating function. In R. R. Roberts & H. Northen (Eds.), *Theories of social work with groups*, New York: Columbia University Press.

Schwartz, W., & Zalba, S. R. (1971). *The practice of group work*. New York: Columbia University Press.

Seeman, M. (1959). On the meaning of alienation. *American Sociological Review, 24,* 783–791.

Semrad, E. V., & Arsenian, J. (1951). The use of group process in teaching group dynamics. *American Journal of Psychiatry, 108,* 358–368.

Shader, R. I., & Meltzer, H. Y. (1968). The breast metaphor and the group. *International Journal of Group Psychotherapy, 18,* 110–113.

Shaffer, J. B., & Galinsky, D. (1974). *Models of group therapy and sensitivity training*. Englewood Cliffs, N.J.: Prentice-Hall.

Shambough, P., & Kanter, S. (1969). Spouses under stress: Group meetings with spouses of patients and hemodialysis. *American Journal of Psychiatry, 125,* 928–936.

Shapiro, D., & Birk, L. (1967). Group therapy and experimental perspective. *International Journal of Group Psychotherapy, 17,* 211–224.

Shellow, S. R., Ward, J. L., & Rubenfeld, S. Group therapy and the institutionalized delinquent. *International Journal of Group Psychotherapy, 8,* 265–275.

Shepard, H. A., & Bennis, W. G. (1956). A theory of training by group methods. *Human Relations, 9,* 403–413.

Sherry, P., & Hurley, J. R. (1976). Curative factors in psychotherapeutic and growth groups. *Journal of Clinical Psychology, 32,* 835–937.

Shulman, L. (1979). *The skills of helping: Individuals and groups*. Itasca, Ill.: F. E. Peacock.

Silbergeld, S., Thune, E. S., & Manderscheid, R. W. (1979). The group therapist leadership roles: Assessment in adolescent coping courses. *Small Group Behavior, 10,* 176–199.

Singer, J. L., & Goldman, G. D. (1954). Experimentally contrasted social atmospheres in group psychotherapy with chronic schizophrenics. *Journal of Social Psychology, 40,* 23–37.

Slater, P. E. (1966). *Microcosm: Structural, psychological, and religious evolution in groups*. New York: Wiley.

Slavson, S. R. (1951). *The practice of group therapy*. New York: International Universities Press.

Slavson, S. R. (1955). Criteria for selection and rejection of patients for various kinds of group therapy. *International Journal of Group Psychotherapy, 5,* 3–30.

Smith, A. J. (1960). A developmental study of group processes. *Journal of Genetic Psychology, 97,* 29–39.

Smith, P. B. (1979). Changes in relationships after sensitivity training. *Small Group Behavior, 10,* 414–430.

Smith, P. B. (1980). Personal causality and sensitivity training. *Small Group Behavior, 11,* 235–249.

Smith, W. M. (1966). Observations over the lifetime of a small isolated group: structure, danger, boredom, and vision, *Psychological Reports, 19,* 475–514.

Snortum, J. R., & Myers, H. F. (1971). Intensity of T-group relations as function of interaction. *International Journal of Group Psychotherapy, 21,* 190–201.

Spitz, H., & Sadock, B. (1973). Psychiatric training of graduate nursing students. *New York State Journal of Medicine,* June 1, 1334–1338.

Standish, C. F., & Semrad, E. V. (1951). Group psychotherapy with psychotics. *Journal of Psychiatric Social Work, 20,* 143–150.

Stava, L. J., & Bednar, R. L. (1979). Process and outcome in encounter groups: The effects of group composition. *Small Group Behavior, 10,* 200–213.

Stevens, J. O. (1971). *Awareness: exploring, experimenting, experiencing.* Moab, Utah: Real People Press.

Stock, D. (1962). Interpersonal concerns during the early session of therapy groups. *International Journal of Group Psychotherapy, 12,* 19–26.

Stock, D., & Thelen, H. A. (1958). *Emotional dynamics and group culture.* Washington, D.C.: National Training Laboratories.

Stone, W. N., Blaze, M., & Bozzuto, J. (1980). Late dropouts from group psychotherapy. *American Journal of Psychotherapy, 34,* 401–413.

Stoute, A. (1950). Implementation of group interpersonal relations through psychotherapy. *Journal of Psychology, 30,* 145–156.

Taylor, F. K. (1954). The three-dimensional basis of emotional interaction in small groups. *Human Relations, 7,* 441–71.

Taylor, F. (1958). The therapeutic factors in group analytic treatment. *Journal of Mental Science, 96,* 976–999.

Taylor, S. W. (1980). Using short-term structured groups with divorced clients. *Social Work, 61,* 433–437.

Thelen, H. A. (1952). *Dynamics of groups at work.* Chicago: University of Chicago Press.

Thelen, H. A. (1959). Work-emotionality theory of the group as organism. In S. A. Koch (Ed.), *Psychology: A study of science.* New York: McGraw-Hill, pp. 544–611.

Thelen, H., & Dickerman, W. (1949). Stereotypes and the growth of groups. *Educational Leadership, 6,* 309–316.

Thelen, M. H., & Harris, C. J. (1968). Personality of college underachievers who improve with group psychotherapy. *Personnel and Guidance Journal 46,* 561–566.

Theodorson, G. A. (1953). Elements in the progressive development of small groups. *Social Forces, 31,* 311–320.

Thorpe, J. J., & Smith, B. (1953). Phases in group development in treatment of drug addicts. *International Journal of Group Psychotherapy, 3,* 66–78.

Tindall, J. (1979). Time-limited and time-extended encounter groups: Descriptive stage development. *Small Group Behavior, 10,* 402–413.

Tolor, A. (1970). The effectiveness of various therapeutic approaches. *International Journal of Group Psychotherapy, 20,* 48–62.

Tompkins, D. S. (1972). Group effectiveness as a function of leadership style moderated by stage of group development. Doctoral Dissertation. Columbus, Ohio: Ohio State University.

Trecker, H. (1955). *Social group work: Principles and practices.* New York: Association Press.

Tropp, E. (1972). *A humanistic foundation for group work practice* (2nd ed.). New York: Selected Academic Readings.

Trotzer, J. P. (1977). *The counselor and the group: Integrating theory, training, practice.* Monterey, Calif.: Brooks/Cole.

Trotzer, J. P., & Kassera, W. J. (1973). Guidelines for selecting communication techniques in group counseling. *The School Counselor, 20,* 299–301.

Truax, C. B. (1961). The process of group psychotherapy: Relationships between hypothesized therapeutic conditions and interpersonal explorations. *Psychological Monographs, 75,* 1–35.

Truax, C. B. (1968). The process of group psychotherapy: Relationships between hypothesized therapeutic conditions and intrapersonal explorations. *Psychological Monographs, 75,* (Whole No. 505). (a)

Truax, C. B. (1968). Therapist interpersonal reinforcement of client self-exploration and therapeutic outcome in group psychotherapy. *Journal of Counseling Psychology, 15,* 225–231. (b)

Truax, C. B, & Carkhuff, R. R. (1967). *Toward effective counseling and psychotherapy: Training and practice.* Chicago: Aldine.

Truax, C. B., Carkhuff, R. R., & Kolman, F. Jr. (1965). Relationships between therapist-offered conditions and patient change in group psychotherapy. *Journal of Clinical Psychology, 21,* 327–329.

Truax, C., & Mitchell, K. (1971). Research on certain therapist interpersonal skills in relations to process and outcome. In A. Bergin & S. Garfield (Eds.), *Handbook of psychotherapy and behavior change.* New York: Wiley, pp. 521–540.

Tucker, D. M. (1973). Some relationships between individual and group development. *Human Development, 16,* 249–272.

Tuckman, B. W. (1965). Developmental sequences in small groups. *Psychological Bulletin, 63,* 384–399.

Tuckman, B. W., & Jensen, M. A. C. (1977). Stages of group developmented revisited. *Group and Organizatonal Studies, 2,* 419–427.

Van Dyck, B. J. (1980). An analysis of selection criteria for short-term group counseling clients. *Personnel and Guidance Journal, 59,* 226–230.

Vorrath, H. H., & Brendtro, L. K. (1974). *Positive peer culture.* Chicago: Aldine.

Ward, P., & Rouzer, D. L. (1974). The nature of pathological functioning from a Gestalt perspective. *The Counseling Psychologist, 4,* 24–27.

Wayne, J., & Avery, N. (1979). Activities as a tool for group termination. *Social Work, 24,* 58–62.

Weigert, E. (1960). Loneliness and trust: Basic factors of human existence. *Psychiatry, 23,* 121–131.

Weinberg, S. B., Hall, L. M., Samuels, P. & Dale, J. R. (1981). Common group problems. *Small Group Behavior, 12,* 81–92.

Weiner, M. B., & Weinstock, C. S. (1979/80). Group progress of community elderly as measured by tape recordings, group tempo and group evaluation. *International Journal of Aging and Human Development, 10,* 45–55.

Werner, H. (1964). *Comparative psychology of mental development.* New York: International Universities Press.

Whitaker, D. S., & Lieberman, M. A. (1964). *Psychotherapy through the group process.* New York: Atherton Press.

Whitaker, J. D. (1972). Models of group development: Implications for social group work practice. *Social Service Review, 46,* 308–322.

Wile, D. B. (1972). Group leadership questionnaire. In J. W. Pfeiffer & J. E. Jones (Eds.), *The 1972 annual handbook for group facilitators.* La Jolla, Calif.: University Associates, pp. 91–106.

Williams, M., Roback, H., & Pro, J. (1980). A geriatric "growth group." *Group, 4,* 43–48.

Winter, S. D. (1976). Developmental stages in the roles and concerns of group co-leaders. *Small Group Behavior, 7,* 349–362.

Wise, T. (1977). Utilization of group process in training oncology fellows. *International Journal of Group Psychotherapy, 27,* 105–111.

Wogan, M., Chimsky, J. M., & Schoeplein, R. N. (1971). Stages of group development in an experimental ghetto program. *American Journal of Orthopsychiatry, 41,* 659–671.

Woods, M., & Melnick, J. (1979). Review of group therapy selection criteria. *Small Group Behavior, 10,* 155–175.

Yalom, I. D. (1975). *The theory and practice of group psychotherapy* (2nd ed.). New York: Basic Books.

Yalom, I. D. (1980). *Existential psychotherapy.* New York: Basic Books.

Yalom, I. D., Houts, P. S., Zimerberg, S. M. & Rand, K. H. (1967). Prediction of success in group therapy. *Archives of General Psychiatry, 17,* 68–73.

Yalom, I. D., & Moos, R. (1965). The use of small interactional groups in the teaching of psychiatry. *International Journal of Group Psychotherapy, 13,* 242–246.

Yalom, I. D., & Rand, K. (1966). Compatibility and cohesiveness in therapy groups. *Archives of General Psychiatry, 13,* 159–168.

Zenger, J. H. (1970). A comparison of human development with psychological development in T-groups. *Training Development Journal, 24,* 16–20.

Zimpfer, D. G. (1967). Expression of feelings in group counseling. *Personnel and Guidance Journal, 45,* 703–708.

Zimpfer, D. G. (1968). Some conceptualizatons: Some conceptual and research problems in group counseling. *School Counselor, 15,* 326–333.

Zinker, J. C. (1970). Beginning the group therapy. *Voices* (Summer), 29–31.

Zinker, J. (1977). *Creative process in Gestalt therapy.* New York: Brunner/ Mazel.

Zinker, J. C. (1980). The developmental process of a Gestalt therapy group. In B. Feder & R. Ronall (Eds.), *Beyond the hot seat: Gestalt approaches to group*. New York: Brunner/Mazel, pp. 55–77.

Zurcher, L. A. Jr. (1969). Stages of development in poverty program neighborhood action committees. *Journal of Applied Behavioral Science, 5,* 223–258.

Zweben, J. E., & Hommann, K. (1970). Prescribed games: A theoretical perspective on the use of group techniques. *Psychotherapy: Theory, Research, and Practice, 7,* 22–27.

Index